Anthropology of the Performing Arts

Madame Ludmilla Shollar in Schéhérezade, *souvenir program of the Russian Opera and Ballet season, 1914, courtesy of the Harry Ransom Humanities Research Center, The University of Texas at Austin.*

Anthropology of the Performing Arts

Artistry, Virtuosity, and Interpretation in a Cross-Cultural Perspective

Anya Peterson Royce

A Division of
ROWMAN & LITTLEFIELD PUBLISHERS, INC.
Lanham • Boulder • New York • Toronto • Plymouth, UK

For Ron, again,
and for performers,
past, present, and future

ALTAMIRA PRESS
A division of Rowman & Littlefield Publishers, Inc.
4501 Forbes Boulevard, Suite 200
Lanham, MD 20706

Estover Road
Plymouth PL6 7PY
United Kingdon

British Library Cataloguing in Publication Information Available

Library of Congress Cataloging-in-Publication Data

Royce, Anya Peterson.
Anthropology of the performing arts : artistry, virtuosity, and interpretation in a cross-cultural perspective / Anya Peterson Royce.
p. cm.
Includes bibliographical references and index.
ISBN 0-7591-0223-6 (hard. : alk. paper) — ISBN 0-7591-0224-4 (pbk. : alk. paper)
1. Performing arts—Anthropological aspects. I. Title.

PN1590.A58R68 2004
791'.01'03—dc22

2003025785

Printed in the United States of America

⊗™ The paper used in this publication meets the minimum requirements of American National Standard for Information Sciences—Permanence of Paper for Printed Library Materials, ANSI/NISO Z39.48–1992.

CONTENTS

ACKNOWLEDGMENTS

In the making of this book, I have incurred debts too numerous to list in the short space dedicated to acknowledgments. The experience and scholarly reflection on which it is based spans a lifetime and two quite different careers—performer of classical ballet and anthropologist. Madame Ludmilla Shollar and Anatol Vilzak were the two teachers who shaped me most as a dancer. I can never repay their kindness and eagerness to share their love for ballet. Anatol Oboukhoff and Pierre Vladimiroff were two others who instilled a sense of pride and passion when I was a young student at the School of American Ballet. Only now after these four wonderful mentors are gone do I begin to understand the importance of the tradition they lived and shared so freely. They danced in a period of enormous ferment in the world of classical ballet, and their classes embodied that.

In New York, I was a member of the Brooklyn Ballet in the early 1960s and am grateful for the opportunities I had there to dance both the classical and the more contemporary repertoire. Along with our own performances, we provided all the dance interludes for the opera in its regular season there at the Brooklyn Academy of Music (BAM). That experience took my naive love of opera and gave it a more knowledgeable base. I shared the BAM stage with the likes of Zinka Milanov and Robert Merrill. On nonperformance nights, I continued this fascination with opera by getting standing-room tickets at the old Met where I heard some of the most glorious voices of all time. Torn by my dual loves, I spent some nights watching the great dancers of New York City Ballet performing at the City Center. Violette Verdy was one of them. I was grateful then for her enormous gift and more grateful now to be her colleague. It was also in New York that I first met the great mime Marcel Marceau. We have been friends for some forty years and I have learned much about artistry and performance from him. You see his influence throughout the pages of this book. I owe him an enormous debt.

Sol Hurok was the master of impresarios then, and I remember fondly those evenings when he would motion to me or another dancer hanging over the back rail in the standing-room space of the Met to come sit in the two orchestra seats he always had. He loved all dancers and performers, even those just beginning their careers, and treated us kindly and with respect. Similarly, Anatol, the longtime maître d' of the Russian Tea Room, would bring us special cakes when all we could afford was the tea.

Both the Bolshoi Ballet and the Kirov came to New York on their first American tour while I was there. To see Galina Ulanova in Lavrovsky's *Romeo and Juliet* was to see artistry at its absolute highest. Natalia Makarova, Rudolf Nureyev, Yuri Soloviev, and Irina Kolpakova each in a different way opened up the world of classical dance. The beauty and artistry of these and other dancers did not discourage me; rather, it showed me a way of serving an art proudly whether you were in the corps or the most respected of soloists. They reminded me of lessons with Madame Shollar. If you did not dance well, she never scolded; she would simply put her white silk handkerchief over her face. Not dancing well almost always meant dancing self-indulgently, sliding into excess, putting yourself forward rather than the choreography. I am grateful for the models I had.

Coming to Indiana University opened another world of performance and colleagues in the arts. I have been transported by their performances and stimulated by conversations, master classes, lessons, and recording sessions. Coaching soloists and judging competitions has let me share my own training with a new generation of dancers, all of whom have been filled with a love for dance. Singers from whom I have been learned much about the human voice and the artistry of which it is capable include Virginia Zeani, Margaret Harshaw, Martha Lipton, Constanza Cuccaro, Giorgio Tozzi, James Mumford, and Nicola Rossi-Lemeni. György Sebok was the most magical of pianists, whose playing displayed the highest artistry.

The proximity of great teachers on the cello faculty allowed me to satisfy both a personal desire and a scholarly interest. I studied the cello with Helga Winold for three years, realizing that I would never have the intimate knowledge of music making as I did of dancing, but wanting to have some understanding other than theoretical. Professor Winold was a superb teacher and a researcher, too, into the mechanics of cello playing. I learned much from her as I did, indeed, from all the cello faculty, who are like a close-knit family—Janos Starker, Tsuyoshi Tsutsumi, Helga Winold, and Emilio Colón. Sitting in lessons, master classes, conversations, hearing the great artists who were honored by the Eva Janzer Memorial Cello Center annual gatherings, listening to performances—I am grateful for the generosity of those who were willing to share their extraordinary knowledge and passion. Closely connected and generous, too, have been wonderful musicians like David Baker, Franco Gulli, James Campbell, Leonard Hokanson, Shigeo and Reiko Neriki, Joseph Gingold, Imre Pallo, and Kim Walker. It was Walker who organized the replay of a discussion on artistry and virtuosity with a panel that included Starker, Pallo, and Verdy, which led me to think in some new ways about these fundamentals of performance. The initial discussion with Starker and Verdy was part of an international conference on Comparative Arts and Literature, Bloomington, April 2001. My thanks go to its organizer and a valued colleague, Professor Giancarlo Maiorino. In addition to the discussion, I gave one of the keynote addresses, "Virtuosity: The Masque of Nonchalance," now the core of chapter two.

Two colleagues and close friends, Fran Snyyg and Emile Snyder, taught me more than I can say about dance, the arts in general, and the meaning of friendship. The three of us taught a class together, Dance, Society, and the Other Arts, which Emile characterized as a *pas de trois*. It was exhilarating. I miss them very much and the dance community is the poorer for their passing.

Another colleague and friend, Janos Starker, has for many years been the exemplar of the best in musicianship. More important for me has been his willingness to share his vast experience and knowledge about music, artistry, virtuosity, and teaching. He has been a kind but firm critic whose influence has shaped what and how I think about performance, especially music. I am grateful for the joy of his music, the strength of his intellect, and the solid ground of his friendship.

Students, too, have shaped the way I understand performance and have made me optimistic about the future. All of these passionate and disciplined anthropologist–dancers and many more in the classes I teach force me to think new ideas, explore new areas, consider new technologies, and for that, I am grateful.

Many institutions and foundations have supported both my research and my writing. Indiana University has been generous with sabbaticals and leaves, but also with grants and fellowships, especially from the Office of Research and the University Graduate School and the College of Arts and Sciences. Research into mime and the commedia dell'arte was supported by the John Simon Guggenheim Foundation (1981–1982), the Gladys Krieble Delmas Foundation (1983, 1985), and the American Philosophical Society (1986). An International and Area Studies Fellowship from the American Council of Learned Societies, the National Endowment for the Humanities, and the Social Sciences Research Council (2002) allowed me to refine my ideas about healers as performers, especially the Isthmus Zapotec healers with whom I have been working.

The time and place for writing much of the first draft of this book was provided me by the Bogliasco Foundation for the Liguria Study Center (2001). It is fair to say that being in that fairy-tale place on the Ligurian coast of Italy, looked after by a wonderful staff and having a group of witty, serious, creative colleagues with whom to share ideas, freed me from all responsibility except to write. For all their kindness, I want to thank Anna Maria Quaiat, director of the Liguria Study Center; Ivana Folle, associate director; and Alan Rowlin, associate director. For many kindnesses and conversations, I am grateful, too, to Gianni Migone and his wife, Rita Migone, and to Gino Crovetto. In New York, Lucinda Rosenfeld, director of administration, made innumerable details flow smoothly. Heartfelt thanks to my fellow Fellows: Benjamin Anastas, Andrea Bruciati, Emanuela Celauro, Terence Gower, Robert Hahn, Carlo Ivaldi, Françoise Jaunin, James Matheson, Minna Proctor, and Nicole Rafter; a livelier and more supportive group could not be found.

The following archives and libraries provided fertile ground for research: Bibliothèque de L'Arsenal, Bibliothèque de L'Opèra, Bibliothèque National, Bibliothèque de la Ville, Bibliothèque Trocadero (Paris), Museo Correr, Casa Goldoni, Archivio di Stato Marciana (Venice), Biblioteca Estense, Archivio di Stato di Modena (Modena), Archivio di Stato di Parma, Victoria and Albert Museum, British Library, Theatre Research Centre, Royal Academy of Music, Public Records Office (London), Institute of Arts and Sciences (Warsaw), Lilly Library, Huntington Library, Harry Ransom Humanities Center, Bancroft Library, and the Performing

Arts Research Center of the New York Public Library (United States). Thank you to all the staff of these institutions.

To my family and friends, in Juchitán, Mexico, who helped me learn how to listen and to see and so to appreciate the commonality of interpreters whether they are performers or ethnographers or wise people, *binni guendabianni*, my love and gratitude always. A special acknowledgment is due to my closest family, Sra. Rosinda Fuentes and Delia Ramirez Fuentes, and to Ta Feli, healer of healers.

Alfredo Minetti, a graduate student in anthropology at Indiana University and a fine musician, provided comments on the manuscript, articles I might have missed, and his insights on virtuosity. He also did all the reformatting and bibliography checks that are so time consuming. I am grateful for all his help.

Colleagues and friends who read various portions of the manuscript and responded with helpful suggestions include Elizabeth Colson, Raymond DeMallie, Paula Girshick, Giancarlo Maiorino, Paul Parish, Nicholas Radelmiller, Janos Starker, and Violette Verdy. I appreciate their keen insights very much. Moya Andrews introduced me to Dr. Hiroya Yamaguchi and we had an enlightening conversation about Kabuki, especially the *iemoto* system of training. My thanks, too, to Justin Foster, senior editor of the *Ryder*, a Bloomington-based magazine of arts, entertainment, and popular culture, who has invited me to write essays on dance, always a good way to try out your thoughts. Robby Barnett, a Pilobolus veteran, graciously helped with photographs.

It is rare to have an editor who also shares one's own experience and passion. Mitch Allen of AltaMira Press was a dancer in his former life and, like all of us in that distinguished category, is still a dancer at heart.

Ronald R. Royce, as always, has influenced the shape, content, and writing of this book. He can see the possibility of coherence even in incomplete first drafts. Sometimes in the writing of a book like this, you feel rudderless, taken by the stream wherever it wants to go, or seduced into exploring all the tributaries. It is good, essential, to have a pilot who is not swept away. For his clear vision, his critical sense, and his acknowledging when I have to wander down paths that may not lead to paragraphs or chapters, I am most grateful. For all that and more, this book is for him, again.

CHAPTER ONE
TOWARD AN ANTHROPOLOGY OF PERFORMING ARTS

Performing arts, especially music, dance, theatre, and all the combinations of those genres, offer us a view of the world in which our ordinary understanding of who and why we are is brought to a heightened consciousness.[1] Those profound questions are held up for us to apprehend and appreciate in a set-apart place and time. We experience art in the most intimate way through the bodies and creative intelligences of performers who have refined themselves and their crafts so that they are mediums of presentation and transformation.

I offer this book as an extended exploration of the interpretive role of music, dance, and theatre, and of the requisite technical mastery, virtuosity, and artistry that make that role possible and transformative. Anthropologists are most at home working from the observable, painstakingly building up a narrative of meaning. We are also inveterate comparativists. Cross-cultural comparison has long been a hallmark of the field and, more recently, we have added cross-temporal comparison. The selection of genres and cultures that I have made—Japanese theatre and dance in the forms of Kabuki and *Butoh*, Tewa Indian dance and music, the commedia dell'arte, artists and choreographers of the Ballets Russes, the musical artistry of cellist Janos Starker, mime as presented by Marcel Marceau, the performance of individuals during altered states of consciousness, and the creative collaborations leading to new genres or at least new performance styles—is representative of both kinds of comparison.

Anthropological Approaches

Because of the embodied nature of the performing arts, any discussion must attend to the form of the art and the rules that define particular genres.

Moreover, we must examine the ways in which form is acquired and mastered, the degrees of mastery, the nature of interpretation, and the ability of audiences to understand and appreciate what they see and hear. This brings us to questions of virtuosity and artistry, aesthetics and appreciation. Those questions and the approach through form to arrive at shared characteristics are not common in anthropology, although the foundation is certainly there in the work of some of the most significant early figures in the field. For example, Franz Boas approached the visual and literary arts and material culture through analysis of form. In his essay on representative art of primitive people, Boas is unequivocal about technical mastery: "When we speak of art, we have to bear in mind that all art implies technical skill" (1955:535). For Boas, virtuosity in technique is the very essence of artistic skill. Finally, Boas clearly believed in the role of play and the play of imagination in artistic endeavors. Many of the objects or spoken genres he investigated were either utilitarian or part of larger ritual complexes. Nonetheless, he recognized their aesthetic dimension and the creativity of their makers or performers.

This notion of the license to play within the confines of technique is fundamental to any definition of art, regardless of time, culture, or genre. Art is a transformation of the mundane, of the ordinary goal-oriented processes that characterize our workaday world. In its form, art is freed of purpose other than to exist in and of itself. It engages in elaborations of form and process. It plays with form, no matter the genre, and in so doing grants the exercise of the imagination to its creators.[2]

Virtually all of the early theories about art grew out of work with visual or oral genres. While dance and music were recorded, they did not seem to prompt the same drive to generalization or comparison that the visual arts did. Boas, for example, recorded Kwakiutl music on wax cylinders and filmed Kwakiutl dance with the crude technology of the time, but he did not speculate about universal elements in music and dance the way he did with Alaskan needlecases. Nor did Claude Lévi-Strauss, whose work on the structural analysis of masks and other decorative art (1967) points toward common elements that characterize these forms. Elsewhere, I have written about why the performing arts are relative newcomers as subjects for analysis, comparison, and theory building (Royce 1977, 2002a). The larger category of performance, however, has been tackled by a number of scholars utilizing many different approaches.[3] Victor Turner places this attention to performance within a general move in anthropological theory from structure to process and from competence to performance (1987:21). He credits Milton Singer and his notion of "cultural performance" for promoting this trend. In his own work, Turner describes what he calls the great genres of ritual, carnival, drama, and spectacle as being composed of both requisite and variable features, allowing for variation and improvisation in any given performance. The variation and improvisation of which Turner speaks correspond to what I would call the style of individual performers, on the one hand, and their interpretive function, on the other. Turner, while not ignoring form, has concentrated more on what he calls "text in context," the "living context of dialectic between aesthetic dramatic processes and sociocultural processes in a given place and time" (1987:28). In his exposition of the evolution of cultural genres of performance from liminal to liminoid, Turner focuses almost entirely on the process and place of communicative acts, the status of individuals and groups with regard to authority and communitas, and the separation and reintegration of participants. The examination of such questions is, without question, essential to understanding what performance does and why it is significant for human societies. I argue, however, that if we are to understand the nature of the performing arts, including the categories of ritual and spectacle, we must also understand all their formal aspects.

Another shift within anthropology has been toward acknowledging the body, embodiment, and embodied knowledge as important ways of being and of knowing. Referring specifically to embodiment, Andrew Strathern has noted that as terms such as these become more popular, their meanings are stretched in different directions. Some scholars have focused more on the physical and material aspects, while others have explored the more mental and abstract implications (1996:196). The distinction is similar in many respects to the continuum of performance and performance studies—at one end, performance and text are metaphors for human social strategies; at the other, they define actions. Throughout most of the history of the anthropology of dance, the baseline focus has been upon the irreducible physical body moving in patterned, rhythmical ways through space and time. Being anthropologists, scholars in this field moved from that baseline to examinations of the place of dance in the larger cultural context. Only recently, however, have those scholars taken embodied knowledge as an explicit focus. Sally Ness is representative of this new direction. In order to fully understand what performing a choreographed movement means, one must have "some appreciation of how getting oneself physically through a choreographic movement can affect a human being, and how it can affect one's own cultural understanding" (1992:2).

A year before Ness's book appeared, Yvonne Daniel, in a panel at the American Anthropological Association meeting in Chicago, argued for the legitimacy, sometimes superiority, of dance as a window onto culture, referring to dance as "embodied knowledge" (Royce 2002a). Daniel (1995) working in Cuba, Barbara Browning (1995) working in Brazil, and Julie Taylor (1998) and Marta Savigliano (1995) working in Argentina all speak about a corporeal intelligence, acknowledging the existence of a wholly other order of meaning to which access may be only through a body that holds its insights close.[4]

Beginning with the body but moving to issues of power and cultural reproduction, the work of Pierre Bourdieu (1977) and Michel Foucault (1979) has had a major impact on the field of anthropology and raised issues that have changed the way we see human society and individual actors. Body and embodiment have also been central to understanding illness and healing, shamans and healers (Desjarlais 1992; Katz 1982; Stoller 1989). Even more broadly, this concept of body has generated important scholarship on the senses. In *Sensuous Scholarship*, for example, Paul Stoller (1997) argues that we must turn our attention to all the senses through which people experience and explain their world, rather than privileging the body as a text that can be read and distinguishing the visual as the most important in a hierarchy of senses. Whatever issues we define as worthy of examination, in order to understand them fully we must pay attention to their embodiment as part of the cultural repertoire of individuals and societies. And we cannot get to the heart of that place without committing ourselves to embodied ways of knowing. We have recognized ritual and social drama as condensed presentations of and commentary about institutions and values. Now we must recognize movement, dance, theatre, and performance as forms that are at once the most and the least resistant to distortion and misappropriation. They provide subtle and multivocalic entryways to cultural understandings and artistic expression, both in the actual embodied performance and in the memory of it. It is that sense of embodiment that lies at the heart of this examination of artistry and interpretation.

Aesthetics

While general theories of human behavior have come in and out of fashion in anthropology, I am persuaded of some fundamental commonalities in the structure and interpretation of performing genres. While acknowledging the variation of techniques across genres, I find the same elements and characteristics occurring first in the areas of performing ability, that is, virtuosity and artistry, and then again in the ways in which performers and audiences present and understand performance. Perhaps we might call this an aesthetic of performing arts. In its most simple meaning, *aesthetic* refers to an appreciation of what is pleasing to the senses. We often think of it in its more narrow application where it deals with the nature of beauty, art, and taste. While we are more comfortable referring to aesthetics in a clearly delimited realm of art, aesthetic sensibilities also characterize the imaging, crafting, and play of individuals with and within their own cultures. In chapter six, the Tewa Indians provide a fine example of clear, aesthetic judgments about a complex ritual cycle of dance, song, and music. Similarly, the discussion of altered states demonstrates that the role of the healer in cultures scattered around the world represents the choice of individuals to live highly crafted, dedicated, aesthetic lives. That decision is recognized, respected, and supported by the communities of which the healers are a part.

Robert Desjarlais carries the usage of aesthetics one logical step further, referring to it as "aesthetics of experience," meaning "the tacit cultural forms, values, and sensibilities—local ways of being and doing—that lend specific styles, configurations, and felt qualities to local experiences" (1992:65). In his work with the Yolmo people of Nepal, particularly in his examination of their notions of illness, well-being, and healing, he identifies aesthetic leitmotifs of harmony, purity, and wholeness that, among others, shape the constructions of bodily and social interaction. This is similar to Clifford Geertz's analysis of Bali in which he talks about grace and composure as being part of high aesthetics (1973). My own thirty-five-year experience with the Isthmus Zapotec of southern Mexico has convinced me of the imaginative, playful, artful dimension of human behavior, which cuts across all aspects of activity and thought. The Zapotec core values of balance, community, and transforming wisdom provide an aesthetic that governs not only the visual and performing arts for which the Zapotec are well known, but also the events, large and small, that compose everyday life. In short, artfulness and intentionality are embedded in the very fabric of Zapotec culture (Royce 2002b).

It is striking to me that the qualities named as part of the aesthetic experience in these three quite distinctive cultures are so similar—balance, harmony, being settled in one's self, wholeness, and purity. Moreover, as we see in the chapters that follow, they are qualities that performing artists hope to achieve and audiences recognize, whether explicitly or implicitly. They are qualities of artistically satisfying performance.

Virtuosity and Artistry

To be able to perform consistently at the highest levels, performers in all genres must have mastered the technique of their art to the point where they are freed to think about interpretation and perhaps transparency. Virtuosity and artistry refer to levels of mastery that support great performance, and we begin to understand them through an analysis of the form of each genre. Virtuosos are masters of a finite body of technique. This kind of mastery implies a degree of nonchalance and ease, one of the defining characteristics of virtuosity since the Renaissance. Artistry, on the other hand, while assuming virtuosity, goes beyond it. A great artist must be open to being transformed and accept the role of transformer. The artist must understand that artistry opens the way for those who wish to follow to be changed, to dream, and, if only for the moment, to glimpse what lies outside the realm of the everyday. Artists must do all this by giving the spotlight over to the art, rather than drawing attention to themselves.

Virtuosity is a simpler concept to grasp than artistry. It appeals to our attraction to what we can see, hear, and comprehend. It can create a universe built to our measure—small enough to comprehend, bounded so that there are no ambiguous middle territories, no spaces that remain undefined or without labels. We can describe it in words that have a commonly understood currency. Virtuosity is based upon mastery of a technique described by a codified vocabulary. For everything except the highest levels of virtuosity, there exists an uncontested vocabulary. Alongside a technique and its vocabulary comes a set of standards by which to judge performance. Even those extra-technical elements that define the highest levels of virtuosity can be categorized in terms of aspects of musicality or phrasing or as part of the practice of economy.

Virtuosos are very good at something we can define and about which we can talk. We can count the number of *pirouettes* or *fouettés* dancers can do; we can measure how high they jump or count how many notes musicians can fit into one impulse. By that, we think we know how good they are. In fact, this is precisely the sort of thing that competitions measure and reward. What these virtuosic performers do is certainly off the charts compared to our own abilities but it is not incomprehensible. We have words with which to describe and know them. They have a kinship with us, and perhaps that is why we sometimes attach negative connotations to virtuosity. If we had the opportunity, we might have been virtuosos, too. It is not beyond the realm of imagining.

Technique, or the rules of a genre, is what one must master. Techniques are specific to genres. They are created from very different selections of elements out of an almost limitless number of possibilities. They also elaborate a system of rules for combining those elements. While each performing art genre has a distinctive and codified technique, at the next levels—extra-technical elements, style, and artistry—we find patterns common across genres. Of course, genres themselves are often problematic (Kallberg 1996), serving variously what E. D. Hirsch calls a "code of social behavior" and Hans Robert Jauss a "horizon of expectation" (Kallberg 1996:5).

Techniques appear to be exclusive and slow to change, while extra-technical elements are much more fluid. In chapter ten, I examine this notion by presenting examples of innovation, continuity, collaboration, and change in a number of genres. Those elements that are held in common (musicality, phrasing, economy) become especially clear in collaborative works in which techniques are radically different.

It would be interesting for someone to examine the issue of literature and the visual arts, which, at one level, do not change by virtue of multiple performances. Does the viewer or the reader stand in the place of the interpreter or performer? Is the painting or the literary text re-created each time it is viewed or read? Are genres defined by their manifestations? Certainly they differ from each other in the way in which they are seen, heard, or otherwise absorbed. What is the role of technique in all this? is the question we must ask ourselves.

Performance implies a certain level of competence. What happens between that technical competence and interpretation has to do with style and with artistry. Here, we must shift from a codified to a metaphorical vocabulary. Style implies individual choices about interpretation. We may speak of style in two ways. First, we can identify style in the sense of those choices that make an individual performer immediately recognizable. Second, we can speak of style that tries to carry out the intention of the creator so that the performer becomes simply the medium, although by no means a passive one.[5] Artistry, at its best, creates an interpretation in which not only is the artist transparent but the interpretation itself seems inevitable. Performance at this level is rare. These are individuals who can let the work flow through them, an old story finding a disciplined and open vessel that can give it form. Artists move us into the realm of magic. They are more difficult to pin down than virtuosos because their language is metaphor and their greatest gift is to disappear so that audience and work come together as if they were not there.

Virtuosos and artists exist in every culture but many cultures do not create a separation between those who practice art and those who farm or make pots or do a myriad of other things. Artists in those cultures—musicians, dancers, people in the theatre, healers, and shamans—set aside their normal activities in order to be artists for an evening, a week, an hour, and then they return to those normal activities. Balinese, !Kung, Zapotec, and Siberian shamans and healers, even those acknowledged to wield great power, fill many roles in addition to these crucial ones. The Tewa Indians maintain a full calendar of ritual celebrations and everyone in the community participates in one role or another, as performer or as audience, stepping in and out of their ordinary activities. Even European cultures only began recognizing a special status for artists in the late Renaissance. Before then, artists were on the royal household's payroll like anyone else—the master of horse, the cooks, the gardeners. And they created to order, usually an order determined by a "humanist" also on the payroll. That humanist, knowing the tastes of the patron, would pick a theme, suggest the composition of the painting, dictate the colors to be used, and specify how much and which parts had to be drawn and painted by the master artists and which could be finished by apprentices. The humanist would, in the same way, direct musical or theatrical compositions and performances. Whether a particular society grants a special and exclusive status to artists or performers or embeds them in community roles and activities, technical mastery and artistry still apply to their performance.

Interpretation

Technique, discipline, and artistry create the forms within which performers craft their interpretations. What all performing arts share is their interpretive function.[6] All interpretation is a departure from the original yet it is crucial if we are to forge any understanding at all of things that matter. Humans need more than the living out of their days; they need to understand and reflect. Artists help this process of reflection by telling the truth at a slant, to use Emily Dickinson's wonderful phrase. They read the text of humanity and human creation closely and with the eyes of their heart. This is their gift—reflection and interpretation. Theirs are peculiar vocations: this standing apart from the world, yet understanding straight through to the core in ways that bypass words, then molding the interpretation until it is more real than the reality from which it arises, and giving it back. Georgia O'Keeffe, one of the twentieth century's great artists, acknowledged this reality when she said, "Nothing is less real than realism. Details are confusing. It is only by selection, by elimination, by emphasis that we get at the real meaning of things" (Udall 1996). When artists do this well, people say "Ah, yes" and know it for the truth.

All performing arts share this interpretive function. Dancers interpret choreographers, musicians interpret composers, actors interpret dramatists, or, in the case of the commedia dell'arte, actors interpret commonly understood plots and stories adding the spice of political satire. Indigenous dancers and musicians such as the Tewa interpret ritual and tradition passed down from one generation to the next as well as the new choreographies and songs that become part of the repertoire. Healers read the messages of the spirits and their patients' bodies, interpreting one in the context of the other. Interpretation in all these contexts is active, not passive, and is subject to rules of technique and metaphors of style, using those foundations of the genre to weave interpretations that are true to the sense of the work at the same time that they are meaningful to spectators.

In any performance, many interpretations are possible. Indeed, each performance is a unique re-presentation, or, to use Starker's preferred term, a unique re-creation. There are endless arguments over whether or not an interpretation is true to the intent of the creator of the work. That work, whether a musical composition, a piece of choreography, or a theatrical work, has no existence until it is executed or performed. The creator may have intended that it be done in a particular way but few creators are ever so precise in their notation as to allow only one manner of performance. Whether a piece is historical or contemporary makes a difference as well. If historic, the performer has no opportunity to have a dialogue with its creator except by virtue of knowing the whole corpus of work, what the creator may have written about it or the genre in general, and so forth. In a context in which creator and performer are working together as the piece is created, there can be accommodations between the desire of the creator and the ability, style, and desire of the performer. The problem in that case comes then for other performers removed from the process of creation.

Some creators find the ideal executants of their work. One case is that of choreographer Michel Fokine and his dancers Tamara Karsavina and Vaslav Nijinsky. We could add here the partnerships of Alvin Ailey with Judith Jamison and George Balanchine with Suzanne Farrell in dance, and Mozart with Anton Stadler and Brahms with Joseph Joachim in music. In the case of dance where the body, its shape as well as its capabilities and inclinations, has very much to do with potential interpretations, the reliance upon or relationship between choreographer and performer may be more critical. For example, in his early career, Fokine choreographed for Anna Pavlova. She was certainly one of the great dancers of our time but a long-term collaboration did not materialize, in part because of her style of moving. She was truly a classical dancer of the old Marius Petipa school, comfortable in both its technique and its mode of presentation, which featured the dancer rather than the drama of the work. This made her an unlikely prospect for interpreting the fundamentally different style of Fokine, which reversed the importance of dancer and work. This is not to say that dancers other than the ones chosen by the choreographer cannot create valuable interpretations. Here, Ailey and Jamison provide a perfect example. Ailey created one of his most famous pieces, *Cry*, on Jamison. Her long limbs and tall, regal stature—she was six feet tall—appeared to make the piece. Since Jamison has stopped performing, however, other dancers have made *Cry* part of their repertoire, presenting stunning interpretations, quite different but equally satisfying.

It is clear that some work translates well to different times and different bodies while other work does not. Balanchine's choreography and, before him, the choreography of Marius Petipa seem to have survived the exigencies of changed times and styles. The work of Fokine, a choreographer who revolutionized ballet in the first third of this century, is almost never done well, meaning by that, with the original intention of the choreographer. This is the subject of a later chapter, but, briefly, Fokine's choreography has so few steps that contemporary dancers cannot understand it. Fokine is all fluid movement danced across musical phrases, few steps and no stops. It is mood, drama, and movement. Another revolutionary choreographer, Vaslav Nijinsky, also created works that were essentially lost until 1987 when dancer-scholars were able to reconstruct his original notation of one work. In contrast, Balanchine and Petipa are full of steps that dancers recognize and that, because they are part of the technique of the genre, have changed little. While there is some room for freedom, more than Balanchine and Petipa might have liked, there is not very much.

Part of the explanation for the fragility of choreography has to do with the fact that dance notation is not nearly so common as music notation (despite its existence and continued evolution since 1588) and filming is only a recent option. It also has very much to do with the way in which the codified vocabulary of ballet technique shapes what we remember and how we perform. We remember named steps rather than the metaphorical language of phrasing and musicality. Even if we are learning a piece of choreography from someone who is demonstrating it for us, we see it through the steps of the technique we have mastered. Anything that falls outside that technique may well not be seen. It is a curious attribute for such an embodied and kinesthetic genre and so merits an extended discussion in a later chapter.

From time to time, throughout the history of performing arts, scholars, composers, choreographers, and theatre directors have reacted to the powerful role of the performer as the executor and interpreter of their work. At these points, we see the argument being made for the use of mechanical devices—puppets, automatons, and so forth—to replace the human actor, to put the emphasis back onto the work rather than allowing it to be subverted by the will of the performer. Heinrich von Kleist's essay *Über das Marionettentheatre* is one of the classic examples of this kind of argumentation. Let's use puppets, he proposes, so as not to distort the true meaning of the work. Polish stage directors such as Tadeuszc Kantor tried to implement this notion; Kantor mingled puppets and human actors in many of his plays (*The Dead Class* being one of the best illustrations). Bunraku, a Japanese performance tradition, uses life-size puppets manipulated by humans whose presence is tacitly ignored by audiences. The plays tell the same human stories that compose all good Japanese theatre. The movements of some of the puppet characters in Bunraku are echoed in movements of human actors in Kabuki theatre.

Theatre traditions that use nonhuman actors are scattered all around the world, existing alongside human-based theatre. In order to engage the emotions of the audience as human actors do simply by virtue of their humanness, a puppet theatre has to portray a powerful human story or emotion. An excellent example of this would be the Tbilisi Municipal Studio Theatre under the inspired direction of Rezo Gabriadze. While Gabriadze works on an economical scale in terms of sets and costumes, making many of them out of discarded materials, and while he anthropomorphizes magpies and horses, he presents audiences with sweeping human drama. In *The Battle of Stalingrad*, he delivers the epic story of the German siege in miniature and with understatement, letting the love story of two horses stand for the catastrophic tragedy of that city, indeed, of the civil war that has divided Gabriadze's native Georgia for so long. In another of his plays, *Autumn of My Springtime*, the main character is a magpie named Boris, who falls in love over and over again, and steals our hearts. Sometimes the most tragic and dark human emotions can only be tolerated in a form which lets us keep our distance.[7]

Conclusions

The arts of music, dance, and theatre are ones that exist as designs in space and time. They are manifested in performance, interpreted by performers who have mastered the techniques of the genres. Meaning resides both in the intrinsic qualities of form and the extrinsic qualities of content and context. One must speak of meanings, however, rather than meaning. There is the meaning intended by the creator, the meaning interpreted by the performer, and the meaning that results from the interpretive process of the audience. It would be a rare performance, indeed, in which these were consonant. We could propose that meaning is a separate question from aesthetic principles that derive from virtuosity and artistry, with meaning having more to do with content and context, and virtuosity and artistry more to do with form (Royce 1987b). But I would argue that, by virtue of performance, these genres have meaning embedded in the form or technique and, not insignificantly, in the bodies of the performers themselves.

When we begin to examine meaning from the point of view of the audience, we must raise such issues as critical judgment, an aesthetic sense, and the cues and clues of form, content, and context. The latter, although multilayered, is perhaps the easiest to approach. Marcel Marceau has spoken at some length about how he crafts his performances so that meaning can be found by any audience member, however naive, while at the same time offering more subtle meanings for those who are well versed in his art. We shall see how he does this, working with different kinds of symbols and kinesthetic cues, in later chapters, particularly chapter five. In chapter ten, I turn to the question of genre, what defines particular genres, how they are created, and how they are recognized. Briefly, for a new genre to be successful, it must portray itself with enough clarity and consistency of form for audiences to recognize it. I offer a number of examples that allow us to speak about meaning-filled experiences for audiences. Chapter nine takes up the subject of audience as creator and interpreter directly.

How audiences assess performances involves the reception of meaning but also judgments based upon skill and artistry. Again, as any performing artist knows, audiences come with a range of knowledge and experience from the totally naive to the connoisseur. The latter is someone who understands the technique and principles of an art and who also has a comparative basis for making judgments. Critics certainly fall into this category. When we read their reviews and criticism, we can extrapolate the aesthetic principles on the basis of which they assess performance. There will always be a few audience members with this level of knowledge. But what of the remainder? Is there some consensus about what makes a performance adequate, very good, superlative? On what basis does the average audience member assess a performance?

I argue that consensus is more readily and easily reached at the level of technical competence. There is a comfort and ease of performance that comes from mastery of technique that produces a consistently high level of performance. Without that, performances are likely to lack definition, harmony, and focus. Part of classical mime technique requires the performer to outline and accent each movement, slowing it down, enlarging it. Without this limning, all movements become ordinary, flowing into each other, and present a mush that is unrecognizable to an audience. Even if audience members cannot say why this is a poor performance, they recognize that it is inadequate.

It requires more subtle distinctions to differentiate technically masterful performances from truly artistic ones. Western culture has placed such value upon virtuosity (why else do we value winning competitions so highly?) that we may be satisfied with that kind of performance, our senses blunted to the transformative qualities of great performance. In working with Ta Feli, the Isthmus Zapotec healer, and in reading accounts of healing and shamanistic practice around the world, I believe that communities that rely on this kind of intervention recognize the extraordinary ones among the general class of healers. As I argue in chapter eleven, that recognition does not depend on rates of cures but rather on the power that emanates from such persons, power that comes from their absolute belief that they are channels though which the power to heal and to transform flows. Further, they have made themselves into perfect vessels through mastery of rituals, fasting, and years of experience and practice.

Great performance has this same power to move audiences, even ones who are not connoisseurs. Throughout the book I offer some theories about why this is so and how it works as well as provide examples drawn from a range of genres and times. I invite readers to recall those performances that have moved them, touched their hearts, revealed truths that were made transparent through the medium of the performer.

The genesis of this book lies, in part, with great performances of artists, past and present, scattered across cultures and genres, whose lives have touched mine. Their lives, their performances, their words have provoked and sustained me, have been the cause for tears and laughter, and have transported me out of myself and into those realms of the heart's imagining. Long-ago commedia dell'arte performers came alive in the pages of dusty and bare-bones scripts, in letters—sometimes witty, sometimes heartbreaking—from players to royal patrons, in the account books of theatres who employed them. Almost forty years of seeing Marceau in performance helped me understand what artistry and consistency mean for all those thousands of people who have seen him. Watching Starker teach, listening to him play, talking with him about interpretation pushed me to the point of trying to capture all that thought, craft, and genius for others who have not had the privilege. My own career in classical ballet and following the performances of those great dancers who submit to the daily discipline of class no matter who they are is part of this narrative. Finally, my thirty-five years of working with the Isthmus Zapotec as an ethnographer whose goal is the crafting of their story, making it my own, and letting it take form through me has contributed to the understandings that are the core of this book. Its genesis does not have the economy of great performances but it does share the discipline, passion, and daily commitment.

Notes

1. More often than not, performances are combinations of genres, or "orchestrations of media," as Victor Turner expressed (1987:23). One example from the Western classical realm is grand opera. The equivalent in the East might be Kabuki or Noh drama. For many non-Western cultures, the melding of genres inheres in the language itself. The Zapotec *saa* can be glossed as music, fiesta, and dance. Adrienne Kaeppler describes the collection of actions and genres recognized by Tongans as one category known as "taking the long way around." This collection includes sung poetry, the kava-making ceremony, and the ritual presentation of pigs. Many of the genres I describe in chapter ten that result from collaborations are multimedia as well. In all these cases, however, the respective arts maintain their individual techniques at the level of form. That is, dance continues to be bound by its technique, music by its technical rules, and so forth. The overall presentation may follow its own rules for presentation and the content may be more than the sum of the individual parts. This is an important point because much of the discussion about virtuosity and artistry that follows examines the form of the different genres, rather than meaning, context, or function.

2. These hallmarks of art—elaboration, play, goal-free nature—are characteristics of the form, that is, the rules or technique of the particular genre. Technique is composed initially of arbitrary choices—turn-out in classical ballet, for example—which then become the nonnegotiable basis for all that follows. The arts do play a role in the societies in which they are embedded and, in serving this purpose, are no longer goal-free. What purposes they serve has been debated rather consistently for a long time. The conflicting positions perhaps have been best summarized by Bertolt Brecht, who said that art is not a mirror held up to

reality but a hammer with which to shape it. The important point for our purpose here is to make the distinction between examinations of form and examinations concerned with purpose or use.

3. I concentrate here upon the work of Victor Turner but want to acknowledge other scholars who have worked in closely related areas. Richard Schechner was especially interested in the connection between theatrical and anthropological views about drama (1985). The whole ethnography of speaking focus, which looked at the performative aspect of language rather than the codification of its structure, the *parole* rather than the *langue*, supports the examination of performance in all its manifestations (Abrahams 1983; Bauman 1984; Bauman and Scherzer 1989; Scherzer 1990). The work on play of Don Handelman (1990) and Helen Schwartzman (1978) opens up that ludic and improvised dimension of human activity.

4. These represent only a small number of the scholars of the anthropology of dance and of human movement. To fully appreciate how the field came into being and the powerful insights of which it is capable, one must know the work of such scholars as Katherine Dunham, Judith Lynne Hanna, Adrienne Kaeppler, Joann Kealihinohomoku, Gertrude Kurath, Drid Williams, and Judy Van Zile.

5. *Style* has almost as many meanings as *art* or *aesthetics*. I use it in two ways throughout this book. The simpler sense refers to the defining features of a school or era, so that one might refer to a Ballets Russes style or a Balanchine style. The more complicated sense refers to what a performer (or composer or choreographer) creates out of a number of possibilities. In all genres, technique is one constraining factor, but in the embodied genres the body itself poses limitations simply by virtue of its appearance and its capabilities or inclinations. Voice works within similar bounds. Instrumentalists do not share precisely these constraints; rather, they have to work with the distinctive sound of their particular instrument. Acknowledging then that style is a factor in performance, we observe that some performers call attention to themselves through their style while others privilege the style of the work they are interpreting—John Wayne as opposed to Sir John Gielgud.

6. I would argue that anthropology is, at its heart, interpretive. We spend months and years, sometimes lifetimes, living and working within a society, and our job is to let its stories flow through us. We stand in the middle, between a culture as a continually changing work and other cultures. Sometimes our words help the process of self-awareness and reflection. Like performers, we also proceed from a base of discipline and craft; like performers, our interpretations are neither passive nor mechanical.

7. Clearly, in the case of Gabriadze's theatre, it is he who retains both the creative and interpretive upper hand. It is interesting not only that he chooses pup-

pets as the conveyors of his message but also that he chooses animals and birds to portray very human qualities. His theatre stands in contrast to more traditional puppet theatres such as Bunraku or the *wayang golek* theatre of Indonesia, both in its secular performative mode and in its commentary on contemporary or recent events. Bunraku and especially *wayang golek* have complex rituals associated with their performance, plays that are centuries old, and, in the case of *wayang golek*, puppets who are alive and puppet masters or *dalang* who are mediators between the gods and human beings. Puppet master Tizar Purbaya defined the essence of *wayang golek* in this way: "The *wayang* puppet is not a doll. It follows the *dalang*, but the *dalang* must also follow it. He gives it soul and it, in return, gives life to him" (Herbert 2002:43).

CHAPTER TWO
VIRTUOSITY: THE MASQUE OF NONCHALANCE

Virtuosity is a concept that, like many others, has meanings for the scholarly and creative communities but that also has become the province of the general public. In both public and restricted communities, virtuosity stirs passions and controversies. Understanding it matters because all performing arts recognize techniques and standards that define their particular genre. The mastery of those techniques results, for some performers, in virtuosity. That level of performance is a necessary step toward artistry, another kind of mastery altogether, which even fewer performers attain. We might perhaps compare violinist Nicolò Paganini, without doubt a great virtuoso, with Jascha Heifetz, both a virtuoso and a great artist. We can see equivalent pairs in the world of classical ballet: Fernando Bujones, an impeccable technician and virtuoso, and Mikhail Baryhsnikov, both a technical wizard and an artist of the first rank. I begin this chapter by exploring what I believe are formal qualities of anything we call virtuosic, because you cannot have any art—performing, visual, or literary—without the mastery of technique, which is a requirement for virtuosity.

Virtuosity has a long and varied history as a term connoting a particular kind of mastery. It has variously been seen as a positive attribute and as a negative; in its latter mode, it implies a kind of misplaced pride or an indication of settling for the obvious rather than the more subtle. A remarkable panel discussion on the topic of virtuosity and interpretation took place at Indiana University during Arts Week, 2002. Members of the panel included ballerina Violette Verdy, cellist Janos Starker, and conductor Imre Pallo. As one might imagine from that list, the conversation ranged widely. We began with notions about what virtuosity is. All agreed that virtuosity is bad when it is an end in itself and that it is good and necessary when it is a foundation for serving the art. Imre Pallo mused about whether virtuosity is good or bad and concluded, "Virtuosity is something good if it's serving something good. . . . Where did the description 'virtuoso' get the bad rap? From the people who don't play their instruments well enough. They are envious of the true artists who are virtuosos as well as masters—because a virtuoso is the utmost master of his or her instrument. In conducting, you rely on the virtuosity of the players in the orchestra. . . . I am a better conductor when I let those musicians put their virtuosity in the service of their orchestra as well as in their performing." Verdy added something that expanded the discussion and called attention to yet another dimension. Speaking of ballet, she said, "They [dancers] can push something to the maximum, even a little beyond what has been seen or heard before. But always at the service of the work. The dancers know they fit in a great body of work, and they grow bigger because of the work, but they remain discreet insofar as presenting themselves." Verdy—indeed, all the panelists—understands that drive to make oneself the best possible instrument for one's art. Verdy summarized the implications neatly by noting that "virtuosity is the direct natural result of a drive for perfection."

Drive and going beyond what anyone has done before are characteristics shared by many artists whose names are synonymous with virtuosity. Starker has called some kinds of "going beyond" mechanical feats. If going beyond is informed by taste, a presence of moderation as Violette Verdy put it, then the art is advanced. Among instrumentalists, violinists and pianists are the ones whose names are linked so often with the term virtuosity. Niccolò Paganini (1782–1840) forever changed the nature of violin playing and captured the superstar status previously held only by singers. Harold Schonberg succinctly characterizes Paganini's contributions: "Part of his success was an order of technique previously unimagined and hard to imagine even today. There was absolutely no precedent for the effects he introduced—the left-hand and right-hand pizzicato, the double-stop harmonics, the multiple stops, the ricochet bowing, the unheard-of extensions and rapidity of shifting, the fingered octaves, a new use of the glissando, the octave trills, the solos on a single string, the new kinds of bowings" (1988:105). Schonberg also tells us that Paganini frequently used a *scordatura*[1] tuning to give brilliance and to allow the playing of passages impossible in their original scoring. (Mozart and Kodaly, among others, used *scordatura* tuning.) So successful a showman was

Paganini that stories abounded about his having made a pact with the Devil in return for his phenomenal ability. Whether or not we should attribute artistry to what he did is another matter, one to which we return later in the chapter.

Approaches to Virtuosity

I would like to suggest several ways of approaching virtuosity, which may lead us to a more formal and neutral usage that will allow us to look for commonalities in the performing arts. Most importantly, I would like to examine virtuosity as a necessary part of any aesthetic system, neither more nor less. The aesthetic of dance, and the performing arts in general, is composed of two parts: virtuosity and artistry. These stand in the same relation to each other as do the two components of the formal aspect of dance (and other arts): technique and style.

Webster's Third New International Dictionary, tenth edition, offers the following definitions of virtuosity: "great technical skill in the practice of the fine arts . . . technical brilliance . . . without accompanying artistic insight." The second definition clearly finds virtuosity lacking.

Paul Valéry, in his work on aesthetics, offers an extended and balanced examination of virtuosity. Virtuosity, he writes, is a debatable issue (1964:192). A work of art, and Valéry seems to be speaking of those arts that need performance, is "a check drawn against the talent of a potential performer" (p. 194) and therefore at the mercy of its interpreter. "The case of virtuosity revolves around the essential problem of art, which is the problem of execution, for the virtuoso is by definition an executant of unusual abilities, who may now and then, intoxicated by an exaggerated sense of his technical powers, allow himself to abuse them" (p. 193). Because he admits that works of arts are susceptible to a number of equally valid interpretations, Valéry would argue that there can be any number of equally virtuosic performances or realizations.

Let us examine that set of assumptions. Yes, works of art—performing arts—may engender many quite different interpretations; no one performance is the same as another, not even with the same performer, far less so with different performers. But are these performances different *and* equally virtuosic? The question is whether or not there is variation in virtuosity, or does the fundamental requirement of technical brilliance mean that there can be only one virtuoso performance of a given piece or genre? We have not posed an absolute upper level of accomplishment for a performance to be described as virtuosic, so there could be variation that has to do with levels of mastery. But can there be variations of form apart from that or does that not contradict the very notion of virtuosity as *technical* brilliance? Valéry would say yes, given that the text or score is only a system of conventional signs that, by its nature, must remain unnuanced. We must, at some point, take the measure of virtuosity. I suggest that virtuosity stands at midpoint between technical competence and artistry. Further, I argue that certain components of virtuosity include extra-technical elements, which by their nature are susceptible to different performance. We shall return to this point.

The thoughts of Baldassare Castiglione in his book *The Courtier*, specifically what he wrote about *sprezzatura*, provide a different way of thinking about virtuosity and art in general. *Sprezzatura*[2]—perhaps better, *disinvoltura*—means a kind of nonchalance that characterizes one's behavior and attitude. Castiglione continues then to speak of art, saying that we may call art "true art which does not seem to be art; nor must one be more careful of anything than of concealing it, because if it is discovered, this robs a man of all credit and causes him to be held in slight esteem. . . . Art, or any intense effort, if it is disclosed, deprives everything of grace" (1959:43–44). In order to have this kind of nonchalance, or true art as Castiglione would have it, one must have so mastered the technique of the artistic genre that one does it effortlessly, indeed, artlessly. And is not that kind of mastery virtuosity?

Mikhail Baryshnikov, a dancer whom all would call both a virtuoso and an artist, articulated what Castiglione meant by *sprezzatura* in a conversation about the kind of double vision he has on stage. "Maybe I take it too personally, but that sort of double vision happens to me all the time on stage. One part of me is dancing, the other observing from the side. This control protects you from an overdone, vulgar presentation. You constantly keep yourself under fire, as it were; you watch, with an ironic eye, as if saying: 'Well, well, so you can do it, but don't show it too much!' Nabokov rarely displays his technique, but his prose is masterful. That's the way it should be—be a master but don't show your mastery" (Smakov 1981:125).

Simplicity, understatement, the culling of what is the heart of the performance or interpretation, and the discarding of the nonessentials—all these seem to be part of virtuosity. The last is illustrated by a particularly telling statement by Eugène Delacroix in his *Journals*. "I didn't begin to do anything passable on my trip to Africa until the moment I had sufficiently forgotten small details and so remembered the striking and poetic side of things. . . . Up to that point, I was pursued by a love of exactitude which the majority of people mistake for truth" (1995).

Let me now summarize the several ways of thinking about virtuosity that take us beyond *Webster's* "technical mastery":

1. Virtuosity as that component of a paradigm for aesthetics that focuses on technique rather than style and that is a necessary step toward artistry
2. Virtuosity as the mastery of certain extra-technical elements common across genres (dynamic variation, agogic or rubato phrasing, sustaining of a phrase, and economy)
3. Virtuosity as the manner or level of execution of a particular technique that defines a genre
4. Virtuosity as an attitude—nonchalant, self-critical, limiting

An Aesthetic Paradigm

The first of these four ways of thinking about virtuosity is the entryway to speaking about aesthetics in general and, in particular, to the position of virtuosity within any aesthetic system. The relationships between key elements become more clear in the context of the following paradigm:

Virtuosity [Nonchalance]	Artistry [Transparency]
technical mastery	inevitability
technique	style

Qualities of technique and style:

Technique	Style
codified vocabulary	metaphorical vocabulary
conservative	innovative

Before going further, I would like to propose some working definitions of the terms of the paradigm.

Technique (for dance and movement) is the set of movements, gestures, and steps that is the foundation of the genre; the accompanying vocabulary that names these steps; and rules for combining steps. Technique is the grammar of dance and codified movement.

Style (for dance and movement) is the individual choices about movement and interpretation; the embroidery on the basic technique. Important style elements include impulse, phrasing, variation, density, centeredness, simplicity, and transparency. There is no codified vocabulary for talking about style; stylistic considerations are couched in metaphorical terms. Style should be further viewed in terms of an individual performer's style (choices and practices that make the performer immediately recognizable) and a style that purports to characterize the intentions of the creator (choreographer and composer).

Virtuosity is great technical skill; mastery of the technique of a genre; incorporation of such extra-technical elements as dynamic variation, agogic or rubato phrasing, sustaining of a phrase (subsumed under the heading of musicality), and economy.

Artistry comes from the foundation of a certain level of virtuosity—technical mastery—and involves an interpretation (based on the elements of style) that is so harmonious with the genre and with the piece that it seems inevitable. The highest level of artistry achieves a transparency in performance such that the audience and the piece come together as if the performer were not there.

Continuing with the relationships outlined in the paradigm, is virtuosity necessary as a foundation for artistry? If artistry is an enduring quality rather than an effect and if artistry characterizes the career of a performer rather than an occasional performance, then virtuosity, in the sense of technical mastery, is necessary. Violette Verdy, one of the great ballerinas of our time, sees virtuosity as a tool we use to reach the beyond and, as such, it must be as crafted and polished as we can make it. The beyond, for her, is a deep place of universal recognition.

When artists are able to summon the beyond, it creates a sense of awakening that lasts past the moment. Technique, as performers refine and master it on a daily basis, is a guarantee of order and simplicity. Daily practice is a submission to a particular kind of order, which calms emotions and quiets passions. It does not eliminate emotion, passion, or thought; it converts them, distills them, substitutes the intentional commitment of the ego for the chatter of the unmanaged ego. To use a distinction made by poet Yosef Koumenyaku, craft makes passion possible rather than the sentimentality that results from untutored emotion. Or, as Marcel Marceau once said to me, "feeling without technique is worth nothing."

Mastery of Extra-Technical Elements

Let us shift now to the second way of thinking about virtuosity. This approach isolates elements whose possession moves a performer from the level of technical mastery to virtuosity. The first three elements—dynamic variation, agogic or rubato phrasing, the sustaining of a phrase—can be glossed under the heading "musicality." The fourth, economy, with its related elements of stillness and silence, is that quality of simplicity, unclutteredness, the opposite of overdone vulgarity about which many writers speak in their discussions of virtuosity. I would argue that all of these elements are extra-technical. I have suggested that the realm of technique is described by a codified vocabulary relevant to particular genres. In classical ballet, this vocabulary consists of the names of the steps (*pas*) and the rules for combining them. In contrast, discussions of musicality and economy are couched in metaphorical language or, in the case of dance, demonstrated rather than spoken.

In the case of the general population, it may be that, while virtuosity and artistry are sensed and recognized, there is little articulate naming of them. This is similar to the case of a language of which one may be a fluent speaker: that person may recognize the highest levels of competence but be unable to articulate its rules and elements. The metalanguage that would allow this tends to be the province of specialists. My experience in teaching about performance lets me say with some certainty that the nonspecialist can often recognize differences, not only in virtuosity but also between virtuosic and artistic performance, and articulate those differences in metaphorical terms.

Musicality

Musicality—dynamic variation, rubato and agogic, the sustaining of a phrase—is crucial in examining performances that we might call virtuosic. Two remarkable dance critics have written about musicality: Edwin

Denby and Arlene Croce. Edwin Denby describes a conversation he had with Roger Pryor Dodge in which Dodge describes a men's ballet class he saw taught by Pierre Vladimiroff (most likely at Balanchine's School of American Ballet in New York City). The dancers, he noticed, among whom were some of the finest in the country, "executed the steps and leaps in a sort of one-two-one-two military rhythm. . . . Their action was rapid, vigorous, and fairly neat, but the effect was colorless and undistinguished. But when Vladimiroff himself performed the same sequence, Mr. Dodge could see very clearly a variety of emphasis in the movement" (1986:505). Denby continues, "The dance phrase is formed by variation in speed and variation in stress. Its total length is determined by the length of the musical phrase, its total dynamic range, by the nature of the steps and leaps that are used, by the amplitude that is given them in this particular musical setting. And from these different elements the visual reality of a dance phrase emerges; and, in the course of a piece, the special dramatic characterization of a dance role" (p. 506).

Denby elaborates his thoughts about musicality, using Alexandra Danilova and Alicia Markova as examples. Both, he claims, could give an otherwise homogeneous dance phrase a beginning, a climax, and an end. "The quickening or retarding of motion allows some moments . . . to be seen more sharply than others . . . and these stressed moments become the central images around which the observer's mind groups the rest of the motion" (1986:506). Those images help a long movement passage make emotional sense.

Croce speaks to the same matter in a review of American Ballet Theatre's production of Balanchine's *Symphonie Concertantes*, specifically the performances by Cynthia Gregory and Martine van Hamel. "Gregory . . . with her complacent skill and van Hamel . . . with her gracious imperturbability are as one in their defeat of any technical challenge their roles may offer. They've cracked the code stepwise, and they have more than enough stamina, but the steps aren't very hard. Phrasing and attack matter more. Gregory's sense of these things was especially inert; van Hamel's more sharply defined musicality saved her. It's an odd sight: here are two of the most robust and accomplished technicians in American ballet, and they're unable to cut through the surface of their roles" (1987:85). Phrasing in dance leads to both dynamic and durational variation due to the physics of the body in motion. Limitations on duration deriving from the capacities of the human body can be, and are, stretched by playing with illusion. Such variation, dynamic and durational, has dramatic content. Denby writes explicitly of the function of phrasing, attributing to it the dramatic characterization of the dance role. Croce suggests the same implicitly by saying that, without it, Gregory and van Hamel remained on the surface of their roles. Violette Verdy maintains that emotion, longing, and passion lie in phrasing.

Not all movements in dance are equally important. Pieces performed, as it were, in a monotone, are intrinsically boring. Audiences need to have peaks of energy framed by moments of relative quiet; great dancers not only do this, they know how to call attention to it to increase the audience's anticipation. When Baryshnikov, for example, explodes in *grande jetés* (big leaps), the *pas de bourrée couru* (quick, little running steps), which is the preparation, is small and a time for the ingathering of energy and breath. It is like a cat bunching its muscles for a leap. The subsequent *grande jeté* appears to burst from nowhere. Baryshnikov goes even further by extending his legs and arms and lifting his head at the very top of the leap, thus giving the illusion of suspension. Olympic champion diver Greg Louganis did similar things to make his dives appear slower, his mastery (based quite concretely on certain technical efforts) hidden behind the masque of nonchalance.

Dancers who are known for their musicality, and by this I mean dancers whose phrasing is elastic but not self-indulgent and whose phrasing makes sense within the context of the whole choreography not just dance phrase by dance phrase, feel the beat between the beats. In dance terms, in music, and in the mime of Marcel Marceau, we most commonly refer to this as impulse. It always marks an ongoing, continuous phrase but it also is the anticipatory beginning to actual movement.

In music, the phrasings that play with time are called rubato and agogic. They are a kind of elastic fluctuation applied to tempo such that time is stolen from certain notes and is made up on others in the same phrase. A good example of this usage is documented in Allan Kozinn's review in the *New York Times* (March 22, 1998) of Yo-Yo Ma's *Inspired by Bach*, a set of video recordings and CDs: "He uses rubato to draw melody lines and accompaniments from figures that look metronomically square on the page."

Janos Starker, one of the great cellists of all time, a virtuoso and an artist, defines rubato and agogic as essential to any musical performance.

He also emphasizes that you cannot change the written value of the notes. Such choices of phrasings, he would argue, must be based on melodic or harmonic reasons having to do with the sense of the whole piece. Done well, the use of agogic and rubato adds to the dramatic intensity as well as contributes to what Starker has called the inevitability of the interpretation.

Rubato and agogic produce variations of duration rather than of dynamic level. In ballet technique, however, there is a curious way in which playing with time has a visible dynamic aspect to it. I use an example from class, specifically barre work, because it is clearer to more people. In *grandes battements* (rapidly raising one's leg up high and then down while keeping a straight working leg), the upward lifting of the leg is done faster; it begins, in fact, on the "and." Lowering the leg then has more time left in the musical phrase. Doing the movement this way emphasizes the raising of the leg, which is the more important element. The same is true of *rond de jambe en l'aire à la seconde* (circle of the leg to the side). The working leg is raised forty-five degrees to the side. In the *rond de jambe* (circle of the leg), the leg is brought into the supporting knee faster than it is then extended back out to the side. The effect is to nicely delineate a movement that has thickness about it, at the same time avoiding a metronomic quality.

In Japanese dance, the equivalent of rubato lies in the concept of *ma*, which, simply put, is the time–space between movements or poses. As Masakatsu Gunji defines it, *ma* "is a rubato tempo by means of which a dancer is not ruled by the music but uses the music to give his dance greater expressiveness" (1970:73). Other writers, specifically Kabuki actor Danjuro IX (1838–1903), consider certain ways in which *ma* is used that fall into the realm of artistry rather than that of technique: "There is *ma* that can be taught and *ma* that cannot be taught" (Gunji 1970:72–73). He goes on to argue that rhythm can be taught but "extent" or *hodo* (degree) cannot. No matter how expert a dancer's rhythms might be, he says, true artistic dance does not happen without *hodo*, or the expressive sense of degree.

For the audience, duration and dynamic level may produce the same effect. The potential effects of duration may be multiplied in string playing and voice. There is a role for dynamic variation and voice. The following examples illustrate this usage. One is in Verdi's *Rigoletto*, in which

Rigoletto shifts from full voice to light voice as he pleads with the courtiers for information about his daughter. The second comes from *bel canto,* in which a singer varies the dynamic of a single note while everything else remains constant. The extreme of dynamic variation in string playing is negative sound created by lifting off the weight of the bow on the string. Again, in all of these examples, the effect increases the dramatic character of the piece.

Economy

Economy is the last of these extra-technical elements. Virtuosity does not mean more (although addition, rather than subtraction, is one of the attributes of virtuosity for its own sake). Virtuosity involves taste, judgment, selection, discrimination. It is knowledge reduced to simplicity and you have to have known all the possibilities in order to discard them (Verdy, personal communication). Marcel Marceau speaks about simplicity in mime in similar terms: "For me to have simplicity is difficult because it means I have to throw away what is *bavard*, what is *inutile,* and go to the essence, the *essentiel*" (Royce 1984:105). Another mime, actor, and director, Jean-Louis Barrault, echoes the importance of economy: "The classic teaches *economy*. It makes use of the minimum of means for the maximum yield, and this is because it lives in depth. Economy is after all less a matter of taste than of concentratedness" (Barrault 1951:169). Economy means eliminating confusion and clutter; it does not mean eliminating elaboration, which is a key feature of art. Elaboration itself is restrained by the rules of the particular art form. Confusion and muddiness reign when rules are forgotten or abandoned or never learned. In fact, there is a relationship between increasing emotion and increased control as evidenced in technique. The Polish *metteur-en-scène* Jerszy Grotowski speaks forcefully to this: "The more we become absorbed in what is hidden inside us, in the excess, in the exposure, in the self-penetration, the more rigid must be the external discipline; that is to say, the form, the artificiality, the ideogram, the sign" (Royce 1984:28).

The use of silence and stillness follows naturally the discussion of economy and elaboration (see chapter eight for a more complete discussion). First, silence is not simply the absence of sound, nor stillness the absence of movement, when performed by an artist. Silence and stillness are filled with all the possibilities of sound and movement. They have a texture. Marcel Marceau was eloquent on this subject in a conversation about breathing, or what I have called impulse. "Breathing carries energy, carries the silence and makes the silence musical. Breathing is like a light you switch on. It's a force, an energy force. The energy comes from our breathing; the movement alone doesn't give light. The average dancer just does movement; the average mime just does movement or attitude . . . without the artistic breathing, the lyrical appeal is gone. It's like a symphony without a space between movements. All the other music is paced between silence and sound" (Royce 1984:78). Marceau has referred to this interior, artistic breathing as *énergie intérieure.* The "light" calls attention to movement that occurs in almost a staccato way, which he calls *acuité métallique.*

In dance, the *énergie intérieure* is always there, even in what, to the audience, seem like static poses. Some choreographies and some dance genres use stillness more frequently and perhaps more intentionally than others. Dramatic choreographers like Antony Tudor or Kenneth MacMillan, the latter especially in *Romeo and Juliet*, use stillness to heighten emotions. The *farruca*, a solo dance for men that originated in Andalusia, creates intensity by long stretches of stillness broken by outbursts of movement, often *zapateados*. When you watch an artist such as Antonio Gades, you see the contrast, the density, and the breathing quite clearly—it is, in fact, a good example of Marceau's *acuité métallique*, "switching on the light."

Another virtuosic use of stillness is at the heart of the performances of Sankai Juku, one of the most classical of Japan's Butoh companies. Butoh is a postwar phenomenon representing a break both with Japanese classical dance and theatre—Kabuki and Noh—as well as with Western classical forms. Sankai Juku presents dance in its most existential form, refined and pure, elemental in its absolute economy of movement, indeed of sound. It presents a kind of theatre of Zen, full of paradoxes—sound-filled silence, vibrating stillness, illuminated shadows. In 1990, the company performed *Unetsu* (The Egg Stands out of Curiosity) at the Indiana University auditorium. The stage was a model of simplicity—a pool of water, hanging gongs, a low platform with an egg standing on end, vertical streams of sand and water on either side of the pool. The dancers were equally stark—shaved heads, powdered white heads and bodies, draped white cloths, the red of fingertips the only color. The music was minimal—gongs, conch shells, the sound of falling sand and water. The opening saw Amagatsu, the central dancer and director, crouched at the edge of the pool downstage center, his back to the audience, the stage dark except for the one spot on him and the brilliant blue of the backdrop. The sound was the sound of breathing. With each breath, Amagatsu seemed to unfold until he was standing utterly still yet filled with a sense of contained movement. He slowly raised one foot, heel forward, and stepped into the pool. The ripple reflection of the water was thrown onto the blue backdrop.

At another point in the ninety-minute drama, a spot came up revealing Amagatsu on his knees and elbows on the platform, hands hovering over the then illuminated egg. He is motionless; then his red-tipped fingers begin to move, weaving like sea anemones, holding the audience utterly spellbound.

A related phenomenon from Kabuki is the *mie*. *Mie* are those points at which the actor freezes in a highly stylized pose, holding it for as long as ten or twelve seconds in order to heighten the emotion. Many of the woodcut images we have of Kabuki actors portray them in one or another of the *mie*, simply because they are so dramatic. Breath, tension, the potential for impulse, whatever you might call it, characterizes not only art but also, I would argue, the natural world. There are no full stops in nature; no hard lines, no impenetrable boundaries. Rather, we see flow, points of heightened activity, moments of quiet, shading. Humans somehow have a need to impose clear beginnings and endings, making boundaries to contain fluid entities. We pin butterflies to paper in order to understand them, we say, when the only thing worth understanding about butterflies is their amazing flow between stillness and flight. We analyze but never restore the original. In art, the flow is everything and artists are those who give us back the breath that is life.

The mastery and creative use of dynamic variation; agogic or rubato; the sustaining of a phrase; and economy, stillness and silence, to enhance performance is what moves a performer from technical mastery to virtuosity. That these elements occur in such widely ranging forms—classical ballet, Kabuki, mime, classical music, shamanistic performance—seems to argue for common characteristics of virtuosity. As we see in the discussion of Tewa ritual in chapter six, the Tewa also implicitly recognize and use these embellishments of technique in their song and dance.

CHAPTER TWO

Virtuosity: Definition of Genre

Let us turn now to the question of technical execution. The manner in which one executes the technique that defines a genre reaches the level of virtuosity in some performers, and it may be that this masterful execution is what audiences recognize as virtuosity. Genres are defined and distinguished from each other by specific techniques.[3] These techniques are characterized by a codified vocabulary that is the basis for teaching, evaluating, and maintaining the genre. It is this codification that makes technique so resistant to innovation and that, in turn, makes it so immediately identifiable.

Despite the introduction of video recordings and the increased use of dance notation, dance is usually taught by imitation. This is as true of classical ballet as it is of Balinese dance. Dance students watch and reproduce movement, and are often corrected by the teacher pushing and pulling their bodies into correct positions. They repeat steps and combinations daily until the best have mastered the technique. Dancers devote all their time to technique in the first six to ten years of training. They master it until it is so embedded in their bodies that they do not think about it. Not all, of course, reach this level of comfort. Whether a dancer achieves mastery or not depends on many things—body, physical coordination, musicality, and intelligence. Those who go beyond this stage to artistry are even more rare.

The embodied knowledge achieved by dancers is reinforced by the codified, formal vocabulary that allows it to be taught in a consistent manner. (Not all dance forms teach their technique by means of such a vocabulary. *Nihon Buyo*, Japanese classical dance, for example, does not. Neither does Kabuki, which teaches its art by having students learn complete roles.) Even those elements I call extra-technical, which do not constitute part of the codified technical vocabulary, are learned by imitation and correction. Indeed, I would suggest that it is precisely in those elements that we distinguish between virtuosities. One example illustrates what I am talking about: the famous dance competition between Baryshnikov and Gregory Hines in the film *White Nights*. Both dancers, in their real lives, are virtuosos: more than that, both are artists. And Baryshnikov, more than any other classically trained dancer of this century, moves with fluency in other dance genres. Nonetheless, there is a difference in the virtuosity of execution between Baryshnikov and Hines in this passage with Hines clearly the tap virtuoso. Why does Baryshnikov not convince us as a tap dancer? The answer lies in his basic body involvement and attitude, the weight and looseness, the attack.

To elaborate for a moment on the difference, I want to recall a discussion in Constance Hill's great book *Brotherhood in Rhythm*, the story of Harold and Fayard Nicholas, in which she describes a home movie in which the Nicholas brothers and Fred Astaire break into an impromptu tap dance on the RKO lot in 1934. All three dancers have been described as "classical," usually referring to formality, elegance, ease, and the use of the whole body. Hill comments: "There is a sense of pull-up in Astaire's torso as he dances. . . . While the brothers dance the time steps in vertical alignment, their arms swing more naturally than Astaire's and follow the momentum of the movement which is motivated by the foot rhythms. . . . This film confirms Astaire's smooth elegance and demonstrates the dominance of form over rhythm in his dance style. It confirms what class-act dancer Honi Coles once said of Astaire, that he was not a tap dancer so much as a dancer who used tap steps. While Fayard and Harold were less than smooth, and considerably more angular in form than Astaire was, they integrated the tap rhythm into their bodies. And this rhythm, in turn, determined the form of the movement" (2000:199). The same difference is what distinguishes Baryshnikov from Hines.

What Hill describes and Honi Coles names is the difference between a virtuoso trained in the technique and extra-technical elements of a dance genre and a great dancer of another tradition adapting to a different genre. Baryshnikov, in this case, is Fred Astaire to Hines' Nicholas brothers.

Virtuosity as Nonchalance

Mastery of technique such that performance is effortless is something that audiences recognize even if they are unable to articulate it. Delacroix was speaking of something quite similar when he spoke of having to forget the small details in order to render a more poetic and striking picture. Dancers concerned with technique at a conscious level have not yet reached mastery or that order and simplicity that comes with refinement of technique.

In this last way of speaking about virtuosity, the essential ingredient is nonchalance. The performance must appear effortless, full of intensity and empty of tension. Even though audiences know that they are seeing performance beyond anything they could imagine doing, they still feel that sense of ease that the true virtuoso strives to convey. When the performer achieves the highest level of artistry, this nonchalance becomes transparency.

The performer goes beyond craft to present an interpretation that has a sense of inevitability and, in that presentation, becomes transparent so that the audience and the work come together without the intrusive presence of the performer–intermediary.

This acknowledges the special nature of performance, which is both ephemeral and intimate. It requires space and quietness in which the audience can imagine its own dream. It requires great delicacy on the part of performers who mediate between the intrinsic qualities of form and the extrinsic features of context.

This is what Baryshnikov was talking about when he used the term "double vision," that is, his awareness of one part of himself being a censor that keeps him from calling attention to himself or the difficulty of what he does. It is especially challenging to achieve transparency in dance because it is an embodied art that can have no existence apart from the body of the performer. In classical ballet, it is often in the context of the great partnerships that one sees this kind of transparency—Tamara Karsavina and Vaslav Nijinsky, Alicia Alonso and Igor Youskevitch, Alicia Markova and Anton Dolin, Gelsey Kirkland and Baryshnikov. Indeed, it is interesting to speculate about why this should be. Perhaps it is the partners losing themselves in each other that makes them, as a couple, transparent.

This is a kind of virtuosity that not all performers achieve or even desire. Some call attention to themselves or to the difficulty of what they do—the opposite of *sprezzatura* as used by Castiglione. Their performances become more like those of genres in which the point is to show all the tension and difficulty. The circus is one example where part of the thrill is not knowing whether or not the trapeze artist will fall or the animal tamer will be attacked. Or we might use the examples of gymnastics and figure skating as competitive sports. There, too, the point is to have the audience perceive the difficulty, hence the accomplishment. In those sports, the composition of routines into moves ranked by difficulty illustrates the emphasis on impressing an audience with how hard something is rather than carrying an audience away in its own dream uncontaminated by the "presence" of the performer. André Levinson, a critic and writer at the beginning of the twentieth century, covered every kind of dance, film, and theatre, including music hall attractions. What he said about the latter supports the notion that some genres have a goal of creating tension in the audience. Levinson, in his book *La Danse d'aujourd'hui*, comments, "Intensity, it seems, is one of the fundamental ideas of music hall attractions. Betting against the odds, daring beyond measure, going overboard . . . this is what crowns a good act. The act unfolds in a crescendo up to the final paroxysm. . . . The orchestra falls silent, and it is to a drum roll—just as at an execution—that, at the top of the pole or the bend in the loop, the final wonders are produced. When the acrobat waves . . . , the spectator claps, delighted to be relieved of this delicious but almost painful anxiety" (Acocella and Garofala, 1991: caption of plate following p. 86).

Creating the place and the time for dreaming: this is the reason for the existence of dance and music, indeed, all art. Free of goals other than to elaborate, to imagine, to weave poetic dreams based on mastery of a prose technique—then, and only then, can art move its audience to suspend time and place and share in a special vision of the world.

Notes

1. *Scordatura* refers to an abnormal tuning of a stringed instrument to facilitate difficult passages, unusual chords, and different tone color (Randel 1978:454).

2. *Sprezzatura* is not used today in Italy to mean either "nonchalance" or "virtuosity." Two terms have replaced it: *virtuosità* and *virtuosismo.*

3. Jeffrey Kallberg explores the fluid and fuzzy state of genres in his 1996 book, *Chopin at the Boundaries: Sex, History, and Musical Genre.* He takes the topic up most specifically in chapter one, "The Rhetoric of Genre: Chopin's Nocturne in G Minor," where he outlines what we have imagined to be the characteristics that define *nocturne* and then examines how few of those characteristics are apparent in this piece by Chopin. It raises the very interesting questions of how genres are defined and by whom and how it is that we all agree upon something that appears to each individual as a different entity.

CHAPTER THREE

TECHNIQUE AND STYLE, CONSERVATISM AND CHANGE: MICHEL FOKINE AND THE BALLETS RUSSES

Michel Fokine and his innovations during the time he was the primary choreographer with the Diaghilev Ballets Russes marked a period in the history of classical ballet remarkable for the collaboration of outstanding painters, musicians, composers, librettists, patrons, critics, and choreographers. It marked a shift from ballet as a display of virtuosity that entertained and amazed audiences to ballet as drama. Understanding the implications of that shift, which was one of style, intent, and interpretation rather than of technique or genre, is fundamental to understanding how performance genres endure and change and what the relative roles of the creators and the performers are. In this chapter, I examine more completely the twin concepts of technique and style, which are the foundation of virtuosity, on the one hand, and artistry, on the other. Through that analysis, we can then explore conservatism and change in performance genres. Implicitly, any discussion of these concepts and trends involves the performer as interpreter and executant. As we shall see, certain performers were crucial to the embodiment of Fokine's stylistic innovation and certain techniques were expected, indeed required.

Classical ballet is a highly codified dance form with a long history. It began in the court of Louis XIV of France and crossed national boundaries; today, virtually every one of the world's nations has some familiarity with it. Questions of technique and style, virtuosity and artistry, change and conservatism, embodied knowledge and verbal learning all can be posed within the context of such a form. The specifics of what we learn from this single case have far-reaching implications for generalizations about how the body and the mind know, perform, and learn. It also has much to tell us about the nature of virtuosity and technique, artistry and style.

CHAPTER THREE

In chapter two, I introduced the concepts of technique and style in dance and the importance of distinguishing between them. To remind the reader of those definitions and distinctions, technique is the set of movements, gestures, and steps that are the foundation of a dance genre. It includes the rules for the selection and arrangement of elements into a system. We have a codified vocabulary for speaking about technique that is commonly understood and used. Style, on the other hand, implies choice; choosing ways of moving or interpreting within the framework of the technique that complement the body, technique, and mind. It relies on such elements as impulse, phrasing, variation, economy or simplicity, density, centeredness, and transparency. Style is what moves a performance from virtuosity to artistry, and it is where the performer has the most license to interpret. The language with which we speak about style, unlike that of technique, is metaphorical and not standardized. To use an analogy with language, technique is the grammar and style is the way in which grammar is used to craft a literary signature. Technique is not distinctive to an individual; style is. Virtuosity and artistry stand in the same relationship to each other and have the same relationship to language as do technique and style.

Technique is important in perpetuating tradition, while style fosters innovation. While we find examples of innovation in both technique and style, technique has been much more conservative. I want to explore why that is; what the implications are for sustained change in genres; more broadly, what it tells us about language and embodied ways of knowing; and, finally, what the implications of this discussion are for aesthetics and interpretation.

Throughout the history of classical ballet, innovation has occurred far more often in the area of style than in technique. Only two changes in the area of technique have radically changed the form. The first change, and perhaps the most significant, accompanied the professionalization of dance under Louis XIV with the founding of the Académie Royale de Danse in 1661. This brought the rationalization and codification of positions and steps with the attendant technical vocabulary to describe them. The significance of the vocabulary is clear from the steady production of academic treatises that it made possible, beginning with Raoul Feuillet's *Chorégraphie, ou l'Art de d'écrire la Danse* published in 1700. Being able to describe dance movements also had an early practical application in the printed descriptions of the latest court dances sold to dancing masters who then taught them to people who were not part of the court.

The second change accompanied the introduction of the blocked slipper in the mid-nineteenth century, which elevated female dancers onto the tips of their toes and created the specialized techniques of pointe and supported adagio. While there already were some differences in techniques for women and men, this innovation created subtechniques for each that were clearly distinct.

Innovation and Conservatism

There are variations in technique across the schools—French, English, Russian, Danish (some would argue that Bournonville was really a continuation of the French school under Vestris), and Italian. But these schools have seen little change since the end of the last century, by which time all were established. Indeed, there has been far more change in preferences for the physical body, the instrument of dance, than in the technique that it performs.

One of the arguments I am proposing is that major stylistic change, such as what happened with the Diaghilev Ballets Russes beginning in 1911, can only be sustained if there is an accompanying change in the realm of technique. Michel Fokine, the architect of that Ballets Russes style, did not concern himself with foundational change; indeed, he assumed that the dancers with whom he worked would have solid training in classical technique. Fokine's innovations had, rather, to do with basic elements of style—impulse, phrasing, density, variation, economy—for which there was no common, established vocabulary.

Had Nijinsky's career not been so tragically short, we might have seen both stylistic and technical innovation because he was clearly working toward that goal. His study of Dalcroze eurhythmics was a means to a radical restructuring of classical technique. His work on creating a notation system came from his contention that a new technique required a new vocabulary, which would be manifested in a new notation. Unfortunately, what we have left are notebooks, tantalizingly incomplete, balanced between passages of great lucidity and passages of madness. Some of the painstaking reconstructions of his choreography give us glimpses of where he was trying to take ballet but he was not destined to embody his vision in a lasting form.

The crucial point about developing a technical foundation for a new genre is vividly clear in the contrast between two of the great early modern dancers, Isadora Duncan and Martha Graham. Duncan's innovations were almost purely stylistic, while Graham quite deliberately crafted a technique to support her stylistic innovations. Today, we have only memories of Duncan, sometimes realized in nostalgic re-creations, while Graham's technique has taken on the mantle of tradition, allowing her work to be restaged. It also has allowed the continuation of the Graham school in terms of both training and new choreography. Paired with Graham as the other great twentieth-century influence in dance is George Balanchine. His is an interesting case because, while he clearly shaped his dancers through his school, he did not create a new technique. In fact, for the first twenty years of the school, its instructors were all Russian dancers who had been trained at the Kirov or the Bolshoi. And while Balanchine's ballets are better able to survive his death than were Fokine's because of their density of steps, they are gradually being changed as new dancers trained in different schools perform them.

Modes of Teaching

Important processes are often made most clear by examining the way in which something is taught and learned. In this case, it has further import for the role of different modes of expression—spoken language or embodied learning, to take only two. As we examine the way in which classical ballet is learned by dancers, either in classes or as part of a repertoire, we begin to see how style and technique are differentially taught and reinforced and what implications this has for change. We also see the crucial role that vocabulary—written, spoken, or simply implicit—has had in perpetuating tradition.

Imitation is by far the dominant mode of teaching and learning in classical ballet. It is a process, in fact, that takes the body of the teacher and disembodies it in the sense of making it into a sketch, which is then shown to the dancers, who mark it or sketch it and then finally reembody it in their own bodies. Other dance traditions have not formalized this disembodiment and reembodiment in their mode of teaching. Take, for example, Balinese dance—the teacher stands behind the pupil and moves the latter's body in the appropriate way. Less gets lost in translation.

This process is one reason why ballet genealogies are so critical to those who claim them. Imitation works in this way: the teacher or choreographer demonstrates *enchaînements* (combinations of steps); the dancers watch, mark, and then reproduce them. While demonstrating, teachers almost always face the same way as the dancers; that is, they have their backs turned to them, so that the dancers' right and left are the same as the teachers'. There are variations within this basic form. Many teachers mark the combination. *Mark* here means to show the outlines without doing the steps full-out. In painting, the corresponding phenomenon would be the cartoon which would then be filled in, fleshed out. You may mark with the full body or you may use your hands as if they were feet and legs. Teachers sometimes name the steps as they mark the combination. Finally, they may simply name the steps in the sequence in which they want them performed, giving no visual cues whatsoever.

Music introduces another element. The teacher asks the accompanist for a 2/4 or 3/4 time or whatever, usually explaining the request by describing the "kind" of 2/4, for example, such as "a brisk march" or "a slow lyrical waltz" or "a bouncy square beat." Often the teacher further specifies by reference to a particular piece of music, the mazurka from *Les Sylphides* or the coda from *Black Swan*, humming the piece in illustration. After listening to the music with the combination in mind, then demonstrating it, the teacher may ask the dancers to mark the combination with the music. This further reinforces the combination in the body of the dancer, the music working in the same way as the naming of the constitutive steps.

At the end of this process, and depending upon the teacher, the dancers may be given an opportunity to ask for clarification. The teacher assumes that the dancers know the combination and, dividing them into groups, has them perform it, one group following the other without a break. If it is a combination that does not change from side to side, the dancers are then asked to do it beginning on the other side. There is no explanation or opportunity to mark the other side; dancers are simply expected to be able to make the appropriate transformations. Sometimes the teacher asks the class to reverse the combination and, again, this is done with no explanation or marking. Part of learning a combination is knowing how to do it in all possible directions and to all sides. Dancers do this routinely.

How long are these combinations that dancers are asked to do? They can be as short as eight bars and as long as sixty-four. Anatol Obouhkoff, a legendary teacher at the School of American Ballet, and Anatol Vilzak, an equally renowned teacher at Ballets Russes and San Francisco Ballet, were famous for the length of their combinations. How it is that dancers are able to remember combinations?[1] Knowing the combination through and in the body is part of the answer but other and not so obvious features are equally important. Experience and training, of course, affect learning and remembering. Certain combinations of steps occur more frequently than others simply because of their physical ease and flow and dancers become accustomed to them. Moreover, what we might call "linking" steps, steps like *glissade*, *failli*, *tombé*, and *pas de bourrée*, form a kind of subset of the technical vocabulary that is taken for granted. These steps get you from one foregrounded step to another. Working within the same tradition guarantees that you can depend upon certain preferences; at the very least, you can eliminate some ways of combining steps, in some instances even particular steps themselves. The way the body moves and the desirability for contrast (dynamic variation, for example) create conventions used by both choreographers and teachers. Dancers anticipate these so that, rather than there being an almost limitless set of combinations of steps, *enchaînements* become more or less predictable.

What do dancers do to commit an *enchaînement* to memory while the teacher is demonstrating it? Most dancers name the steps to themselves while they watch, and they make the names of the steps into a kind of sing-song that matches the beat of the music. So, for example, you might have the following eight-bar 2/4 combination: *glissade, assemblé, sous-sous, entrechat-trois, pas de bourrée en tournant, pirouette en dedans, pas de bourrée en tournant*. Singing it might sound like this: *glissade, assemblé, sous-sous, entrechat-trois//pasdebourrée en tournant, pir-ou-ette* (*en dedans*) *pasdebourrée* (*en tournant*). The underlining represents accent and the // represents the end of the first four beats. The second and third *en tournant* are eliminated because they are understood and because they disturb the meter.

It is important to note here that, in most of the classical ballet traditions, the steps that are named in this way, as part of *enchaînements*, are exclusively those done by the feet and legs. *Épaulement* (carriage and movement of the head and shoulders) and *port de bras* (arm and hand movements) are, in some traditions, taken for granted, or, in others, taught in a different manner. As with the steps of the feet and legs, there are conventions about *épaulement* and *port de bras*. In the previous example, dancers would know the appropriate *port de bras* and *épaulement* without being told. If the teacher wanted a different kind of upper body movement, then she would indicate it.

All of these conventions of learning and of technique make it possible for dancers to learn combinations and whole ballets quite quickly. At what cost does this ease of learning come? The most obvious is that students rarely "see" the combination; what they reproduce is the combination of steps they have used as a mnemonic device. Anything that departs from the way in which these steps are routinely done tends to disappear unless the teacher has called especial attention to the difference. And it is not sufficient simply to name the difference; the teacher must say something like "while we normally do it this way, I want you to use *these* arms in this combination," demonstrating the different arms for emphasis.[2] All the nuances of style that depart from how the dancers have been trained to move are lost with this privileging of basic technique that comes from its ability to be verbalized in a commonly accepted vocabulary. Anything that is not a named step tends to drop out. Michel Fokine's description of the changes in his *Firebird* between 1914, when he was last with the Diaghilev troupe, and 1937, when he saw a production of it, illustrate this point: "I recognized all my steps. Only the groupings had disintegrated, and the climax seemed to be entirely different. . . . Everything seemed to have lost its former force, characteristics and expressiveness, and its former consistency" (1961:176). The steps, or the building blocks of technique, remained; all the stylistic innovation had disappeared. Watching older dancers from the Kirov school coaching today's young dancers in repertoire impresses the same phenomenon on the viewer. The young dancers reduce everything to the level of technique, moving from named step to named step. In the process they lose any sense of the piece as a whole with its phrasing, its stylistic integrity, its basic signature. *Épaulement* and *port de bras* are particularly likely to be changed or disappear because they do not have a separate vocabulary in the same way that the movements of feet and legs do. In a wonderful film of Natalia Makarova coaching a young American dancer, we see her demonstrate again and again and we see the dancer's complete inability to "see" what Makarova is doing in a way that would allow her to reproduce it. Finally, in frustration, Makarova says, "make body like snake," to convey a sinuous movement that has the shoulders and the hips in opposition to each other, one arm crossing the midline of the body while the opposite leg crosses it in the other direction. Even with this "illustration," the young dancer continued using the parallel shoulder–hip placement.

Technique, then, always exerts a powerful and conservative shaping effect on classical dance. First, it is what dancers devote all their time to learning in the first six to ten years of training. They master it until it is so embedded in their bodies that they do not think about it. This embodied knowledge is reinforced by the codified, formal vocabulary that allows it to be taught in a consistent manner. That dancers also use the vocabulary as mnemonic devices to remember combinations only serves to reify its importance. Style, on the other hand, has only an impressionistic vocabulary. Remember Makarova's "make body like snake" to indicate a sinuous way of moving. Little or no intentional teaching takes place in this realm where elements such as phrasing, impulse, weight, and so forth allow dancers and choreographers to move beyond technique or virtuosity into the area of artistic statement.

Let us turn now to this question of technique and style in contexts where a particular style is desired. Whether it is new or it comes from an older tradition with which the dancers are not familiar, it requires the dancer to move in new ways. This was the case with the repertoire that Michel Fokine created for the Diaghilev Ballets Russes.

Michel Fokine

Michel Fokine (1880–1942), one of this century's most influential choreographers, was trained at the Imperial School of the Marinsky Theatre, St. Petersburg. He entered in 1889 and made his debut, a kind of graduation performance, in 1898. His teachers, in the order in which he worked with them, included Platon Karsavin, Nicolai Volkov, Alexander Shiraev, Pavel Gerdt, Nicolas Legat, and Christian Petrovich Johannsen.

The reigning choreographer at the time was Marius Petipa (1818–1910), well into his fourth decade of dictating ballet fashion for St. Petersburg. By this time, many critics were calling him old-fashioned and out-moded. He silenced them, at least temporarily, with *The Sleeping*

Princess (*Sleeping Beauty*), which premiered in 1890, his last great three-act ballet. Although Fokine professed admiration for Petipa, his ideas about what ballet should be departed rather radically from the tradition of the grand old man. Fokine believed that dancing should be interpretive, not merely gymnastic, and that for it to realize its full potential, it had to be composed to music that was equally inspired. This certainly was a change from Petipa who, when choreographing *The Sleeping Princess*, had given Tchaikovsky a libretto that specified the kind and numbers of waltzes, gavottes, and minuets that he needed. When he discovered in rehearsal that the scrolling Vision-scene backdrop was too short to accommodate his choreography, Petipa sent word to Tchaikovsky that he needed another twenty-five yards of Vision music. Tchaikovsky complied. Quite a different attitude is revealed in Fokine's comment about collaboration: "The most absorbing system of creating a ballet is that of close collaboration between the choreographer and the composer, when two artists work out the content of each musical moment together. For this, full cooperation is essential and conditions must exist whereby one can be inspired by the other" (1961:162).

Fokine trained himself in music and painting as well as dance so that he might be prepared to realize his ideas about what dance should be. George Balanchine, another pupil at the same school, was to do the same thing ten years later. Fokine methodically worked out a philosophy of dance and movement focused on stylistic elements and relationships among the arts. This allowed him to articulate a new kind of classical dance to dancers and composers in ways that foregrounded it, that is, its new style, precisely as technique had always been foregrounded. In his autobiography, Fokine talks about what he was trying to achieve in teaching advanced ballet: "I tried to give meaning to the movements and poses; I tried not to make the dance resemble gymnastics. I endeavored to make the student aware of the music so he would not treat it as mere accompaniment. I tried to make the student not content with having just a superficial connection between the movements or a measure of the music, but to seek to interpret the phrases, the accents, the musical nuances and whole phrases. I stressed the extension of the lines of the body. . . . I elongated the attitude which was in total accord with the tradition of the old classical school. I noticed that . . . the head failed to participate in the movements of the body. The arms were curved in a stereotyped circle, the body was invariably straight and always directly facing the audience. Without trying to create something new, I developed the *épaulement*, which is the art of presenting one's position to the audience not flatly but in perspective, with one and then the other shoulder to the audience [this kind of *épaulement* allows the arms and upper body to move around the vertical axis of the spine, something that Fokine used wondrously well in ballets like *Schéhérezade*]. I tried to find the opposing relation of position between the body and the head" (1961:70). This is quite radical in the context of Petipa.

We may use *Les Sylphides* as a model of how Fokine translated his philosophy into a ballet. This ballet, originally called *Chopiniana*, was given its second première March 8, 1908, at the Marinsky Theatre in St. Petersburg. The cast was spectacular: Anna Pavlova in the Mazurka, Olga Preobrajenska in the Prelude, Tamara Karsavina in the Waltz, and Vaslav Nijinsky as the Poet. It was a ballet without a plot set to music of Chopin. Both these characteristics already set it apart from any of the extant repertoire. It was a whole, each part connected to every other part. Fokine's instructions to his dancers emphasized the connectedness and the expressiveness: "Do not dance for the audience, do not exhibit yourself, do not admire yourself. On the contrary, you have to see, not yourself, but the elements surrounding you, the ethereal Sylphides. Look at them while dancing. Admire them, reach for them! These moments of longing and reaching toward some fantastic world are the very basic movements and expressions of this ballet" (1961:132). Fokine is not talking at all about steps here. You have to imagine the dismay of dancers raised on *enchaînements* of steps and the regular pace of Petipa when confronted with Fokine. As we shall learn, it was perhaps even more difficult for those dancers who were the first interpreters of Nijinsky's ballets.

In contrast to the classical way of expressing feelings, which relied upon pantomimed recitative, Fokine required the dancers to express feeling with their whole bodies. In terms of elements of style—impulse, phrasing, density, variation, economy—this meant that movements originated in the center of the back and flowed outward. In *Sylphides*, the difference internally motivated movements rather than externally initiated ones make is particularly noticeable in the *port de bras*. What appears, for example, to be a very small hand gesture actually originates not in the hand but in the shoulder blades being pressed together and down.

Michel Fokine in Schéhérezade, *courtesy of the Harry Ransom Humanities Research Center, The University of Texas at Austin.*

Breathing was intimately related to impulse, beginning movements and extending them. Every movement had an impetus, an impulse, and this gave it meaning. Fokine's phrasing also departed from the classical tradition; he phrased movements across the musical bars, and he used agogic and rubato, that is, he would save space and time with one movement in order to lengthen another. Moments that, under Petipa, would have been static poses became way stations—Preobrajenska frozen on pointe kept the movement and the line going with gaze, breathing, and impulse. There are literally no full stops in this ballet. Related to the use of *épaulement* and impulse was the sense of sculpted movement or density of body and space. Fokine's dancers did not make pretty patterns in a two-dimensional space; they moved through three dimensions, sculpting the space around them, their bodies freed from the constraints of having to always present themselves flat to the audience. Variation similarly flowed from this new kind of phrasing. Economy came from movement being pared down to the essentials, made possible by the locus of all movement in the center of the back, and movements that flowed outward rather than remaining isolated gestures of arms, hands, and feet. Natalia Makarova, trained in the same tradition as Fokine, wrote eloquently about the demands of *Les Sylphides*: "In *Les Sylphides* there is a unique style. While still, one must always be on the brink of movement. The ballerina, holding an arabesque on pointe, is not poised like a statue, but must seem to be leaning forward, resting in this position only momentarily to flow almost immediately into the next movement" (Makarova 1979:118).

If we try to name any part of this ballet in the way that dancers name *enchaînements* and variations, we immediately confront the absence of steps. In the first eight bars of the Prelude, for example, we have only two clearly named steps—*arabesque* and *failli*, despite the fact that these bars are filled with movement and expression. I have, for many years, taught the variations in *Les Sylphides*, which I learned originally from Madame Ludmilla Shollar, a contemporary of Fokine. My first attempts failed miserably because the students built up the variation from named step to named step, leaving out all the important in-between movement. They simply did not see the flow or the movements, which seemed to them to be "just walking." Then I began teaching it by having them first listen to the music, and then breathe through the whole variation. Only after that did I demonstrate the choreography. It was marginally more successful, but Fokine's style eluded all but the most intuitive. The haunting appeal of the ballet lies in the qualities of the Fokine style, not in a choreography full of virtuoso technique, and we may have returned to a time in which virtuosity has once again become the point of performance.

Clive Barnes, in his August 27, 1967, commentary in the *New York Times*, quite appropriately described Fokine as a revolutionary and as the first modern ballet master: "Before Fokine, choreographers—even the greatest such as Petipa—had been regarded as mere arrangers of dances, no more important than the director of a play or an opera. It was Fokine who elevated the concept of a choreographer to that of a major creative artist."

However brilliant Fokine's philosophy of dance, it was dependent for its realization on the dancers and composers he had at his disposal. Here he was blessed by the bodies and abilities of two dancers in particular—Tamara Karsavina and Vaslav Nijinsky, both products of the Imperial School but extraordinarily gifted in their abilities to absorb a new style. Contemporaries describe the eerie experience of watching Nijinsky backstage as he *became* what he was dancing, his body metamorphosing as he and the role became one.

In their ability to adapt to a dramatic form of ballet, Karsavina and Nijinsky differed from Anna Pavlova, for example, who found her métier in the earliest of the romantic repertoire and in the solo pieces choreographed specifically for her unique abilities. It was not that Fokine was unsuccessful in choreographing for Pavlova. For example, their first collaboration was *The Swan*, about which Keith Money had this to say: "He [Fokine] went with Pavlova to her studio and began to shape the imagery of a swan, moving about as he hummed the music, with Pavlova stepping behind him. Then she tried a sequence on her own, and he made modifications in her arms and carriage. . . . As with all their work together, the two dancers progressed in an easy way that was not exactly improvisatory but more the result of an intuitive accord between them. Fokine had but to give the merest hint of the image in his mind for Pavlova to take that thought and flesh it out with an ineffable physical signature" (1982:71).

Karsavina and Pavlova were equally intelligent and equally able to absorb nuances of movement. The crucial difference lay in Karsavina's ability to interpret Fokine's choreography as part of an ensemble whereas Pavlova always needed to shape it to her own advantage. Her dramatic intensity certainly suited the role of star, and she created a company for herself in which she, not the choreography nor the ensemble, would be the main attraction. Chameleon-like, Pavlova was able to give Fokine the flesh and blood evocation of his choreographic desires but she was, at heart, rather more like the dancers whom Fokine railed against in describing the state of classical ballet at the beginning of the century: "Everything was focused on the dancer himself—his dancing, his technique, his personal appearance—instead of on the dancer's transformation in the creation of a new type [each time]. All the artistic requisites . . . were replaced by inartistic ones" (1961:51). Indeed, the Petipa formula for his ballets included the showstopping variations in which dancers stepped out of their characters to display their virtuosity, and then returned to the story line. This mode was, of course, quite standard for singers throughout the seventeenth and eighteenth centuries when they would sing an aria two or more times if the audience wanted it, or they would insert favorite songs or arias into whatever work they were singing simply because it showed them to their best advantage. Fokine needed exquisite dancers for his ballets to have their maximum impact but, more than that, he needed dancers who understood the importance of the unity and coherence of the choreography.

Karsavina shared Fokine's principles about the integrity of the choreography; as important, she knew the relative significance of technique and artistry in any interpretation. In 1912, she spoke about her credo, as she called it: "Great technique—the craft—is absolutely indispensable in order to create something marvelous but it is only a means to an end and one must never have the bad taste or the vanity to show it. The best, the true technique is that which is unnoticed. And, that great technique is not accessible to the agreeable talents of dilettantes." She continues by responding to a question about what school she represented, the French or the Italian. She talks about what she likes in each and then concludes with this thoughtful statement: "Neither one nor the other is worth anything without the help of a true artistic personality, without the help of an element of art, discrete, perhaps imponderable, and which almost always escapes analysis."[3]

Within the framework of his philosophy of dance, Fokine created very rapidly—*Les Sylphides* was finished in three days, *Carnaval* staged in three rehearsals. He came to rehearsals having thoroughly absorbed the music, planned the dramatic content of the ballet, and settled upon the movement motifs of the ballet and of individual roles. Then he worked quickly, demonstrating what he wanted and seeing it take shape in the bodies of the dancers. Nijinsky, according to Fokine, understood quickly and completely what Fokine wanted; he caught each movement detail that was important to the style of the piece and he remembered everything. No speeches or theories were necessary (Fokine 1961:133).

Evidently, the corps was as eager, if not quite as talented, to work with Fokine in the creation of what they felt was a new approach to ballet—they became grotesque creatures, leaping and crawling in *Firebird*, or they danced Russian folk dances; they were peasants, acrobats, giant animals, and loose women in *Petrouchka*; they danced with turned-in bare feet in *Daphnis et Chloé.*

The music of these ballets, by Igor Stravinsky and Maurice Ravel, was as much of a challenge for the dancers as was the choreography. In reflecting on the fate of his ballets when he was not there to supervise their staging, Fokine commented on the issue of music: "It is one thing to learn a ballet while it is being created, when its rhythm is being perfected slowly, gradually, and clearly, and it is being thoroughly assimilated as something inseparable from the music, and quite another thing to learn a ballet hastily in conjunction with a number of other ballets in the repertoire" (1961:173). It is not just haste or the number of ballets one must learn that makes it more difficult; it is also that the context is no longer that heady one in which the choreographer and the dancers are working *together* on a piece, each giving to the other. I think, too, that coaching dancers in an already choreographed and performed work tends to rely on the shortcuts and mnemonic devices I discussed previously, which are the standard mode of teaching. In professional companies it is worse because they are on rigid rehearsal schedules and neither time nor money usually permit an expert to spend more than a few days staging a ballet. The dancers get the bare bones (steps) and then the choreography is cleaned in subsequent rehearsals without the costly presence of the expert. The focus, of necessity, becomes the technique and not the style. Most interpretations miss the original sense of the work.

How much Fokine's choreography grew from and with the music is seen perhaps most clearly in his masterpiece *Petrouchka*, which had its premiere June 13, 1911, in Paris. Stravinsky had composed the score, working on it and the story in collaboration with Alexandre Benois. Its conception owed much to a number of sources and movements that were very much part of the cultural ferment of the time. The Russian Symbolist movement, the theatrical ideas of Stanislavsky and Meyerhold (the latter, in fact, was the Pierrot in Fokine's *Carnaval* and supposedly a model for Nijinsky's *Petrouchka*), the commedia dell'arte, and the great Russian

Shrovetide festivals and fairs (see Wachtel 1998 and Ritter 1989). Both music and characters were established when Fokine began working on the ballet. Musically, the score is full of variations of tempi, signaling the charged and ever-changing emotional states of the characters. Asymmetry keeps the listener further off-balance, enough so that Fokine used square, angular rhythms in many of the group dances. The three central characters—Petrouchka, the Ballerina, and the Moor—all have their own musical motifs. "For the dancers in the leading roles, I tried to create puppetlike, unnatural movements and, at the same time, to express in these movements three totally different characters and to convey the plot of the drama—so that, in spite of the puppetlike movements, the audience would be forced to respond and sympathize" (Fokine 1961:191).

Those first three dancers included Vaslav Nijinsky, Tamara Karsavina, and Adolph Bolm. Fokine thought of the Ballerina as attractive and stupid and, indeed, she rejects the clumsy but loving Petrouchka for the self-satisfied, extroverted Moor. Fokine created a role that was simplicity itself, no extraneous puppet gestures, no personality, yet only Karsavina was able to perform it exactly as he wished. He realized later that, as other performers added their own interpretations, they lost "that economy of movement which excludes all the unnecessary, leaving only the essential" (1961:192). The choreography for Petrouchka and the Moor was based on turned-in positions for the former and turned-out positions for the latter.[4] With that one fundamental choice, Petrouchka's movements become awkward and pathetic, the Moor's self-confident and bold. Fokine went further in order to demonstrate Petrouchka's lack of will—each of his movements begins just a fraction of a second behind the beat of the music. For audience members, this manipulation is too small to identify, but we feel ourselves, in empathy with Petrouchka being, quite literally, pulled along. Subsequent stagings have layered on interpretations, imposed the personalities of the dancers, and rationalized the relationship of movement to music, putting everything back squarely on the beat. Today's Petrouchkas dance from the outside in, character put on like the Fool's costume, more like automatons wound up tight than all-too-human puppets.

A similar fate has befallen all of Fokine's ballets, that is, the few that remain in the repertoire like *Les Sylphides* and *L'Oiseau de Feu* (*The Firebird*). They are done as period pieces but with no sense of what Fokine did in his choreography. Ballets are reduced to those steps that can be named and taught to dancers trained in a different school. Dancers use mannerisms to stamp their own personality on roles, destroying the inner motivation and simplicity. Musical sense is restored by counting beats, and those great spanning movements disappear. Subtle ballets are made more virtuosic at the expense of artistry.

Fokine had moved ballet from the display of technical brilliance, which had been its purpose under Petipa and Ivanov, to an internally motivated, artistic form grounded in principles of simplicity, phrasing, *épaulement* rather than *en face* (face front) positions, harmony with the music, density, and inner impulse.[5]

While he was creating ballets, collaborating with composers, and working with dancers such as Karsavina and Nijinsky, he was able to make those principles come alive. After he was no longer there as an active choreographer or stager and new dancers filled the familiar roles, the subtlety of his style gave way to the certainties of a technical vocabulary. Steps appeared where there had before been movement. Poses marked the end of *enchaînements*. The ballets were no longer integrated wholes but rather pieces to fill out a program. Dancers needed to learn the choreography, and they learned it in the familiar way, by naming steps and counting beats, creating a role and telling the story.

Vaslav Nijinsky

Ironically, the same fate befell Nijinsky's choreography. *L'Après-midi d'un Faune (The Afternoon of a Faun)*, his first ballet, was premiered in 1912. When he returned to the Diaghilev company in 1916, he refused to dance in it because it had been so changed. When he did finally perform it, the critics' commentary indicate that he changed it (restored it, to his mind)—the arms were not angular but rather smooth; the jerky timing more regular. Ann Hutchinson Guest, one of the reconstructors of Nijinsky's original intent, comments: "Because the detailed choreography for the nymphs was forgotten at an early stage in the ballet's history, the faun's actions were given greater emphasis and additional movements incorporated to add interest. As can be seen from existing film and videos [I have studied one of these closely, and agree completely with Guest], the gesture in which the faun lifts his arms forward as he rises on half toe in fourth position has become more strongly marked. In Nijinsky's score, the arms move directly up from having

Michel Fokine in Schéhérezade, *courtesy of Cliché Bibliothèque Nationale de France, Paris.*

Michel Fokine in Schéhérezade, *courtesy Cliché Bibliothèque Nationale de France, Paris.*

been down. In the 1931 film one sees a slight over curve added by dancer William Chappell for emphasis. Later this over curve was progressively exaggerated until, in the Joffrey version in which Rudolf Nureyev dances the faun, the arms are raised overhead on their way down. The size and force of the movement give the impression of a chopping action close to the chief nymph's head. The hard, forceful gestures which appear to hit the air, the jerky head movements . . . are not found in Nijinsky's score" (Beck 1991:31). Guest goes on to write about the differences in other gestures; the walk, for example, which today is done with a very flexed foot, heel first then rolling onto the flat of the foot, but which is nowhere found in Nijinsky's notation. All the changes lie in the direction of adding to the choreography or making steps and gestures larger and more exaggerated. The discovery of a score written by Nijinsky shortly after he choreographed *Faun* makes it possible to see exactly how later versions changed the original. Those changes, I would argue, are consistent with the influence of a codified technique, which tends to make all choreographies accommodate themselves to its rules for the genre. This power inherent in a codified technique is reinforced by the imitative manner in which ballet has been taught and passed down. Had Nijinsky been able to continue his work, especially with respect to his notation, we might have seen more faithful representations of his choreography. As it was, his work suffered the same fate as that of Fokine.

While Fokine's style, as embodied in specific ballets, has ceased to exist, elements of it persisted in some dancers. The most eloquent of these was Rudolf Nureyev (1938–1993). He was trained at the Kirov, the same school that produced Fokine, Karsavina, Nijinsky, and others, but was so independent artistically that only the patronage of Natalya Dudinskaya, the reigning ballerina, saved him from dismissal. Still pursuing that artistic freedom, Nureyev defected in 1961. His dancing, whatever the repertoire, was characterized by an instinctive sense of line that flowed from one extension to the other, a feeling of mass, of sculpting space rather than making designs across it, musical phrasing that crossed bar lines and played with rhythm, great dynamic variation, movements that began in the upper back and spread outward, and the ability to dance in slow motion, sustaining a legato throughout very difficult technical passages (Bland 1976). If he were a courtier in Castiglione's Italy, he would be the embodiment of *sprezzatura*, the nonchalance that comes from having so mastered an artistic genre that you can do it effortlessly.

His artistry was exactly that; it took virtuosity and raised it to that sense of inevitability and transparency. That transition he made on his own, though it had its roots in the Kirov training under Pushkin. Natalia Makarova, another of the great artists who found her freedom in the West, comments on a colleague of theirs who never made that change from virtuoso to artist. Yuri Soloviev, she says, was an impeccably schooled dancer whose dancing was beyond reproach. But there was "nothing moving in his execution; he did not astound with his strangeness or extravagance. . . . This was a Stradivarius that played beautifully, but never sang" (Makarova 1979:72)

George Balanchine

Ironically, it was another Russian, also a Kirov-trained dancer, who founded the school of classical ballet that has dominated the last half of this century. George Balanchine returned ballet to its classical vocabulary and a kind of academic austerity. Retaining the importance of music that Fokine had pioneered, he rejected the Ballets Russes emphasis on sets and costumes that had made ballet a form that went beyond the vocabulary of ballet itself. Bare stages and black leotards replaced the extravagant materials and vibrant colors of Léon Bakst and Alexandre Benois. Along with this stripping away of external distractions, Balanchine also stripped away all but technical virtuosity. Emotion and personalities had no place in the ballet Balanchine created (although even Mr. B had to bow to Suzanne Farrell). Dancers were trained in his school to be the perfect instruments for his choreography. During the panel on virtuosity during Arts Week 2002, Violette Verdy made a very interesting comment about Balanchine and dancers' personalities: "The material was virtuosic, important, challenging, pushing you to the limits of your technique, and he expected that you would tackle the material first and be true to [it] before you would decide to be whoever you are. He wanted to delay the onrush of the personality. . . . He said to me, 'I'm not worried about personalities. You can't get rid of the human personality. It will come back, but it will be better if it is filtered by the discipline of sticking to the orders and the material.'" Elements that were foregrounded in Fokine's open-weave choreography, especially phrasing and impulse, were impossible in the tight, fast-paced vocabulary of Balanchine. Balanchine replaced Fokine's flow and phrasing with a spare elegance.

It will be intriguing to follow the fate of the Balanchine style now after his death. Will dancers continue to be trained in the technique so closely allied with the choreography? Will the prevalence of named steps allow the continuity that Fokine's more metaphorical choreography did not have? Will the twin, new recording technologies of notation and video preserve the sense of the choreography beyond the steps themselves? Finally, will the Balanchine Trust ensure fidelity to the master's intent? Jennifer Homans, a former dancer and writer on dance, presented her analysis in a May 26, 2002, review in the *New York Times*. She concludes that Balanchine's ballets, as performed by his company, the New York City Ballet, have become "boring, pompous, and passé." She presents a review of how Balanchine's style came to be—a melding of classical Russian technique and love of drama and American energy. She observes that Balanchine's intimate acquaintance with the Russian Orthodox Church and its majestic rituals carried over into his choreography and the bearing of his dancers who "had regal bearing, exquisite manners and uncompromising taste." She describes quite correctly the very Russian world of the School of American Ballet. It was certainly exotically Russian in its teachers, its staff, its whole atmosphere in the late 1950s when I was a student there, studying with Anatol Oboukhoff, Pierre Vladimiroff, and Antonina Tumkovsky. Homans notes that it continued in this character into the 1970s. So what has happened? Balanchine died, but so also did that wonderful generation of Russian dancers and teachers who taught not just technique but a style and a musicality and a passion. More than that, many of those dancers trained in this heady atmosphere are now elsewhere. In her review, Homans mentions Allegra Kent, Melissa Hayden, Violette Verdy, Suzanne Farrell, Patricia McBride, Jacques D'Amboise, and Edward Villela who are staging lively and fresh versions of Balanchine's repertoire. She calls them aristocrats of art, in contrast to the new, young dancers who never saw Balanchine's work in those exciting times and who have "flattened" his ballets into "step-driven, one-dimensional" forms.

Commedia dell'Arte

I have limited this chapter's discussion to classical dance because that is my area of embodied expertise. It is worthwhile, however, raising the parallels offered by the transition of Italian commedia dell'arte from a primarily improvised form to a scripted one. While earlier actor–dramatists, like Luigi Riccoboni, wanted to shift the focus from actor to author, none was successful in doing so until Carlo Goldoni. Happily for Goldoni, and unhappily for the improvised commedia, Goldoni began writing at about the time that the great commedia players were getting too old to play and the new generation had not yet found its footing, its *salta im banco* (jump on the trestle). The old style commedia relied on the barest of scripts, three-page sketches that were little more than stage directions, character lists, and the faintest hint of a plot. These *scenari* were usually posted backstage before a performance and the players read through them, those who were literate passing on the information to those who were not. Low, masked characters like the comic servants, male and female, the *Pantalone* and *Dottore* characters, and the Captain invented their patter from a rather wide inventory of spoken dialogue in dialect, and a hefty catalogue of physical humor or *lazzi*. The high characters, like the young lovers, had a storehouse of memorized dialogue in more elegant language. But performances were improvised on the spot. There were few actual plays because each was completely different in each performance. What distinguished players was their style, their choice of accent, dialogue, *lazzi*, and their ability to incorporate current political happenings into the evening's play.

What Goldoni did was to write out the entire play: dialogue, stage directions, props, costumes, characters, sets. He wanted his players to memorize the play and not depart from the script. He was fond of saying that players were simply an unfortunate necessity for performance but that the play was the thing. The number of plays in a company's repertoire grew from eight to ten to twenty-five under Goldoni. In improvised comedy, the same plots looked different at each performance; with scripted comedy, the large number of plays was necessary because there was little variation from performance to performance.

In the language of the previous discussion, players now had to learn the technique of the genre. And that script-based technique guaranteed the survival of the commedia dell'arte as Goldoni had created it. It also allowed companies composed of actors who had not spent years playing together. In the improvised form, actors needed the familiarity with each other in order to anticipate and respond. With a script, an actor had simply to follow the dialogue. So, as with Fokine, where you can scarcely ever see a performance faithful to the original choreography, so too have the old commedia dell-arte plays disappeared because there are none who know the style, and the plays themselves never existed except in performance.

Performers understand that there must be a fluidity and a freedom within which they re-create a work. The nature of the genre, especially its technique, can push us toward a false sense of the genre as fixed, comprehensible, and definable. Critics especially, as Harold Schonberg would have it, "seem to regard music as a Platonic ideal—an Idea, bloodless, bound up in form and content, the written note sanctified, all adding up to some objective patterns in sound. If they had their way, . . . they would abolish the performer" (1988:xi–xii).

In the case of dance, the mode of learning itself contributes to this false precision and regression toward the named steps of technique rather than the metaphorical imaginings of style. But great performers continue to emerge, defying all attempts to constrain, restrain, or define them. In them, the work is embodied and has its only, albeit ephemeral, existence.

Notes

1. Schools do exist where combinations do not vary and are prescribed for certain days of the week or in which particular subsets of ballet technique—turns, small allegro, big jumps, adagio—become the focus of classes on particular days. These schools and techniques include the Cecchetti, the British Royal Academy of Dance (RAD), and the Danish Bournonville.

2. In Julie Taylor's book, *Paper Tangos*, she describes her experiences learning the tango and records the following comment of her teacher: "You must take care . . . not to repeat in order to memorize the steps in your head. If you do that, you will dance automatically. In the tango you mark steps in order to become sensitive to the music and to the particular circumstances of your partner at any given moment. And all the moments will be different. You must remember how the step felt, not what the step is" (1998:107). This provides a different perspective on learning a dance genre that has a technique and a vocabulary with which to speak about it. This is a perspective that does not revert to language nor does it reify steps.

3. The following is the French original of my translation in the text. "J'ai la conviction absolue que la grande technique—le métier—est absolument indispensable pour parvenir a la réalisation de ce qui paraît merveilleux. Mais il faut se servir de cette technique comme un moyen d'attendre un but et n'avoir jamais le

mauvais goût et la vanité de la montrer, de 'l'étaler.' La meilleur, la vraie technique est celle qu'on ne remarque pas, celle que supprime tout effort visible. Et cette grande technique est un domaine qui demeure inaccessible aux agréables talents des dilettantes. . . . Mais ni l'une ni l'autre ne valent rien sans le secours d'une véritable personnalité artistique, sans le secours d'un élément d'art, discret, parfois impondérable et qui échappe presque toujours à l'analyse" (Karsavina and Nijinsky 1912:416).

4. In the West, since the Greeks of antiquity, these two postures have had the same associations. Turned-in feet and hands, shrunken chest, downcast head—these indicate someone who is insecure, pathetic, of low status, a fool, perhaps. All the depictions of the inept, foolish clown, from the Italian Pedrolino to the French Pierrot, show this posture. A turned-out, wide, hands and arms extended, chest and head up stance indicates strength, confidence, and high status, and this characterizes depictions of strong figures throughout history.

5. When I use *épaulement* in describing the differences between Fokine and Petipa, I am using it as I think Fokine meant when he said that he was developing *épaulement.* Not inventing it—it was already part of the classical technique with *écarté, éfacé,* and *croisé* alignments of the body, adding variation to the face-front position—but rather, elaborating it. In the illustrations in this chapter, it is very clear what Fokine had in mind: bodies in which the shoulders and hips were not aligned but were turned in opposite directions, head turned back and away from the line of the arms, the whole body facing to the back of the stage with the head looking back at the audience over the shoulder. The photographs of Fokine are excellent examples of the kind of spiraling body—twisted torso and legs, all parts facing in opposite directions—that Fokine used to such advantage in creating his new style. Many of today's choreographers use bodies spiraling around a central core but it was Fokine who made this departure from the nineteenth-century classical form.

My thanks to Paul Parish, dancer, dance critic, and friend, for his close reading of this chapter and his helpful comments.

CHAPTER FOUR

ARTISTRY: THE EMBODIMENT OF TRANSPARENCY

In Louisville, in the early 1980s, Mikhail Baryshnikov was featured with Patricia McBride in a performance of Jerome Robbins's *Other Dances* to music of Chopin. In one of his solo passages—a mazurka, if I remember correctly—he did a series of *pirouettes en dehors* (turns to the outside *en attitude*). On the fourth or fifth turn, he let his head fall back and follow its natural weight. It was a simple gesture that set an ingenuous, wholly endearing mood. And it was a moment of the highest artistry. Most dancers would hold the head erect throughout. A virtuoso might let the head describe a backward arc while maintaining control of its movement. Letting it fall of its own weight is more than risky in terms of balance; it is folly for virtually anyone except Baryshnikov. His choice to do it was not made simply because he could, however; it was because it was the absolutely perfect, inevitable gesture for that moment. That is what I mean by artistry.

In any discussion of aesthetics, especially of the performing arts, artistry occupies a place of major importance. This is true whether we name it or not because it is always there in its shadow self. In this chapter, I would like to go beyond naming it to propose a series of qualities and processes that define the phenomenon of artistry. First, however, we must be clear that, while artistry is always there as the match to virtuosity in the aesthetic paradigm I outlined, it is not realized by all or even most performers. Similarly, virtuosity lies beyond the reach of many performers. Baryshnikov is one of those rare beings who embodies both. From the beginning of his career, Baryshnikov submerged his ego to the demands of dance. He has lived his belief that dancers are instruments, no more, no less.

Unlike the case of virtuosity with its foundation in techniques that define each genre, artistry does not have a codified vocabulary with which it is defined, taught, or evaluated. Style stands in the same relationship to artistry as technique does to virtuosity but the language we must use to speak about it is a metaphorical one.

Virtuosity and artistry differ significantly in degrees of latitude about the form of performance. At the beginning level of technique, in any genre, there is no choice in the manner of execution. Dance, music, and theatre have grammars as well as standards that can be clearly articulated; performance is judged in those terms. This is not to say that everyone looks the same in dance or sounds the same in music. In the case of dance, bodies differ and create different impressions even though the technique remains the same. For classical ballet, the original and arbitrary choices about its technique were made in the court of Louis XIV and the only subsequent change, as I noted earlier, was the introduction of the blocked shoe, which created a subset of the basic technique exclusively for female dancers. The male technique was reified in response, becoming more dependent on jumps, *batterie* (beating movements), and turns. Instruments in music are comparable to the body in dance. On the one hand, changes to the instrument itself—for example, from gut strings to steel or the addition of the end-pin to the cello or all the metamorphoses of the piano—made possible new technical feats. On the other hand, the instrument itself has its own sound and capabilities. Performers are bound by the same technical grammars but the resulting sounds vary because of the qualities of the instruments.

When one approaches virtuosic performance as contrasted with technical mastery, then there is more variation and more choice, especially in the extra-technical elements involving musicality and economy. And here, there are major differences among schools of ballet. The Russian school, especially the Kirov before and during Vaganova, is immediately recognizable by its musicality, its great flowing legato movement and line. This is something so rare in American ballet as to be nonexistent. The English, especially the Royal Academy of Dance with its emphasis on the correct execution of steps and squared placement of the hips, is very close to the American school. The French are somewhere in between. The technique, meaning the repertoire of steps, is the same among schools but the way in which the extra-technical elements are used creates quite different approaches. But, regardless of differences across schools, technique and virtuosity are inherently conservative, so we see few major or long-lasting changes.

Artistry and style, on the other hand, are all about choice. Style is the sum of individual choices about movement and interpretation. It is embroidery on the basic technique; at moments, it may abandon the technique altogether. Makarova speaks implicitly of style in contrast to technique when she compares American Ballet Theatre dancers with Russian-trained dancers: "Their [ABT's] purely rational approach to movement was highly economical in comparison with the Russian school, as their dancing was based only on a necessary set of technical skills that guaranteed the needed theatrical effect. . . . The guiding principle of the Russian school, by which a dancer must sense a movement with his entire body, was foreign to them; for them a movement was just a mechanical task assigned to their bodies. . . . In their movements I did not feel that abandon that makes it possible to 'transcend' the movement, to step out into a new dimension. . . . Like athletes, they were after spectacular effects that utilized only the external resources of the body, ignoring its inner potential" (1979:112).

Elements of Style

This distinction between external and internal resources underlies many of the specific qualities that compose style. These elements include impulse, phrasing, density, centeredness, simplicity, and transparency.

Impulse

The external–internal distinction is especially true of impulse, the first of the elements of style. In music, *impulse* can refer to the beat between the beat. Good musicians feel it in their bodies even while marking the beats that the listener hears. It is in this sense that one can say that silence in music hums with the potential of sound. In dance, impulse is that ingathering of energy preparatory to a movement and it cues the audience to anticipate a movement or a gesture. It is what limns a movement, giving it meaning and power (Royce 1984:77). Otherwise, movements are just designs in space. I want to provide two examples here, one from *Les Sylphides*, one of the most famous of the Fokine ballets, and the other from *Sleeping Beauty*, one of the last great ballets of Marius Petipa. I do this to illustrate that impulse is a quality of the performer rather than of the choreography. In both these examples, the choreography could be performed without the alternation of energy or impulse; indeed, it often is, because today's dancers have training quite different from the earlier Russian school.

As Fokine has said about *Les Sylphides*, the ballet is a series of long and fluid phrases without poses or stops. One way to create this sense of continuous flow even when the body is between movements is through impulse. Starting a change from a position of the hands and arms in fifth position over the head (fifth *en haut*) by an intake of breath and a slight extension upward of the arms before carrying them downward to second position at the side creates a feeling of never stopping. It provides an accent that adds variation to normal phrasing, a kind of rubato.

In Aurora's first act variation from *Sleeping Beauty*, there is a beginning sequence of *glissade précipité, piqué* into first arabesque, *failli, glissade précipité, piqué attitude en arrière croisé*, finishing in fourth *en plié* on the front leg.

Arabesque and attitude en croisé *to the back, Aurora's Act I variation in* Sleeping Beauty. *Drawing by Della Collins Cook after drawings by Selene Fung in Laurencia Klaja,* A Ballerina Prepares Classical Ballet Variations for the Female Dancer *(Garden City, N.Y.: Doubleday, 1982).*

The *port de bras* begins with the arms low, then moves into first arabesque. On the *failli*, the back arm moves slowly down and up to the front across the body at the same time that the front arm rises above the head and is carried back in an extended position. On the second *glissade*, the arms meet in middle fifth *en avant* (in front) and move into fifth above the head for the attitude. As the working leg drops to the floor in the extended fourth position, the arms drop to a low second position. The sequence, when done in the Russian style (the style I was taught by Ludmilla Shollar) is a beautiful series of nicely contrasting qualities—a strong, sharp movement (the two *glissades piqués*) followed by a soft, delicate one (the *failli* and the dropping from the *attitude*). Breathing helps emphasize this pattern—in and with a premovement impulse on the strong and out on the soft (Royce 1984:81).[1]

What is it, then, that impulse contributes to performing arts? It is perhaps closest to being part of technique in the sense of being recognized and commented on in the arts of music and mime. In the latter, Marcel Marceau speaks about impulse as if one were switching a light on; it is a sharp gesture that precedes the gesture proper. It signals to the viewer to pay attention; it gives a gesture shape so that it is, in fact, visible. Marceau teaches this quite consciously, using terms like *ênergie intérieure* and *acuité métallique*. Each movement that his students do is preceded by an impulse that Marceau reinforces by using the syllable *tak* to signal that sharpness or accent. In mime, everything has to be extraordinary in order to portray the ordinary, and impulse is part of creating the illusion.

In music, impulse is essential for creating an interesting performance; it generates the opposite of a monotone. Again, as in mime, it signals that something important is coming. It attracts the listener's attention even though the listener only knows of its existence by the effect it produces. When Janos Starker teaches, he stresses how you must begin a piece: the bow arm is already making a small circle in the air even before the upbeat in order for the sound to begin confidently. Gestures such as this for the bow arm are joined with gestures of the head but all the gestures are used in order to help the player embody the impulse or inner pulse.

Phrasing

Phrasing is the second element of style and is closely related to how the performer uses breath. Musicians often sing a phrase to feel how it should flow because singing and breathing are interdependent. This is interesting because you sometimes see dancers holding their breath while the same happens with musicians. This is impossible to do when you sing. Not breathing does not work very well with dance and instrumental music either but stress or simply forgetfulness sometimes causes it.

The simplest, and most uninteresting, kind of phrasing faithfully follows the bar lines. This is true of dance as well as music, and even of mime and other kinds of theatre. The most intriguing artistic phrasing takes into account the whole piece. Having made a decision about how the whole piece needs to flow, the performer then makes choices about subsets of the piece so that they all contribute toward to the vision of the whole. In this sense, there is no bar or phrase independent of any other. The standard definition of phrase—to divide into units so as to better convey the meaning—supports this view of phrasing in performance. Meanings, as I have suggested, may reflect the ideas of the creator, the performer, and the audience. The person mediating those meanings is the performer, who examines the "text" and calculates the level of understanding and interest on the part of the audience. That individual may decide that neither creator nor audience should determine an interpretation or may weight one or the other. And certainly, the performer's interpretation is fluid. Starker, for example, has recorded the entire Bach suites for solo cello five times and each recording is unique. One may prefer one over another but for this listener, each interpretation presents a performance that seems inevitable, as if there were no other possible interpretation. Starker has clearly stated his feelings about re-creating Bach: "All the observable changes, whether they involve notes, ornaments, phrases, dynamics, or tempi, should be attributed to the personal expressive desire of each player and the validity of each approach will rest solely on the communicative power of its deliverer. No tradition or truth can be invoked to justify any attempt which does not satisfy the needs and requirements of the already accepted standards of instrumental playing of our time" (Jacobi 1999). Commenting on his last recording of the Bach solo suites, Starker said: "[to play Bach] is a never-ending quest for beauty as well as in some sense the truth. One only hopes to get near to it, and as the years and the decades go by, the understanding grows while the technical means weaken. Let me say that I meant it to be my last statement about the suites but certainly not the ultimate" (Jacobi 1999:236). His last recording won him a Grammy for best solo instrumentalist in 1997 and this thoughtful, perceptive review by Lon Tuck of the *Washington Post*: "One of the keys to Starker's approach is the pure and simple incisiveness of it. He has a marvelous command of the rhythms, never lagging. And he has an unsurpassed capacity for playing on pitch, regardless of contrapuntal rigors. His dynamics are pretty glorious, especially in those spots where he chooses to lighten the sound, without its sounding in any way frayed—not easy on the cello, which is one of the most magnificent of instruments but not one of the most flexible" (Jacobi 1999:236).

There is no question that phrasing contributes significantly to meaning across all the performing arts. In ballet, for example, the ability to think in terms of an entire variation, or better, an entire ballet, changes the way in which you phrase and, hence, the meaning you are able to convey. Again, American dancers, especially when dancing the choreography of Balanchine or any of the nineteenth-century classical choreographers, think in terms of steps rather than linking movements for phrasing, and think in terms of adopting a character from the outside-in rather than internally motivated meaning. Russian-trained dancers think more broadly and tend to dance from the inside-out. This notion is conveyed succinctly in the comparison of Mimi Paul and Makarova in *Les Sylphides* made by Arlene Croce: "That meaning is what Mimi Paul toyed with in her Prelude but couldn't project because her arms kept losing tension in a step-by-step definition of the dance instead of sustaining that tension like a charged current throughout the dance as a whole. It was Makarova's ability to do this at both fast and slow tempos that gave her dancing its sculptural grandeur, its sense of a smooth, unbroken relationship to the architecture of Fokine's choreography" (Royce 1984:136). John Martin, in his October 8, 1961, *New York Times* review, came to the same conclusion reviewing the Kirov on its first tour of the United States: "which brings us to another admirable characteristic of the Kirov method—its authoritative use of slow tempos. How much more satisfying . . . to see a phrase danced with an awareness of its shape and content all the way to the movement's natural muscular and spatial completion than to watch hurrying and scrambling feet, the throwing away of hands and arms, and along with them, the shape and validity of the composition."

Musicians use different phrasings in order to vary the sound of repeated note phrases. For example, in the opening of the Dvořák Cello Concerto with its two four-note phrases, the musician will phrase them differently each time they occur. How a cellist phrases them is a matter of interpretation rather than any clear indications in the score. On other matters, Dvořák had very strong preferences and made them clear in his instructions to his publisher.

Singer Maria Callas explains the effect of phrasing in the *bel canto* school in which she received her first training: "You learn how to approach a note, how to attack it, how to form a legato, how to create a mood, how to breathe so that there is a feeling only of a beginning and ending. In between, it must seem as if you have taken only one big breath, though in actuality there will be many phrases with many little breaths" (Ardoin 1987:3). Her conception of breath and the illusion that all is sustained on one breath is remarkably like Fokine's notion of dancing across the music and phrasing that encompasses the whole piece.

Dancers vary phrasings of the same step sequences to achieve different effects. Prokofiev's *Romeo and Juliet*, even across the distinctive choreographies of Lavrovsky, MacMillan, Ashton, and Cranko (Royce 1984), uses runs for the ballerina throughout the three acts of the ballet. No one run is phrased the same as any other, even when the tempi are the same. This is because the context calls for different meanings—breathless love, anguish, hope. And these runs vary not just in terms of fast and slow, but also in the shortening and lengthening of the phrases.

Related to phrasing in the sense of an entire work is the concept of *ma* found in Nihon Buyo, the classical dance of Japan. *Ma*, roughly translatable as "time–space," refers to the interval between one pose and the next, which must be artistically crafted. This flow of time–space as an overall rhythm governs the dance as a whole. Tewa Indian dance has a similar built-in pause called *t'an*, a slight hesitation that allows dancers to shift from duple to triple meter in a smooth, unhurried way.

Density

Let us move now from phrasing, essentially time-centered, to density, which in dance has most to do with space and how it is filled. Density is not a concept that is talked about or taught in classical ballet yet it distinguishes fine dancers from good ones and is one of those elements that can provide variety in a performance. The surest way to describe it is to say that when present, the body takes on a three-dimensionality. Density allows the moving body to sculpt space rather than fill it, something that Marceau has said about mime. There is a difference, however, between density in dance and density in mime. In mime, the performer creates the illusion of a thick space filled with objects and other people. In ballet, the dancer's body itself is the object with mass. This does not mean only in movements that are on or into the ground but also in jumps and other "light" movements. There is still a sense of roundedness and weight that makes the movement three-dimensional. The dancer then is defined and carries more of a sense of intentionality and presence. Indeed, it is the quality of weight or density that signals to an audience that movement continues even when it seems as though the dancer is still. It is this quality that gives texture to the stillness.

Dancers with this kind of quality include the three former Kirov dancers—Nureyev, Makarova, and Baryshnikov. Nureyev has been described by many critics and by former colleagues as being possessed of a dense legato, dancing slower than anyone might think possible and then shifting instantly into high gear. This is clear in the following commentary on Nureyev's version of *La Bayadère*: "The slowness of some sections [is] emphasized until they become as dramatic as speed, exploiting the tension of a long-held balance and poised, circling turn. The movements of the head and torso are stressed, and the extended phrases . . . nursed into a singing legato sustained through the whole work" (Bland 1976:90). Others speak of him as a big cat preparing for a leap. It may have been the three-dimensional quality of his dancing that made him appear to hang in the air or to appear to perform a ménage of leaping turns in slow motion. Dudinskaya, with whom he partnered before he left the Kirov, spoke of his ability to devour the stage, and it may be that she was referring to the illusion given by that quality of weight—it just made him seem everywhere, in the same way that Baryshnikov fills the stage.

Density then, in classical ballet, creates a number of illusions—of suspension, of slow motion, of covering the stage, of hanging in the air. It also creates drama. The dancer appears to have something important to say, even in storyless ballets. Makarova's arms in *Les Sylphides* convey a kind of melancholy and elemental sense that is completely missing in the performance of any American dancer. The impression conveyed through density or weight is that the dancer is not just making graceful designs in space. One can see this quality even in still photographs. The Martha Swope photograph of Baryshnikov in Balanchine's *Four Temperaments* is an extraordinary example. Baryshnikov is in a line with the other dancers all in the same pose but his arms and legs have a feeling of solidity that is completely missing in the other dancers (Royce 1987).

The various photographs of Tamara Karsavina are similarly revealing, especially in the arms and upper body, in particular in ballets such as *L'Oiseau de Feu*, *Russian Dance*, *Narcisse*, and *Schéhérezade*. That density and quality of three-dimensionality becomes a doll's two-dimensional rigidity in photographs of her as the Ballerina in *Petrouchka*. This contrast highlights the importance of density as a conveyor of meaning.

Modern dance, created at the beginning of the twentieth century, especially in the form given it by Martha Graham, is all about weight. So many have written about modern dance originating as a reaction to classical ballet that it has begun to take on the aura of a true story. In reality, it is much more complicated than that. But, if individuals assumed that the ballet in general was all about lightness and creating pretty designs in space, they were certainly wrong. American ballet had scarcely begun so what most people knew would have been French or Russian. Isadora Duncan traveled widely and spent time both in Russia and in France. But foreign dancers also toured the United States. The first foreign ballerina to take the country by storm was Fanny Essler, who visited in 1840 and in 1842. But it was Anna Pavlova, who toured every small town and every big city from 1909 until her death in 1931, who really brought classical ballet to Americans.

Perhaps it was the subject matter of Pavlova's ballets that prompted Duncan and Graham to create a new genre. As both of them said, there were serious matters to be presented and the dance medium should undertake that task. Flowers, butterflies, national dances, sylphs, and swans were too inconsequential in comparison with all the drama of Greek myth. Duncan, at least, spoke of the contrast between her vision of dance as rooted, coming from and into the earth, and that of classical ballet, which was all froth and no substance, hovering above the ground, blocked shoes adding an ethereal quality when her own dance relied on bare feet.

In fact, the Russian dancers did have that quality of weight and density though they used it in different ways and toward different ends. This truth was apparent in the reaction of the American public to the visits of the great Russian companies, the Bolshoi in 1960 and the Kirov in 1961. In response to programs of the full-length classics, especially to the three-act *Romeo and Juliet* to music of Prokofiev, Americans fell in love with these Russians.

Though Balanchine claimed to have created a ballet that the American public would understand, that public never took him to their hearts and his ballet remains the province of intellectuals. Perhaps the intellectual rather than popular appeal of Balanchine has to do with the fact that his choreography leaves no room for the elements of style, which are the special province of the dancer, rather than the choreographer. His choreography is so dense in the relationship between technique and music—it is filled with steps—that dancers have little space in which to contrive an interpretation; no space certainly if we mean room for phrasing, impulse, density, centeredness, and so forth. If we return to Robbins's *Other Dances*, we can see the contrast quite clearly, especially in the performances of Makarova, on the one hand, and Balanchine ballerina Patricia McBride, on the other. Unlike Balanchine's, Robbins's choreography is like a loose weave; there's always room in it for interpretation. Makarova speaks to this: "There is always, between the body and his choreographic design, a 'clearance' that guarantees the necessary freedom to develop nuances and stylistic colorings. . . . The space between the threads [of the lace] is filled with pauses, the hesitations, the subtle nuances, that fine understatement of movement that for me is the most precious feature of . . . any ballet" (Makarova 1979:155–56).

When McBride danced *Other Dances*, she filled the spareness by creating a persona. Of course, in Balanchine, she was perfectly adapted to the speed and density of the choreography itself. She was in the perfect place, she felt: "I would be on my own if I left the company. I wouldn't be in such marvelous hands" (Lyle 1977:79).

Violette Verdy, on the other hand, felt the limiting impact of Balanchine's choreography: "I'm not being used in the full range of my emotional powers. I haven't been asked to use what might become my best quality as a dancer; a sense of interpretation rather than a technical, aesthetic demonstration" (Lyle 1977:68).

It is not surprising that none of the three former Kirov dancers—Nureyev, Makarova, Baryshnikov—were successful in their attempts to dance for Balanchine.

One way to appreciate the centrality of a stylistic element is to see it taken to an extreme in order to create comedy. In the case of weight or density, we have the example of ballet in drag as in Les Ballets Trocadero, an all-male company that does the classics. As Arlene Croce comments, the comedy arises from having men impersonating women, that is, something heavy trying to be light. The reverse does not make people laugh. Matthew Bourne, in his 1995 *Swan Lake,* achieves a serious examination of the potential impact of reversing traditional gender roles. Odette is danced by a male swan and the entire corps of swans are male as well. The choreography plays on the power and strength of male dancing and is very effective. Odile is danced by a powerful male and both function as alter-egos of Prince Siegfried.

Twyla Tharp also plays with density to create humor. In *Sue's Leg*, a ballet that recreates the dances of the 1930s—marathon dancing, tap, and so forth, she slows everything down and makes it dense as if the dancers were moving through molasses. You recognize the original genre but it is stretched out and heavy and so becomes funny.

Centeredness

Centeredness, that quality of being placed, is different from the preceding elements of impulse, phrasing, and density. Those three, among other things, serve the important function of creating variety. In contrast, centeredness provides an anchor point, a sense of continuity and calm. In dance, we can speak of it in a technical, physical way but we can also speak of it metaphorically. In terms of technique, a dancer's *center* refers to the point from which all movement originates. In Russian ballet, that center is in the upper back, the point at which the shoulder blades come together. In modern dance, especially in the Graham technique, the center is in the stomach. In gymnastics, the center is found in the upper chest. So the center varies from genre to genre but, once chosen, it is no longer arbitrary or a matter of choice and everything else flows from it, quite literally.

Metaphorically, being centered or being placed gives both the dancer and the audience a sense of comfort, of familiarity. Choreography that is always everywhere but centered is very uncomfortable to watch, just as an unplaced dancer projects a sense of unease. Good choreography goes out from and returns to a center. It is in the relationship of periphery to center that nuance arises and, for the dancer, the possibility of interpretation. For the dancer, that center is also the physical balance point but only in the tension manifested in stretching beyond it. For example, in an arabesque, a dancer's ability to stay on balance depends on the counterpoint between the front arm or arms and the extended leg. Making the longest line possible between these two points leads to the most stable balance. Perhaps speaking metaphorically, you have to leave the center or place of comfort in order to stay there. It is certainly what generates excitement in a performance, this abandoning the center, either in extensions or jumps or grande allegro. It is what Baryshnikov did in that performance of *Other Dances* that made it so exciting.

Some choreographers play with center–periphery and the tension between being centered and being off-center in order to cultivate interest. Twyla Tharp is one of the best examples, especially when she aims for comedy. *As Time Goes By* is one of the funniest "classical" pieces by any choreographer. It is nominally storyless, but Tharp makes a comedy out of it by having the dancers always dancing at the edge of what is normal for the classical genre. Arabesques are held just a bit too long with the weight just forward of center, until the dancers fall forward out of them, or pirouettes are not finished in a neat fifth or fourth or, indeed, any recognizable position—they just seem to trail off, or, when performed by Baryshnikov, they stop on half-point and just hang there. What Tharp does better than anyone else is play with that particular canon of the genre, that of centeredness or being in balance, which sometimes translates to bringing a movement to a satisfying conclusion—in its place. It is in Tharp that we can appreciate the metaphorical as well as the technical uses of this element.

One cannot speak seriously about centeredness, however, without engaging the choreography of American-born dancer William Forsythe. Forsythe was trained in ballet by Maggie Black and Finis Jhung at the Joffrey Ballet School and danced with the Joffrey company from 1971 to 1973, when he moved to the Stuttgart Ballet. He was that company's resident choreographer until 1981. In 1982, he became choreographer for the Frankfurt Ballet and since then has been a prolific and creative choreographer. His work is distinctive for its patterns that arise from what he calls "kinetic isometries," a way of body placement and movement that first appeared in his ballet *Interrogation of Robert Scott* (1987), as the choreographer explained during a visit to the Brooklyn Academy of Music for his Frankfurt Ballet's performances in November 1998. As Sulcas points out in her December 9, 2001, *New York Times* review, Forsythe describes these isometries as "learning to develop a feeling for transferring the shape or form of one part of the body to another part, so, for example, the curve of an arm might be translated onto the whole body or the line between waist and neck." Sulcas, in the same review, describes the ballet *Enemy in the Figure*: "The dancers move in angled, disjointed configurations, their ballet-trained limbs mutating into entirely unexpected shapes, their bodies appearing as polyphonous instruments that can generate movement from any point, rather than taking impetus (as ballet teaches) from the legs and arms around a vertical body."

Forsythe has had an almost twenty-year period in which to build a company and a body of work that describes a whole new set of possibilities for dance. In a November 29, 1998, *New York Times* review, Sulcas called his work idiosyncratic, rooted in classical ballet but building upon it to create a new physical language. His dancers move with enough force to almost knock themselves off balance; their bodies assume extraordinary angles and postures, sometimes moving in such a disjointed way as to isolate one part of the body from another. Clearly, Forsythe does not accept the classical notion of centeredness as a given, except perhaps as a place to which his dancers can occasionally return.

In the mime of Marcel Marceau, we can see the significance of being centered. Center is the origin of all impulse to gesture. Just as for a dancer, it is the point of equilibrium. The mime often finds himself off center, too, as when he pushes against an invisible wall or leans on an invisible mantelpiece or the rail of a ship. It is precisely that off-centeredness that creates the illusion of wall or mantelpiece or railing.

It is interesting to compare mime and ballet in the way in which being centered is intentionally taught as part of the genre. When Marceau teaches, every movement not only begins with an impulse but it also begins from the center and moves outward. Most of the technique of mime is verbalized in class, which makes it much more intellectual than the manner in which ballet is almost always taught. All the elements of dance that I have classified as extra-technical, including those that define virtuosity as well as those that compose the style elements of artistry, can be spoken of only metaphorically. They are usually not articulated verbally but rather are demonstrated. And sometimes even then, they are raised only when a dancer does a movement without those elements that define it. I have rarely experienced classes in which the notion of movement originating from a center is verbalized. One exception was classes I had in New York City with a Kirov-trained teacher, Vladimir Konstantinov. He would give long adagios at the barre which included balances that seemed both interminable and impossible. He would stand behind me and other dancers and thump us at that point in the back where the shoulder blades come together, saying in his loud and heavily accented voice, "Find spot!" I understood none of what he was trying to convey until one day in class, I felt that spot, and realized that it was not only the secret to balance but was also the place from which all movement and gesture originated.

The difference in the approach to the teaching of dance and mime may go back to the techniques that define the two genres. In ballet, technique is made up of positions and steps, each of which has a name. You could, in fact, recite a piece of choreography without a single metaphorical or narrative reference. In mime, this is not possible, because each gesture does not have a unique name; rather, the gestures are coded in terms of what they represent—for example, "walking against the wind," or "climbing the stairs." Hand positions are various, as one might imagine, but again, the names are descriptive. Some balletic terms are descriptive as well, like *pas de chat*, literally, "step of the cat," though it would be very difficult to imagine or perform the step if all one had were the descriptive term.

The difference in approaches may be one of degree, but it is significant in terms of the intentionality and thoroughness in the mode of teaching. It may explain, too, the inherent conservativeness of ballet technique in contrast to the innovation we have seen in twentieth-century mime. Finally, it may reflect the underlying difference between the genres in that mime is essentially narrative while ballet relies on the kinesthetic patterns of movement for its definition. It may have a narrative but this is not essential for its self-definition (Royce 1984). So what do center and periphery have to do with dancers' interpretations? They may be everything or nothing, depending upon the dancer. Makarova explicitly recognizes style as a component of ballet, and by it, she means finding the inner state of each role. For her, this is finding something in the role she is to perform and a counterpart in her own psychological being; there is no such thing as dancing without that central impulse or tacking on a role from the outside—adopting a character, as many dancers do. She talks about this eloquently: "Movement does not exist outside the human body, and if a dancer's body is incapable of filling movement with *meaning*, in order to convey to the audience an equivalent mood, a sense of life, in order to *disturb*, then such a body has no place in the ballet. For me, dancing means overcoming that formality of movement, it means spirituality—otherwise what good is it?" (1979:34).

To return to *Les Sylphides* for a moment, Makarova has thought through the central motivating sense that conveys the meaning she wants in this particular ballet. Everything then follows from that so that the head, arm, and hand gestures contribute to her interpretation, too. The important difference here between Makarova and other dancers is that she has found a core of meaning and has crafted the entire ballet in order to convey it. There are no out-of-place or casual movements. The most an audience will be able to articulate is that it was a moving performance. That anyone might be able to recognize the way in which every gesture fits with every other is unlikely unless they happen to be an experienced dance critic like Arlene Croce, a connoisseur.

The same all-encompassing motivation for an interpretation is true of Baryshnikov. He is the only dancer I have seen who is capable of performing the role of Petrouchka in Fokine's ballet of the same name the way that Fokine intended and which Nijinsky captured. What Baryshnikov achieved was an empathy that emerges from within: "The characterization is extremely clear but difficult to make natural. The use of a puppet-like style must, first of all, be clearly designed and then performed with a seamless, fluid ease so that it becomes its own standard, so that the audience doesn't feel that the dancer is 'playing a doll'" (Baryshnikov 1978:277). Another telling observation of Baryshnikov comes from John Fraser's comments about the *Giselle* that was filmed in 1986 (released under the title *Dancing*). Baryshnikov, then thirty-eight years old, was dancing Albrecht, feeling all the frustrations of filming take after take and the accumulated punishment of years of pushing his body to the limit. Fraser observes, "To have seen the black mood of the morning deployed on the awesomely haunted face of Albrecht, struggling between reason and guilt, and pleading for redemption, was to have understood the technique and process of stage metamorphosis. To have witnessed the suffering technician swallow his pain and accommodate physical limitations was to have explored the intimate structure of professional and personal courage. Most dramatically, to have stepped back and found oneself swept away by the beauty and pathos of what some might consider an archly romantic fairy tale, simply through the willful determination of one man's unyielding commitment, was to travel into the heart of a hundred mysteries that bind the very substance of art and the human condition" (Fraser 1988:28–29).

Simplicity

Simplicity is perhaps the only element of artistic style that seems straightforward and appropriate. Dance genres vary tremendously as do musical genres. Some are more ornate than others. Simplicity must be seen within the defining features of the genre. Excessive ornamentation or elaboration within the genre precludes an artistic performance. In ballet, excess usually occurs in hand or arm gestures or when a dancer puts on a role from the outside, like a coat, and feels the need to "make it clear" by elaborating gestures that go along with that role. Or it might happen that a dancer wants to show off a brilliant technique by adding difficult steps to a variation or choreography. In string playing, excessive vibration destroys the sense of the music, not to mention the purity of the intonation, but it is a common occurrence. Most solo or chamber works have opportunities for individual players to demonstrate their virtuosity. The most effective, in terms of artistry, do not hide real merit under the weight of too much ornamentation.

In performance, simplicity can be achieved through a number of means. Choreographers, for example, may choose simplicity to make their point. A new young Broadway choreographer, John Carrafa, in an interview with Jennifer Dunning in the *New York Times* (April 19, 2002), had this to say about his choreography for the new *Pajama Game*, originally choreographed by Bob Fosse: "*Steam Heat* is pure theatrical dance. By that, I mean it has the greatest impact while employing the simplest compositions. The goal is to create a powerful theatrical dance with the simplest of tools. No counterpoint, clever spacing, or large groups of dancers."

Costume is another obvious means to achieve simplicity. One of the major shifts in ballet costuming came in tandem with the increasing professionalism. The latter meant an increasingly difficult technique, which could not be danced with the heavy costumes of the court. Dresses were shortened to give legs and feet room to move; the multiple layers were shed so that dancers could do allegro with jumps. Another major revolution in terms of costume came under Fokine and others of the Ballets Russes. The Imperial Ballet under Petipa was still clothing dancers in abbreviated court costumes no matter what the ballet. The fairies in *Sleeping Beauty*, for example, wore short court dress that had the symbols of what each fairy represented. Fokine created a furor when he wanted to clothe the dancers in his projected *Daphnis and Chloë* in Greek tunics and, worse, have them dance barefoot. Balanchine took costuming even further by having dancers wear leotards and tights or simple short tunics for many of his ballets.

In other forms of dance, we can see much the same evolution. Butoh, for example, a form of modern dance developed in Japan in the 1960s, perhaps in reaction to Nihon Buyo or Kabuki or Noh, stripped its dancers to an absolute minimum. Its creators, in some forms, used the convention of removing all the dancer's body hair to create a sense of economy, purity, chastity even. With all the hair removed, they then powdered the whole body white. Costumes were minimal strips of white cloth. I speak here specifically of the company Sankai Juku. That simplicity of costuming, together with the minimalist movement, creates a performance honed to its essential elements. It is especially striking in contrast to the other forms of Japanese theatre in which costumes, headresses, and makeup are extremely elaborate.

In the case of Sankai Juku, the messages of costume and movement are consonant. This is not always the case. Balanchine's economy of costume was not matched by an economy of movement; rather, his choreography was extraordinarily dense, especially compared to his contemporaries—Fokine, Jerome Robbins, Léonide Massine. In the case of Balanchine, the stripped-down costumes meant that nothing detracted from his choreography.

Simplicity, as an element of performance style, allows the choreography or the music to be presented without a lot of interference from the performer. It, and the other elements—impulse, phrasing, density, and centeredness—all have primarily to do with form.

Transparency

The last element of style and artistry is different. Transparency is a quality of performance itself and involves the intimate relationship among creator, performer, and audience.

Transparency refers to that state created by the performer in which the audience comes together with the performance directly, without the presence of the performer intruding on that experience. This signals the highest kind of artistry and is not achieved by many. I do believe that people recognize it, although I also understand that there is a big market for virtuosity, and even beyond, to those genres that use tension rather than intensity to generate an effect.

One dancer, who has been an inspiration for many, achieved that state of simplicity and transparency. John Martin, in his July 1936 *New York Times* review, wrote of La Argentina, Antonia Mercé: "Her dancing struck that perfect balance between form and content which the classic arts have so often aimed at and so often missed. . . . Every dance in her large repertoire attached itself to a particular dancer, of whom none was La Argentina, yet all were she. As she delighted to show the dances she had created, so she seemed also to delight in showing the characters she had made to fit them. She did not pretend to be the characters; she preferred merely to present them and to point out all their quirks and graces. To dance simply in her own person seems never to have occurred to her. There was for her a complete unity between form, music, and characterization."

It is entirely fitting that La Argentina should have been the subject of Japanese dancer and choreographer Kazuo Ohno's most famous Butoh work, *Admiring La Argentina*. He created this piece in 1977 when he was seventy-one. The unity of music, dance, and interpretation that Martin so aptly describes spoke to Ohno's ideas of what movement should be—transparent.

Perhaps the most important factor in whether or not transparency characterizes a performance has to do with the stance of the performer toward interpretation. Interpretation is active; it is neither a passive nor pristine re-presentation of something else. Our common notion of interpret is to explain the meaning of something. There is a more specific meaning of interpretation if we are referring to a work of art; in this case, the definition of *interpret* goes further, in the acting upon sense, meaning "bring out or represent [stylistically] the meaning of [a role] according to one's understanding of the creator's ideas" (*The New Shorter Oxford English Dictionary,* s.v. "interpret").

Whether performers reach the level of virtuosity or beyond to that of artistry, they nonetheless engage in interpretation. It may be minimal, as in the case of dancers in Balanchine's company performing his choreography, or it may be more than that, as in the improvised commedia dell'arte, depending on the performer, the genre, and on how clearly one can reconstruct the intention of the creator.

The difficulty of achieving an artistic performance of the highest level lies in having mastered all the craft, having studied all the possibilities, having learned all one can about the creator of the piece, and then stripping oneself down to what is essential, the essence of the piece and the performance. There is, on the one hand, a pride in the genre and, on the other, a humility about one's own performance. The performance is about the genre, music, dance, and theatre, not about the performer, although it is only in the performer's body or hands or talent that music, dance, and theatre are manifested. Ego has everything to do, in the beginning, with becoming the most perfectly crafted instrument possible. Then it must disappear as soon as one begins to craft an interpretation. That is when the voices of everyone else—composers, choreographers, dramatists, critics—have to be heard.

A commentary on Uday Shankar, one of the great classical South Indian dancers, by dance critic Edwin Denby speaks to the dancer's personal modesty and his ability to make the dance the focus for the audience. Denby describes Shankar's masterful presentation of dance as different from but equal to any in its complete expressiveness. He continues, "Although he shows us all this in his own person as a dancer, we do not feel that he is showing us himself; he is showing us something that is beautiful quite apart from his own connection to it. He is a friend of ours who thinks that we will enjoy too what he would enjoy so much if he were a spectator. . . . Considerations of accuracy, of form for the group, of personal projection or style for the star are not secondary, they are an integral part of the artist's life. But they belong at home in the routine of preparation; they are his private life. In the studio the artist is more important than the whole world put together. On stage he is one human being no bigger than any other single human being, even one in the audience. The big thing, the effect, is then at an equal distance from them both" (1986:33–34).

What Denby articulates so well is the proper place for ego: in the studio when a performer is mastering the craft. Sometimes, ego is the only thing that keeps performers coming back again and again, striving for that perfection that can never be attained. On stage, ego has no place. It has done its job in making the performer the best possible medium for the re-creation of the work.

It is a peculiar vocation, this one of being an interpreter. In one sense, you have all the power to bring a work into being; without you, there is no work that the public can see or hear. In another sense, it is not your work; you are simply the medium. You spend your life perfecting yourself as an instrument and, in the moment that counts, that moment of re-creation, you must disappear.

In the chapters that follow, we see the evolution of performers and genres as techniques are crafted and mastered, as creators and performers hone their work in the context of each other, the genre, and the audience and as styles blossom and then fade. The work of both creators and performers demands all and the moments in the spotlight are ephemeral. In our explorations, let us walk with the performer's sense of curiosity and humility.

Note

1. For the reader who wants to examine this variation and others in greater detail, a book that is a classic of painstaking description and notation is *A Ballerina Prepares: Classical Ballet Variations for the Female Dancer*, as taught by Ludmilla Shollar and Anatole Vilzak and notated by Laurencia Klaja (Garden City, N.Y.: Doubleday, 1982). It includes other variations from *Sleeping Beauty*, as well as from *Nutcracker, Coppélia, Raymonda, Swan Lake,* and *Sylvia.*

CHAPTER FIVE

CODIFIED AND METAPHORICAL VOCABULARIES: THE CREATIVE ARTISTRY OF VASLAV NIJINSKY AND OF MARCEL MARCEAU

Performing arts are, by their nature, ephemeral. We have developed audio and visual technologies for recording them, to be sure, so we have recordings of musical performance for much of the twentieth century. We have begun to film dance performance only in the last forty years. But these are, in a very real sense, only records, not the performance itself.

Whether or not a performing art lasts across generations or centuries depends on many things: an audience, continuing generations of performers, the ability of the genre to change—either in its form or content or in its audience—with the context, and the nature of the vocabularies, codified or metaphorical, with which the art is described, defined, and inherited.

In chapter nine, we have examples of two highly codified genres, commedia dell'arte and Kabuki, which were successful for several centuries in adapting to and drawing audiences. The commedia, at least in its original slapstick, improvised form, disappeared with the advent of scripted comedy about the time of Goldoni in the early eighteenth century, although, from time to time, we see revivals. It remains to be seen what will be the fate of Kabuki. Even the most celebrated performers are exploring different avenues to make it appealing to the public.

Tewa dance will last as long as the Tewa community maintains a sense of identity and coherence. It is a mutually supportive relationship—the ritual reinforces Tewa identity and the community is necessary for the ritual to exist. It has happened that a group that has lost its sense of coherence suddenly decides to revitalize itself. Often in these cases, it is the ritual, the music, and the dance that are reconstructed at the very beginning in order to provide a visible symbol of identity (Royce 1977).

In the case of Michel Fokine's choreography, we saw the failure of a particular style to survive the retirement of its creator. The gradual fading of the Fokine style had very much to do with the absence of a codified technique to accompany the stylistic changes. Classical ballet survives because it has a codified technical vocabulary. It does not matter what part of the world you may be in, a ballet class will use exactly the same vocabulary, and, in all cases with which I am familiar, will use it in French, the language in which it was originally created.

Such is the force of that vocabulary that, I think, even had there been films of Fokine's ballets, we would have been unable to reconstruct them—the style was too much a break with the classical tradition and there was no way we could talk about it or teach it. Dancers would have looked at the films and then danced what could be put into words rather than what they saw.

Vaslav Nijinsky

A contemporary of Fokine—actually, a rival, at the urging of the great impresario Sergei Diaghilev—was one of the most perplexing and tragic figures in the world of dance: Vaslav Nijinsky. His work, ended abruptly by the schizophrenia that put him in an institution, pointed to a brilliant new conception of classical ballet, which, had he completed it, would have changed the course of dance in this century.

Nijinsky was born in 1889 in Kiev. Like many others from the provinces, he came to the Imperial Ballet School in St. Petersburg at the age of nine. With his incredible physical gifts, he soon became the school's star and in 1909 joined the Imperial Ballet. Diaghilev had been collecting the most brilliant dancers, choreographers, composers, artists, and librettists for his Ballets Russes, a company whose home was primarily on the Continent. Fokine was the resident choreographer for the company when Nijinsky joined it in 1911. Fokine spoke enthusastically about Nijinsky's intuitive understanding of what was wanted and used him in all of his ballets, the most well-known of which include *Petrouchka*, *Schéhérezade*, *Le Spectre de la Rose*, and *Carnaval.* Nijinsky's most frequent partner was Tamara Karsavina, another one of those intuitive dancers. Karsavina said of her partner that, standing backstage with him, you could see his body metamorphose into the particular role he was dancing.[1] We have very little from which to reconstruct Nijinsky's dancing—only photographs, drawings by virtually every one of the artists of the day who surrounded Diaghilev, reviews, and comments by those he danced with and those who saw him.

Rodin, for example, wrote to a Paris newspaper in defense of Nijinsky after the terrible scandal occasioned by his *L'Après-midi d'un Faune*: "Nijinsky is distinguished by a perfect body, harmonious proportions and the extraordinary ability to translate various emotions into movement. . . . The harmony of mimicry and physical expression is perfect: his entire body is the representation of the will of the spirit." This praise by Rodin was included in a *New York Times* essay (November 9, 2000) by Alan Riding, "Arts Abroad: At the Altar of Nijinsky, Elusive Firebird and Faun."

At Diaghilev's insistence, Nijinsky began choreographing. Like the other choreographers to come out of the Imperial School, Fokine and Balanchine, Nijinsky devoted himself to learning all he could about music, art, and literature. He was to create only four works but they were startlingly new in conception, movement, and music. The first premiered in 1912, with Nijinsky in the title role and his sister Bronislava

Vaslav Nijinsky in Daphnis et Chloé, *courtesy of Cliché Bibliothèque Nationale de France, Paris.*

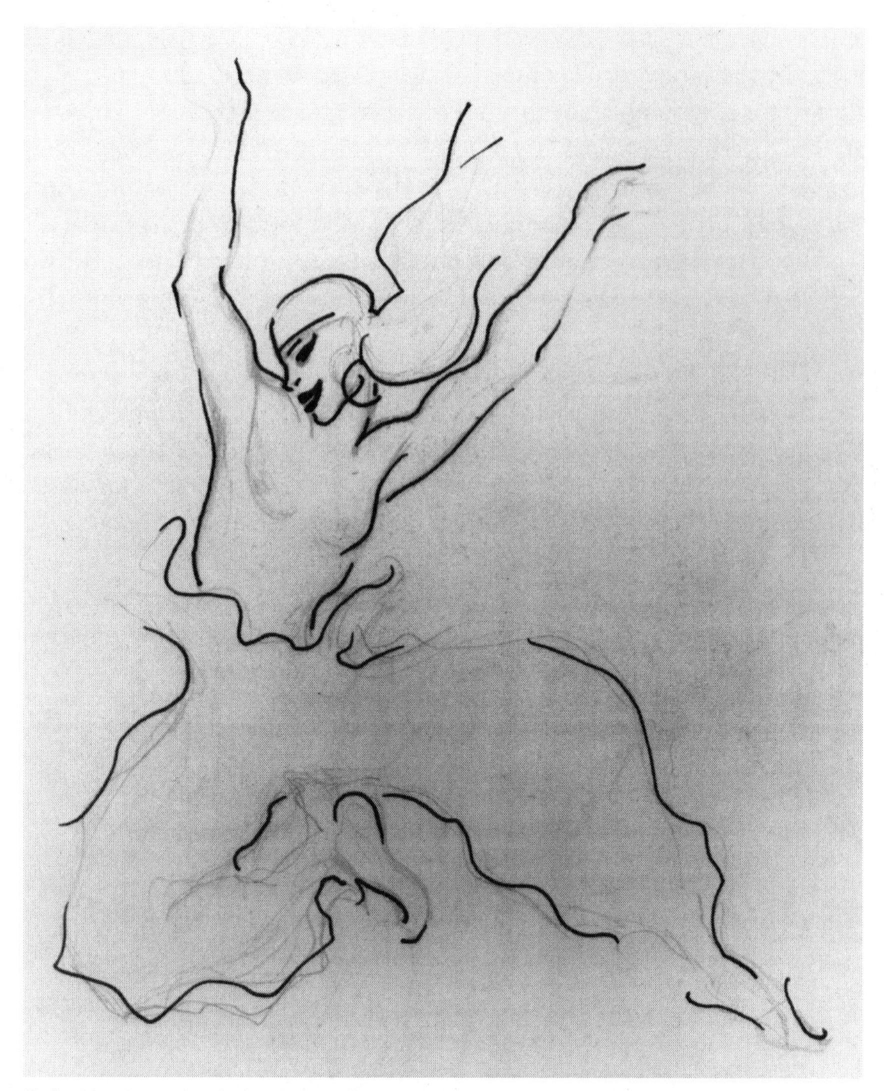

Vaslav Nijinsky as the Golden Slave in Schéhérezade. *Sketch by Joseph Rous Paget-Fredericks, courtesy of the Bancroft Library, University of California, Berkeley.*

as one of the first maidens. This was *L'Après-midi d'un Faune*, the first of two ballets he set to scores of Debussy. It was severely criticized—the dancers wore tunics instead of tutus; they were barefoot or sandaled; they walked with their feet turned in and parallel; and, perhaps worst of all, the Faun was overtly sexual in his fascination with the scarf dropped by one of the maidens. Tamara Karsavina, the partner who knew him best, wrote that, while Fokine had opened ballet to a plastic, fluid line, harmonious and sweet, Nijinsky had declared war on all that, on Romanticism, with his broken and brusque movements (Karsavina 1934:252). We have a series of rather good photographs of the ballet from which we can surmise what the movement might have been like. These are the photographs taken by the Baron Adolf de Meyer at one of the dress rehearsals and published in 1983. *Faune* is also the only one of his ballets that Nijinsky recorded in his system of dance notation. It was also the only ballet of his that was maintained after Nijinsky was no longer either dancing or choreographing. Ballet Rambert of London maintained it for several decades. There have been several reconstructions of it, including the one in which Rudolf Nureyev, that other charismatic Russian, appeared.

Nijinsky's Reconstructions

The history of the reconstructions is significant because it tell us much about the effects of the way ballet is normally remembered, the relevance of notation for continuity, the role of photographs, reviews, and contemporary accounts. Early stagings, such as those performed by the Ballet Rambert, were based on firsthand recollections of individuals who danced in it or were intimately associated with its production. Two of the most important of those were Bronislava Nijinska, Nijinsky's sister who not only danced in the early productions but was also his sounding board as he choreographed it, and Marie Rambert, who was Nijinsky's assistant for *Le Sacre du Printemps* and who subsequently danced in the corps of Diaghilev's company.

In 1979, the Joffrey Ballet included *Homage to Diaghilev* in its season. The three major Nijinsky ballets were restaged, *L'Après-midi d'un Faune, Le Sacre du Printemps,* and *Jeux*. Rudolf Nureyev danced the Faun, finally realizing the inevitable parallels made by the public between him and Nijinsky. He looked the part but, according to critic Arlene Croce, lacked the ability to sustain an unbroken line, instead moving from one pose to another. She also observed Nureyev's inability to see the motivation behind the movements and relationships in the ballet, so his interpretation was inconsistent, staying always on the surface (Croce 2000:251–52). The irony is that *Faun* was the one ballet that Nureyev felt comfortable dancing as he grew older. He said it was like *Dying Swan* was to Pavlova; he could dance it anytime and he was grateful for that. In fact, he danced it for his last performance only six months before he died (Anawalt 1996:320).

What Nureyev did was typical of other re-creations of *Faune*—turning a long line into blocks of static poses; turning soft, fluid, feminine movements into choppy, heavy ones; making the walking steps too intentional, like a Kabuki *onnagata*. Ann Hutchinson Guest, the dance scholar who has given us a *Faune* reconstructed from Nijinsky's notated score, hazards a guess about why this might have happened so consistently. People were just becoming accustomed to Fokine's fluid lines and phrasing—the soft arms, the curving torsos, the tilted heads—and so, to them, Nijinsky's deliberately flat, linear frame and body orientation must have seemed rather far away from these characteristics (Guest 1991). Even Karsavina describes Nijinsky's choreography as brusque. Guest's surmise has merit but I would also suggest that what happened to Nijinsky's choreography is part of the unavoidable retreat to known steps and poses, to adding outlines to what was blurred, all part of our heritage of classical dance training. Nijinsky himself, as early as 1916, argued that people were not dancing *Faun* the way he had intended.

More recently, we have had a reconstruction of *Faune* quite unlike any of the others. This is the work of Ann Hutchinson Guest and Claudia Jeschke (1991). The primary source for their reconstruction is the score notated by Nijinsky in his modification of the Stepanov notation he learned in St. Petersburg. While *Faune* was choreographed and premiered in 1912, Nijinsky only committed it to notation in 1915 while under house arrest in Budapest as a foreign national. After Nijinsky's death, his widow, Romola, gave the score to the British Library. There was considerable interest in this notation system and Romola enlisted the aid of a number of people, including Madame Nicolaeva Legat, Noa Eshkol, Ann Hutchinson Guest, and Claudia Jeschke. This was a crucial step forward in unraveling the mysteries of Nijinsky's notation because Eshkol and Guest were both innovators and practitioners of two of the major systems of dance notion—Eshkol–Wachmann and Labanotation. The score by itself resisted decipherment. It was only with additional notated materials given by Romola to the library of the Paris Opera that Guest and Jeschke were able to unlock the secrets of *Faune*. These documents included Nijinsky's notation of Cecchetti classroom exercises as well as notation of poses from Luca della Robbia's *Cantoria*. Since these were clearly known, it was possible to use them to decipher the notation system. Supplementing Nijinsky's score were the Baron Adolf de Meyer photographs, extensive historical research, interviews, and contemporary commentary. A final working Labanotated score of *Faune* was finished in 1988 and tried out at the Royal Ballet School of London and the Julliard School in New York. The ballet was staged and performed in 1989 for the Nijinsky Centenary Program in Naples and, in the same year, by Les Grands Ballets Canadiens, where it has become a permanent part of the repertoire. As Guest has commented, these productions reveal "the degree to which dramatic inner tension is an important part of this gentler, more subtle version of the ballet" (1991:11).

Nijinsky's Experimentations

Nijinsky continued to experiment with what he perceived as a totally new kind of movement with his second ballet. *Le Sacre du Printemps* was given its first performance in Paris on May 29, 1913. The music was the young Stravinsky's. The combination of music and movement proved too much for the crowd at the Théâtre des Champs-Elysées on opening night. They shouted, drowning out the music so that the dancers had to count in order to be able to continue. At the end, they stormed the stage and ripped away the rail. The descriptions we have of the actual choreography make it seem closer to what modern dancer Mary Wigman was doing in Germany than anything out of the Russian tradition.

In that same year, Nijinsky set another ballet to a Debussy score. This was a *pas de trois* with Ludmilla Shollar, Karsavina, and himself—*Jeux*, loosely telling a story of love, jealousy, and desire in the context of a tennis game moved off court and into a closed garden. Critics were not kind to this ballet either, thinking that the use of a sports theme and contemporary popular social dances was not appropriate. But, in the juxtaposition with *Sacre*, *Jeux* was cast as Nijinsky's most modest work. We can reconstruct enough of the choreography to see that Nijinsky was continuing to explore all the movement possibilities, bringing in contemporary social dances and other nonclassical movements. He was also raising the issue of homosexuality, suggesting a relationship between the two young women who encounter the young man at a tennis game.

Also that year, Nijinsky married during the company's stay in Buenos Aires. Diaghilev, ever the jealous lover, threw him out of the company and, from 1914 on, he had to freelance. In 1916, he was allowed to dance as a guest with his former company and to produce his fourth and last ballet, *Till Eugenspiegel*, to the tone poem of the same name by Richard Strauss. In some ways, it was a self-referential ballet and quite ambitious in terms of sets and costumes. Nijinsky created many sketches for these, and there are sketches of Nijinsky in the ballet drawn by talented California artist Joseph Rous Paget-Fredericks as well. The latter give the viewer a sense of the power and shape of the movements that Nijinsky created for *Til.*

This was yet another addition to his repertoire for a new genre of movement. In that same year, Nijinsky gave his last stage performances with the company—*Spectre* and *Petrouchka*. He was twenty-seven. Just as Fokine carefully articulated his new vision of ballet and embodied it in his choreography, so did Nijinsky think through what he was trying to create. He read about all kinds of dance as well as nondance movement. This led him to send a fellow dancer, Marie Rambert, to Switzerland to work with Émile-Jacques Dalcroze (1865–1950) and his then-emerging system of eurythmics. Dalcroze was a Swiss music teacher and composer who developed a system of rhythmical body movements that could express the content of a piece of music or poetry. Dalcroze saw its uses primarily in educational or therapeutic settings, but Nijinsky was convinced that it could be the basis for a new technique of dance. As he developed new technique, Nijinsky also worked on his dance notation system. By itself, the notation system is an interesting glimpse into what Nijinsky intended and how he worked, and it demonstrates his keen analytical skills. As Guest suggests, his work on the notation system invites consideration of his choreographic choices made on the levels of dramaturgy, movement style, and musical interpretation (1991:11).

The most extended piece of Nijinsky's writing that we have is his diary. He began it in January of 1919, working on it feverishly for seven weeks, trying to finish before he was institutionalized. His wife edited it, removing what she considered offensive material, and published it in 1936. That was the version we had until 1995, when three of the four

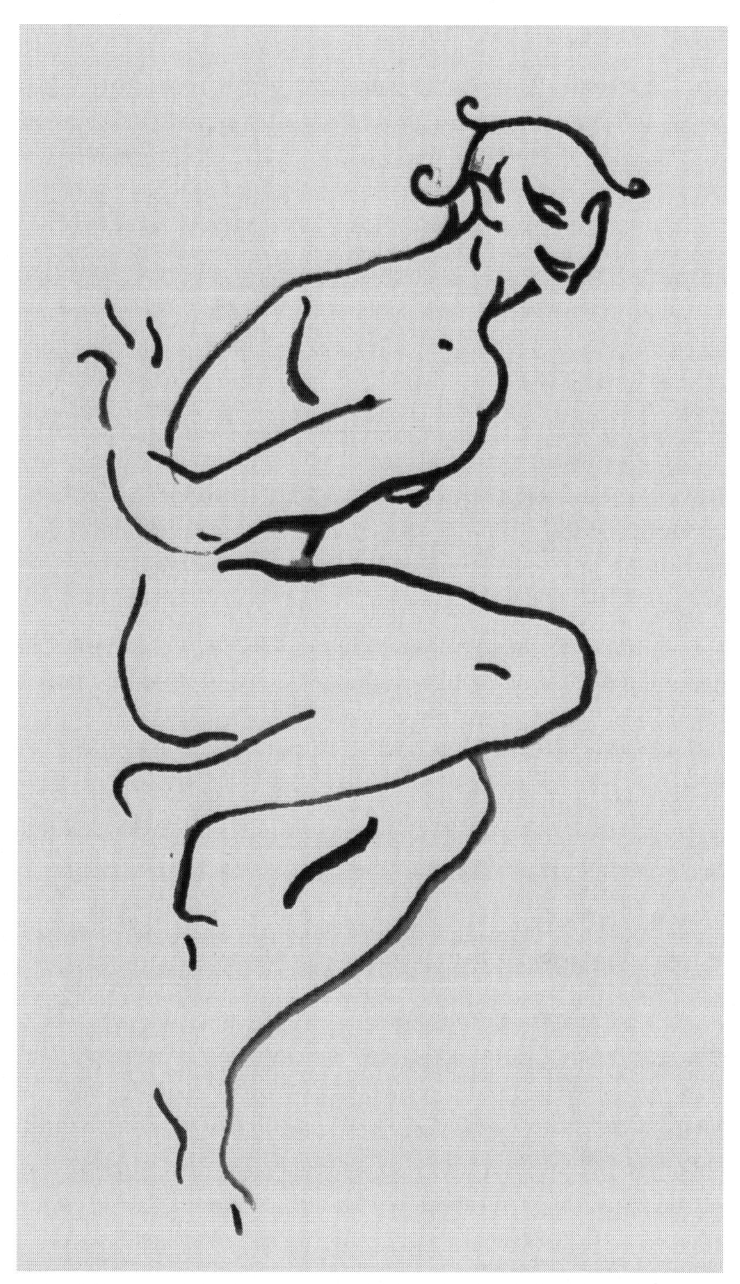

Vaslav Nijinsky as Till in Till Eugenspiegel. *Sketch by Joseph Rous Paget-Fredericks, courtesy of the Bancroft Library, University of California, Berkeley.*

books were published in full in a French edition. The complete 381-page manuscript, housed in the dance collection of the New York Public Library since 1994, was translated by Kyril FitzLyon and published in 1999 with an introduction by Joan Acocella, a most knowledgeable writer on dance. While it provides the best guide we have yet to discover Nijinsky the man, the diary has little to offer in terms of his choreography or ideas for a new dance. Nijinsky was clearly on the track of a new dance with its own technique and vocabulary. One can see patterns and directions emerging across the four ballets he created. At that point, he knew where he wanted to go and was acquiring the various skills and knowledge to get there. Sadly, whatever he imagined was locked up with him in 1919 and died with him in 1950.

His would have been the first major innovation in ballet technique since the introduction of the pointe shoe. Had he succeeded in codifying a new technique, and especially employing notated scores, at the very least his ballets would have been remembered and performed. As it is, his have suffered the same fate as those of Fokine, made to fit the pattern of the prevailing technique. The Joffrey Ballet of Chicago presented new reconstructions in its 2002 season. These were reconstructions of the originals that were done by Millicent Hodson from notebooks, diaries, contemporary accounts, and fragments of musical scores. They have to stand as theatre pieces in their own right since we cannot know how closely they resemble Nijinsky's inspired choreography.

Ballet and Dance Eclecticism

Thus far, what we have learned from the examples of Michel Fokine and Vaslav Nijinsky is that, if radical changes in style or even technique are to endure, they must be codified in technique that is available in some concrete form. In fact, it may be that the natural state of performing arts is one of change. It may be that changes come about in unexpected ways. Dancers today routinely study more than one genre of dance; virtually all companies require ballet training, no matter what their genre. The lines are no longer blurred between genres and there are many more eclectic companies. If one speaks of classical ballet exclusively, there are probably no more than twelve companies known worldwide—three in the United States, two in Russia, and one each in England, France, Denmark, Germany, The Netherlands, Italy, and China. Most of these companies have schools to train future company members and the admission process is rigorous. American Ballet Theatre is a company that had a legendary school in New York until it was closed in 1982. Now, the company has begun to realize the value of a school where dancers from all over the world can work on a common style. It has initiated an intensive summer program, which may just become a year-round school. Last summer, its 242 students had a schedule not for the fainthearted. They take four or five classes a day. At the core are those classes devoted to ballet—technique, pointe or partnering, men's classes, or weight training—but students also have a class in another dance genre (e.g., flamenco or modern) and a non-dance class. Every other evening they rehearse new choreography or something from the ABT repertoire. Every Wednesday, they give two performances. This grueling schedule is described by Laura Leivick in "Dance: Drilling Summer Students in the ABCs of the ABT," a review that appeared in the *New York Times*, August 5, 2001.

After five hundred years, there is certainly still an audience for classical ballet and a seemingly endless supply of those who would be dancers; styles have appeared and vanished, but the technique endures as well as the standards for artistry. There is a growing audience for new diverse repertoires, a few of which have codified their technical base, most of which have not.

In the United States, there are too many repertoires to speak of in any detail. Some, like Alvin Ailey and Garth Fagan, have gone to other traditions for inspiration, primarily the African diaspora. Ailey was directly inspired by dancer, choreographer, and anthropologist Katherine Dunham, who looked to Haitian and other Afro-Caribbean dance genres as a source. Pearl Primus, another dancer and anthropologist, used West African dance materials. Dunham and Primus were really the first to use material other than white, Western movement styles, and, having carved out the territory, made it less difficult for other choreographers to follow. Dunham has developed a technique that some companies use and that she has taught and now is taught by her students. It is not widely or exclusively used, however, so the implications for its continued existence are unclear.

Twyla Tharp, one of the most creative choreographers of this century, was trained in classical ballet and choreographs for a number of ballet companies and dancers, including Baryshnikov. Some of her works play with style features of ballet to create comedy; *Sue's Leg* and *As Time Goes By* are two of the funniest pieces (see chapter four). She has also choreographed *Sinatra Suite* to the Sinatra songs, an echo of Nijinsky perhaps. But, like Fokine, her innovations are stylistic rather than ones that change the basic technique in fundamental ways.

Mark Morris is another contemporary choreographer, quite eclectic both in the materials he uses and the dancers for whom he sometimes sets pieces—here Baryshnikov surfaces once again. Morris also spoofs classical ballet, as in his *Hard Nut*, a very funny version of *Nutcracker*. How serious he can be is demonstrated by his current project—a three-act version of *Silvia*, set to the Delibes score for San Francisco Ballet.

A choreographer who has experimented with ballet perhaps more than anyone since Nijinsky, at least in terms of trying to codify what he proposes, is American-born dancer William Forsythe, discussed in chapter four. A Joffrey-trained dancer, he found his métier as a choreographer, first with the Stuttgart Ballet and most recently as director and choreographer of the Frankfurt Ballet.

Forsythe has been intentional about what began as an idiosyncratic choreographic style. Out of compositional techniques—and here it is important to note that his dancers work with him collaboratively in the choreographic process—came what he calls kinetic isometries, the process of transferring the shape of one part of the body to another. Critic Roslyn Sulcas in "Using Forms Ingrained in Ballet to Help the Body Move Beyond It," an interview with Forsythe in the *New York Times* (December 8, 2001), discusses a 1993 work, *Quintett*, noting yet another characteristic of the way Forsythe has changed traditional balletic notions: "The dancers move on unsteady, buckling limbs, their movements dissolving into and collapsing upon one another in a poignant series of encounters and solos. Their swooping, liquid movements are the result of techniques that trace a muscular process as it goes through the body: here, balletic form is visible but the steps themselves are not, as if their dynamics have been erased, leaving mere vestiges of their shapes." Forsythe, speaking of that same ballet, describes what he is trying to do as "tracing a space around an arabesque rather than doing the arabesque." This bears an interesting resemblance to some of the essential elements of mime, as defined by Marceau. When done well, it allows the audience to see what is not there, although in mime, it is done to convey a narrative while, for Forsythe, it is a way of playing with form.

One might ask, where is ballet and ballet's audience in all this? Forsythe speaks, in the same Sulcas interview, to the first when he talks about another piece, *Woolf Phrase*: "There isn't a real ballet step in it. But it does require a ballet technique." In Sulcas's November 29, 1998, essay, also in the *New York Times*, Forsythe shows that his ideas about the relationship between performance and the audience are remarkably consistent with those of other artists: "I think that it's about shifting frames and perspectives, remaining contexts. In *Eidos* there are sublime moments and grotesque moments; it forces you to keep moving away from and back toward what is happening on stage. But you can always come up with explanations afterward. What I always want to say is that you don't have to understand this, you just have to watch it, and then maybe something will happen to you without thinking."

What is true is that Forsythe's choreography and his dancers are hugely popular everywhere they perform. His works have been performed by other companies, though they are exclusively what he has called his "ballet ballets." He has pushed the boundaries of what we imagine ballet to be capable of doing. It remains to be seen whether his work, other than the "ballet ballets," persists once he is no longer active.

Change also comes from those individual dancers, artists in their own genres, who seem to be able to move across dance genres as easily as they astound us with their leaps and turns. One of the first was Rudolf Nureyev, often described as the new Nijinsky but certainly one of the greatest dancers since ballet became a professional art. He left Russia because he felt stifled artistically and, when he arrived in the West, he was like a child in a candy store, overwhelmed with the wealth of dance styles available to him. He was a perfectionist so whatever he undertook, he did as seriously as he had ballet. He worked with Martha Graham, who choreographed *Lucifer* for him, with Maurice Béjart, and with Murray Louis, who made *Pierrot Lunaire* for him; he even appeared on American television in a much abbreviated *Swan Lake* with Miss Piggy! He was, for most of this time, dancing the classical repertoire with Margot Fonteyn in one of the great ballet partnerships of all time.

Baryshnikov followed a similar trajectory when he left Russia, dancing everywhere and everything, including tap and Broadway. He continues to be an innovative force, first with his White Oak Dance Project, a small company with a very wide-ranging repertoire. In June 2000, he orchestrated a program with Mark Morris and John Jaspers that brought together a number of the original Judson Dance Theater dancers, including Trisha Brown and Yvonne Rainer. The following summer, he presented another program, *PastForward*, focusing on the Judson Dance Theater, some of which harked back to those days of the 1960s when choreographers used everyday objects, nondance movement, and nondancers. But other pieces showed the changes in many of the same choreographers, from the everyday to the virtuosic. Some of his experimentation lies with his restlessness with classical ballet. He said once that, if he had been born in America, he never would have been a ballet dancer, because it is too commercial and not serious.

None of these collaborations and few of the eclectic groups have worked at creating a new movement vocabulary that is codified. Thus far, these exciting new genres of dance come and go in rapid succession. Certainly these collaborations will, of necessity, change, when the stars who prompted them are no longer active. It may be that a few will stay or we may be living in a time in which change is the preferred mode. The context and conditions within which innovation creates a new genre are the focus of chapter ten.

Marcel Marceau

Marcel Marceau offers an example of someone who has created a new genre—modern mime of the twentieth century—who has performed it all over the world for more than sixty years, and who has taught hundreds of students the art of mime in his Paris School as well as in workshops worldwide. The school is reminiscent of ABT's summer program although the course of study is three years. Students take classes in mime, in dance, in fencing and some of the martial arts, in theatrical forms like the commedia dell'arte, in literature, in music, and in history of art. They learn some of the repertoire but Marceau encourages them to develop their own mimes—short pieces as well as mime dramas. The more talented ones go into his company, La Nouvelle Compagnie de Mimodrame Marcel Marceau, or work with him in his solo tours as presenters of the signs, or both. They also may teach at the school. What is important here is that he has created a continuity for mime, not a clone of himself but carried on in the bodies and minds of students trained in all those areas that contribute to Marceau's mime. His mime will change as it is performed by new generations trained by him and by his students, but he has provided a solid technique on which to ground the genre and that will endure.

When Marceau began his career, the only mime was the remnants of nineteenth-century French mime, best embodied in Jean-Gaspard Deburau and derived quite closely from the commedia dell'arte. In fact, mime remained in memory only. As a young man in Paris, Marceau was one of only two students who took mime classes from Etienne Decroux. Mime was not one of the prestigious forms of theatre then, and Marceau and Jean-Louis Barrault were Decroux's only pupils. Decroux's mime was very much *un mime du corps*; in fact, it was called corporeal mime. In it, Decroux saw a hierarchy in the organs of expression: the most important was the body, then the arms and hands, and finally the face. He explained this by saying that the body is large and heavy, the face and arms are small and light; moreover, we are used to looking to the face for expression and rely on conventionalized signs. Finally, in dismissing the face, Decroux says,

Marcel Marceau. Photograph by Roger Pic, 1999.

Marcel Marceau. Photograph by Roger Pic, 1999.

"One may be sublime with a mask, but not with a face. The face has something incurably realistic about it. It's there! But we change the body easily, because the body is made up of large parts. And the moment a large enough stick moves, people see it. The face, however, is made of smaller units, and it's truly difficult to transfigure it" (Royce 1984:73).

Marceau acknowledges Decroux as his teacher and as the founder of corporeal mime but also points to the many, quite substantial differences between Decroux's mime and his own, which he calls illusion mime in contradistinction to Decroux's corporeal mime. In conveying illusions to a public, Marceau says that the mime not only has "to be beautiful esthetically or to show the greatest virtuosities, he has to become what he portrays. If he shapes a stone, he has to be a stone. If he shapes a fish, he has to be a fish; he has to breathe like a fish, he has to become the weight of a fish. You can feel that he sculpts the volume and size of what he portrays" (Royce 1984:71).

In illusion mime, unlike corporeal mime, the face is a critical conveyor of the narrative and of emotion. Perhaps the best example of this is Marceau's famous style pantomime, *The Maskmaker*. It is the story of a maskmaker, sitting in his workshop surrounded by masks. He begins trying them on, one at a time. Marceau's face changes to become the mask—angry, arrogant, foolish, happy, sad; he tries them all on. The last is a happy mask and he cannot remove it. All his efforts fail, and his body shows that he is exhausted and despairing, yet the mask continues to smile. It is a tour de force and, in many ways, a metaphor for the poles of human emotion.

Marceau also uses the face as an indicator of a change of character. He passes his hand down across his face and becomes a different person. The techniques of condensing time and space apply to how he shows the face. For the second half of his October 2001 performance in Bloomington, Indiana, I moved to sit in the back of the auditorium. Among other style mimes, he did *The Maskmaker*. I was astounded at how clearly the emotions were conveyed across that great a distance.

Condensation of time, for Marceau, is an elliptical device that expresses complicated stories or dramatic themes in the space of a few minutes: "Mime cannot take a long time to explain something; it has to make it clear immediately. The mime should not make variations on a theme in movement. He has to go directly to the metamorphosis itself. The process of change has to happen before the audience. Let us give an example: *Youth, maturity, old age, and death.* You have to see the progression of youth, the developing in maturity, old age, and going into death. It's like filming a flower living and decaying in thirty-six hours. If you would do that and put it in a montage, you would have the flower blossoming and decaying in three minutes. This is exactly what the mime does, showing the illusion of time—in four minutes you can show a life span" (interview, April 5, 1981)

From time to timing—Marceau knows that timing is more crucial in comedy. The audience has to get the joke immediately or it will not be funny. In tragedy, time moves more slowly, even in the condensed time of mime, giving the audience more time to absorb the message. *Remembrances of a Past Love* is a marvelous piece in which time seems suspended as Marceau takes us through all the stages of remembering being in love and then brings us back again to the moment.

One of the ways in which mime differs from dance is in its use of narrative. Mime has to tell a story or sketch an emotion; it cannot hold an audience simply by its display of technical virtuosity. Of all the solo mimes, Marceau is most connected to narrative and a dramatic sense. This implies a certain structure to the pieces that allow audiences to understand them. Marceau's mimes are structured around three kinds of symbols that range from the most declarative to the most metaphorical. The first are made up of direct representations of objects, persons, animals, and behaviors out of our lives: fish, birds, a snake, old people, a lawyer, soldiers, playing a violin, or climbing stairs.

The second is more abstract, using metaphor and synecdoche. These symbols convey emotions or moods. Posture contains many implications for mood. Mime comes out of a Greco-Roman tradition, Marceau explains, in which an erect, chest-lifted posture signals beauty and aristocracy; a curved inward, shrunken posture indicates defeat, poverty, ugliness (see note 4, chapter three). Marceau plays with these notions all the time. We understand, without quite knowing why. Speed of movement also conveys meanings. In general, fast movements imply comedy; slow ones, tragedy or sadness.

The third category is altogether different. It is almost never recognized consciously by the audience but without it we would not understand anything more complicated than *The Lion Tamer*. Symbols in this category function like paragraphs in writing and are used to indicate a change of scene or character, or simply the passage of time. Typical markers include passing the hand down in front of the face, closing and opening the eyes slowly, or making one complete revolution in place (around the body's axis). Marceau sometimes uses a rapidly twirling motion with both arms outstretched, accompanied by a dimming of the lights, to signal the end of a piece. Perhaps the audience does not think about how to bring something to a close but performers certainly do—it makes the difference between a professional and an amateur. And audiences *do* recognize a poor ending, even if they cannot articulate why.

This kind of structure is essential if you want to tell a story with none of the usual storytelling devices like spoken or written language. Marceau is a master of telling stories to all kinds of audiences. He varies the program or changes the structure of individual pieces depending on his assessment of the sophistication of the audience. For a less sophisticated audience, he does more mimes that rely on symbols that bear a direct relationship to the objects they stand for; sophisticated audiences are ones for whom he can do the longer, more thoughtful and complicated pieces. But no program has all of one or all of the other. His goals are a good mixture of the desire to entertain and the desire to educate or to move profoundly.

Almost all his mimes, whether comic or otherwise, have a deep understanding of the joys and tragedies of everyday life. Even the tragedies are presented in a loving way. Reviewer Jack Anderson commented in the *New York Times* (March 22, 1999) on this particular quality of Marceau's repertoire: "The works of this great French mime can be whimsical, farcical, bitter, sweet and bittersweet. But most of them are gentle in tone." Marceau's art distills the truth of the everyday, of ordinary people, something that reaches our hearts. As he once told me regarding the "ordinary" nature of his mimes, "All the great tragedies depend on an understanding of the common man. If one understands the tragedy of a child who has let go of a balloon and watches it float away, then one can understand the tragedies of war and death."[2]

His repertoire does not get old. No matter how many times you may have seen *The Maskmaker*, *The Cage*, or *The Birdkeeper*, they continue to touch you because of their commentary on the eternal.

Performing arts, however we preserve them, must be performed to keep alive the conversation between creator, performer, and audience. They are without life as the museum pieces they become in recordings.

But they live a precarious existence in their utter dependence on the public. This is at once their weakness and their great strength. Perhaps nothing else requires the active, creative participation of an audience so much as a performance. If imagination and creativity are essential attributes of a thinking life, then they force us to be alive in all our potentiality.

The Tewa know this; for them, their dance and music is at the very core of who they are as a people. We may say that the arts are really not an essential part of our lives in the same way. Perhaps not, but I would argue that, as they gently force us to exercise our ability to dream, to imagine, to reach beyond ourselves for a glimpse of the eternal, they remind us of the better part of who we are and who we might be. The individuals, companies, even genres that I have talked about here may not continue forever but I am convinced that they will be replaced by performers and arts who will model for us all those qualities of discipline, passion, and transformation, which are reminders of how far we might reach.

Notes

1. Marie-Françoise Christout explores all the ramifications of the ability to metamorphose in her discussion of Nijinsky, comparing him with other dancers and offering contemporary accounts of his uncanny ability to *be* the role he was dancing. Beyond this, she talks about his extraordinary level of energy, of power, quoting Paul Claudel's preface to Romola Nijinsky's *Nijinsky*: "Il n'y avait pas un geste si petit comme par exemple quand il tournait vers nous le menton, quan la petite tête virait subitement sur son long cou, que Nijinsky n'accomplit dans la gloire, dans une vivacité à la fois fëroce et suave et dans une autorité foudroyante" (Christout 1992:123).

2. Marcel Marceau, interview by Anya Peterson Royce, April 24, 1983, New York.

CHAPTER SIX
TEWA INDIAN RITUAL: NATIVE AESTHETICS

> Perhaps no people in North America spend more time in the dance than the Southwest Pueblos.
>
> —Ruth Benedict

The Tewa are one of six groups that together have been called the Pueblo Indians. The Pueblo groups live stretched along the banks and floodplains of the Río Grande River. With the exception of the Hopi-speakers who live in eastern Arizona, all live in New Mexico between Taos in the north and Isleta in the south. Even before the Spanish came into their lands, the ancestors of the Pueblo peoples had built architecturally extraordinary towns. When the Spanish arrived, they found these groups living in farming communities along the river. It was the style of those consolidated communities that led the Spaniards to call the communities *pueblos*, the Spanish word for "towns." The six Tewa villages—Tesuque, Nambe, Pojoaque, San Ildefonso, Santa Clara, and San Juan—are all clustered within twenty miles of each other along the river north of Santa Fe.

Traditionally, the Tewa economy was based on corn agriculture with some hunting and trading. Now, some still farm but most rely on the production and sale of crafts or on wage work. The dances and events that make up the ritual cycle continue to be those that make sense for a primarily farming people, including corn, rain, basket, butterfly, cloud, and rainbow dances. These are supplemented by dances about animals that come from hunting: deer and buffalo. For example, in the 1940s, William Whitman documented a dance for the Tewa pueblo of San Ildefonso led by a hunt leader who calls the animal-masked dancers—buffalo, deer, big-horned sheep, antelopes—from a place outside the pueblo into the community

(1947). This dance is still part of the ritual cycle. There are also dances, like the Comanche, Crow, and Kiowa dances, that signal intertribal relations and knowledge. Finally, many of the Tewa pueblos celebrate the *Matachines* dance, a supposedly Spanish-inspired set of rituals.

Apart from the ritual cycle, whose events take place within the villages, the Tewa now also perform in two more intentionally theatrical contexts. These are ceremonials or large gatherings, the purpose of which is to draw crowds of mostly tourists who buy the local crafts. Some are organized by Anglos; others by the Tewa themselves. Both kinds of theatrical events require a different way of performing the dances. Which dances are done depends upon the organizing group.

What is important to note is that the Tewa make aesthetic judgments about dances, songs, and music; they have choreographers who create new dances; and they recognize and adopt different styles of performance depending on the audience. Although the big ceremonial dances involve a larger number of pueblo members, a certain level of skill and knowledge is expected. For the lead dancers and singers, the expectation is even greater. In other words, all Tewa dance is and has been subject to critical judgment, which, for me, constitutes an aesthetic system.

The other factor that makes the Pueblo ritual, and, in particular, the Tewa Pueblo villages, ideal for this kind of examination of native aesthetics is that we have a long period of documentation. Beginning with H. H. Jackson's 1882 *Atlantic Monthly* piece describing a midsummer festival in San Juan, we move through almost a continuous succession of studies ending with Sylvia Rodríguez's 1996 book, *The Matachines Dance.* This long perspective allows us to separate what is fundamental and not subject to change from that in which change is possible and, indeed, common. Just as we see in the examples of the Kabuki and the commedia dell'arte, changing venues and different audiences have profound implications for the form of any performative art, whether it is closer to ritual or to theatre.

Space and Time

Dance that is embedded in a social system and that provides more than entertainment for the people who support and perform it is affected by more and different factors than theatrical dance done by professionals and performed for paying audiences. Time and space are two important factors for Tewa dance. Since they moved into this area along the upper Río Grande, the Tewa have shaped their life around the physical context and an annual cycle dictated by the combination of physical environment and choices about social institutions and cultural values. Gertrude Kurath, who documented Tewa dance and ritual from the 1940s to the 1970s, comments: "They have developed their way of life, their beliefs, and their ceremonies in accordance with the patterns and happenings on the earth and in the sky. They have created dances, songs, poetry, and ornamental designs expressive of the natural and cultural phenomena" (1970:15).

Cardinal directions (including up and down), sacred mountains, lakes, and hills all shape ritual and dance. For example, San Juan has a sacred hill to the east of the pueblo, which is the starting point for the animal hunt dance. Sun, rain, and earth are all embodied in spirits exemplified in ritual. The creatures who make up the Tewa physical world are featured, too, in dance. The six directions each have an animal or bird symbol—mountain lion, bear, oriole, eagle, water serpent. Other animals—game animals—are featured in ritual: deer, antelope, mountain sheep, elk, buffalo. Finally, the turtle, butterfly, and plants, including spruce, corn, and tobacco, play important roles in sustaining a rich ritual life.

Space determines direction of dances, placement of plazas and kivas, rehearsal space, and beginning and ending points. There is the larger space of the Río Grande plains, valleys, mountains, and hills and there is the space within the pueblo. Each is a reference point for the other and anchors ritual events.

Time remains an important force in Tewa ritual life, although the specific ordering of ritual has to take into account changes brought first by the Spanish with their Roman Catholic calendar and saints, and, more recently, changes having to do with the demands of school and work. What is striking is how tenacious the early patterns are. Winter was originally the season of the hunt and celebration of hunting. It is still the time of most animal dances. Spring, summer, and early fall see corn, rain, and harvest dances. Time, like space, is reckoned along two dimensions. Ritual time that corresponds to the larger cycle of an agricultural and hunting people dictates the performance of dances sorted by genre. Secular time, which can be adjusted to the work and life needs of people, allows the scheduling of specific dances, including those theatrical performances that fall outside the ritual cycle.

When the Spanish brought Catholicism to the Pueblos, they brought another ritual cycle. Pueblo people then and now have practiced selective integration of foreign elements (Sweet 1985:77), not feeling the need to abandon one practice in order to perform another.[1] This has given them a fluidity and resilience that has contributed to the active maintenance of traditions that make them culturally distinct. So, Pueblo ritual dances continue to be performed alongside dances for occasions in the Roman Catholic calendar. And, often, the latter are drawn from the former. This is certainly the case for another Catholic innovation, the feast of the patron saint. The five Tewa saints' days with their dances are San Ildefonso, January 23, San Ildefonso, *konshare* (buffalo dance) and *kwitara* (Comanche dance) in rotation in the two plazas; San Juan, June 24, St. John the Baptist, formerly *konshare* now *kwitara*; Santa Clara, August 12, St. Claire, *xoxeye* (corn dance), *konshare, kwitara,* sometimes *yandewa* (sun basket dance), two or three dances in rotation; Nambe, October 4, St. Francis, *tashare* Elk dance, or *konshare, kwitara*; Tesuque, November 12, St. James, formerly *xoxeye* or *konshare* now usually *kwitara* (Kurath and Garcia 1970:25). Jill Sweet (1985), who worked with the Pueblo people, especially the Tewa, in the mid to late 1970s, documents dances done for saints' days. They seem to include the animal and harvest dances that Kurath, in the late sixties, thought were being replaced and they still retain the popular Comanche dance.

Just as saints' days are celebrated with Tewa dances, the originally Spanish-by-way-of-Mexico *Matachines* dance is a hybrid of European and indigenous dance and musical elements. The characters are European, with the important exception of the clowns. This seems to characterize most versions of the *Matachines* dance as it is performed in the southwestern United States. In the Tewa pueblos, the *Matachines* dance is performed at Christmas, setting it outside the indigenous ritual cycle, although in San Juan, the dancers for the turtle dance are rehearsing while the Matachines are performing. The musical instruments are also European rather than indigenous. They include violins and guitars, with an occasional drum for particular dances, especially the dance of the *toro* (bull). The dance steps themselves fall into the acceptable range of steps that the Tewa have adopted and adapted, making similar aesthetic judgments. The dance patterns, processions, and circuits are also a blend of European and indigenous habits.

Musicians, Dancers, and Other Participants

The questions of who dances and who sponsors the dances are as important in evaluating native aesthetics as are questions directed toward the form of the dances and rituals. Tewa dance was and is a community affair. Indeed, according to Sweet, ritual events are believed to be for the purpose of seeking new life; hence they serve to revitalize the community. In this manner, they bring together community members and reawaken concepts central to Tewa identity (1985:13). This means that every community member is responsible for a good ritual or dance. Such responsibility takes many forms, including that of being a knowledgeable audience member, actively contributing to the communal prayer that is dramatized by the singers and dancers (1985:16).

The first step that sets everything in motion is taken by the village or tribal council, who chooses the dances and sets the dates for their performance. Their choices, of course, reflect tradition and so do not have much latitude. What they propose is augmented by certain dances that must be requested by specific groups; the deer dance is requested by the unmarried men of a village, and the women's society has to request the cloud or basket dance.

With the choices and dates made, the war captains and their assistants go to the composers and ask that they ready the songs. Again, most of the songs are in the traditional repertoire but some dances, such as the turtle, cloud, and basket dances, require new songs each year. The next group to be invited are the lead male singers and they are chosen for their ability. They begin to meet with the composers for practice sessions in the kiva. Other male participants, more singers, and the dancers join in these practice sessions, and the dance steps and choreography begin to take shape. As in the case of songs, many dances are the same from year to year while others have to be choreographed new. Here, it is important to note that the core steps or technique remain the same and characterize the foundation of Tewa dance. It is the choreography or manner of combining the basic steps that contributes the variation.

With all this in place, the war captain and his assistants go to the houses of the women they would like to invite to participate. Participants are chosen for their dance ability and include both married and unmarried women. Those women who agree to dance then join the rest of the ritual participants in rehearsals in the practice kiva. Ability, rather than status associated with a social or political role, is extremely important in selecting dancers for particular roles. Gertrude Kurath and Antonio Garcia speak to this: "For the dancing, especially talented and carefully selected men and women fill the roles of an exclusive nature, as the two Corn Maidens, the Buffalo Mother, the Buffalo Fathers, and leaders of large dances. All eligible males are supposed to participate in *okunshare*, *tunshare*, and *pogonshare*, formerly all males and females in *xoxeye*. All members of Societies, officials, and representatives of both moieties attend the preparatory and final sessions of *tembishare*" (1970:38).

The last group to be involved before the actual dance itself is a group of young men who are charged with gathering the evergreen branches used in the dances to symbolize renewal of life.

Four evenings of practice before an event is the most common and that time is also used to prepare the costumes and paraphernalia. Participants may also have a final practice session on the day of the performance.

The order in which participants are invited signifies the relative importance of their contribution. Composers, of course, are essential even when the songs and dances are traditional because they are charged with remembering and staging them. When new songs are required, they must be able to work within the Tewa style at the same time that they create something different. Singers come next because it is the music that drives the dance and for most Tewa is the most important element in the ritual. Tempo is the most obvious way in which the music determines the dance but it is not the only feature. Phrasing and changes in the beat are cues to changes in choreographic pattern or direction. Both Kurath (1958) and Sweet (1985) write about *t'an* or *t'a*, a pause that allows dancers to shift from duple to triple meter. It is a slight hesitation in the basic *ântegeh* step (stamp, lift the right foot).

In addition to song, music is provided by drummers. Dancers provide percussion music through gourd rattles, sleigh bells sewn to a leather belt, and various noisemakers attached to their legs or leggings such as tin tinklers, deer hooves, and turtle shell rattles. In some instances, the dancers provide their own music. In the turtle dance, for example, the accompaniment is provided by the turtle shell rattles worn by the male dancers.

There are two other individuals whose actions purify the pueblo and who are exceptions to the mostly communal dance style of the Tewa. These are the *tsaviyo* (clowns; not the same as the *kosa*, ceremonial clowns) whose rituals take place during the winter solstice. From December 21 to December 25, the white *tsaviyo* of the winter moiety and the black *tsaviyo* of the summer moiety enact the oldest of rituals in the kivas and plazas and then join the plaza dancers. The white *tsaviyo* appears first, on the twenty-first. The following day, the black *tsaviyo* makes his appearance. Their costumes are white and black respectively, and they speak in Spanish in a falsetto voice. Kurath and Garcia's description of their movements is worth including here because it is so compelling in its detail and because their movements are so distinct from group dance steps: "They tread ghostlike and silently, without musical accompaniment. At times they stop and trot in place, peering about: then they trot ahead and leap soundlessly. They speak in whispers and they lash their whips, which are curative and purificatory rather than punitive . . . their annual solstice circuits make an impression that lasts through the year" (1970:45). In terms of weight and accent, these movements are quite distinct from the other communal dancing. The *tsaviyo* gestures and movements are light, irregular, and away from the ground, while almost all communal dance is weighty and into the ground.

In the four days in which they move about the pueblo, they establish relationships with the officials and they see that the pueblo prepares itself for rituals. On the evening of December 23, they are greeted by the dance officials and enter the pueblo. White goes counterclockwise around the north plaza, ending in front of the winter cacique's house. He strikes the ground as well as the stone pile that represents both the earth's and the pueblo's ceremonial center with his whip. Black goes clockwise through the south plaza to the home of the summer cacique. After they each are greeted by the respective caciques, they go to the big kiva. On the twenty-fifth, after the *Matachines* dance, the *tsaviyo* come from the hills and make the same circuits. On December 26, they announce the *okushare* (turtle dance) and "catch" eligible males, putting them in the dance line. After the dance, they go to the houses, blessing people, saying goodbye, curing people with their whips, reminding children to obey their parents, and receiving presents. At the end, they go to the summer moiety quarters in the big kiva to take off their ritual clothing. As we discuss later, the *tsaviyo* are one of the oldest elements of pueblo ritual and they appear before, during, and after the *Matachines* dance, one of the most European of pueblo rituals.

CHAPTER SIX

Steps and Choreography

In this discussion of the *tsaviyo*, I mentioned the paths each makes through the plazas of the pueblo. These circuits are one of the major features of Tewa dance. They vary in detail according to the geography of each pueblo, but all share the same features of fourfold repetition, entrances from the kivas, movement in a counterclockwise direction (though this is not always the case in practice), circuits of the plazas, or circuits of stations within one large plaza. San Juan pueblo has four plazas, two large ones parallel to each other and running east–west, and two smaller ones running north–south. Some dances may use all four plazas, some only the two larger ones; all begin in the south plaza (see Kurath 1958, Kurath and Garcia 1970 for details of plaza circuits according to pueblo and dance type). As the participants move through the plazas of the pueblo, the women, men, and children who are not performing come outside their homes and sit in the streets, lean out the windows, or sit on their roofs, lending their support to the ritual.

The technique of Tewa dance, or the elements of the grammar one must know in order to perform it correctly, includes choreographic elements such as plaza circuits and group formations. Much of this is determined by past practice; some is choreographed anew each annual cycle. It is within the purview of the composers and choreographers to set, although for those rituals that do not change, they may well consult older musicians and dancers. The other components of the form of Tewa dance include posture, gesture, and steps. Dancers learn the cultural prescriptions for performance, which vary across the different dances and between genders. Much of the learning is absorbed through observation, but coaching and practice also instill proper technique.

The posture for most Tewa dance is an erect torso, perhaps slightly bent forward. Men use more flexed-forward torsos than do women, especially in the eagle dance and the corn basket dance. Men also adopt the flexed and crouched postures when they borrow Plains-style dances. Clowns are the exception to the generally erect, stable torso, and may use highly flexed bodies and extreme extensions.

Gestures often involve objects that the dancers carry—gourd rattles, spruce branches, feather fans, lances, rainbow symbols, baskets. Some are gender-specific: gourd rattles are always carried by men, baskets by women. Spruce branches or cottonwood boughs may be used by both. Kurath refers to these gestures as stylized elements that carry covert meaning. They are "either decorative or symbolic because of the power of the manipulated objects" (Kurath and Garcia 1970:77). While clowns and dancers in the rain and harvest dances gesture with empty hands, all other gestures arise from manipulating ritual objects. In rain and harvest dances, the gestures are mimetic and designed to bring rain and to ensure a good harvest.

Steps take their shape from their dual purposes of locomotion and underlining the beat of the music and the sweep of the gestures. In the case of the animal dances, they are also suggestive of the movement of the particular animal. The Tewa general word for step is *ankhe* and the most common foot-lifting and stamping step is *antege* or *antegeh*. From those words, they create other step names that characterize steps associated with specific dances so *ankhe* for *xoxeye* means the step peculiar to the corn dance. Kurath and Garcia describe the basic *antege*, and Jill Sweet concurs, in the following way: "footlifting, with emphasis on right foot; upbeat of raising right knee, while supporting weight on left foot: accented lowering of right foot, while raising left heel and slightly flexing knees: unaccented raising of right knee while lowering left heel" (Kurath and Garcia 1970:82). This can be done in place or in forward- or diagonal-moving directions. When done by a large group, it conveys the power and the beauty of a unified community. This concentration or commitment of the dancers and musicians is a vital component of Tewa aesthetics. They speak of it as dancing and singing with respect or from the heart, which "makes the meaning straight." Another Tewa said, "You've got to concentrate a lot. Dance with your whole heart in it. Nothing else in your mind—just what is taking place there. Give it all you've got. Singing is the same way. When I sing, I sing from my heart up" (Sweet 1985:26).

One of the variations on the basic *antege* step is used in the fast buffalo dance and imitates a buffalo pawing the ground. The basic step for the buffalo dance, however, does have its own name, *dikonyi*, and it resembles a heavy gait such as would characterize a buffalo. It involves stepping heavily from foot to foot, with a slight lift from the ground on each step. This is also the male's step in *xoxeye* or the corn dance.

Deer Dancer, San Ildefonso. Photograph by Roger Sweet, 1974.

Deer dances have special, named steps as well—*dipenyi*, deer walk.

Those dancers who depict the deer use long sticks as if they were the deer's forelegs. The basic deer walk step is like an ordinary walk with longer strides and straight knees. The torso is bent forward, leaning on the "foreleg" sticks. There is another gait, this one in uneven, iambic rhythm, that gives the sense of a deer galloping. Dancers step forward on the right foot and land on the left at the end of a low leap. The steps may have much to do with the use of sticks. Other deer dances that do not use stick legs, for example, among the Yaqui of Arizona and northern Mexico, use the upper torso and head to mimic the movements of deer. Their leg and foot movements are also different—they cover more ground and are lighter in effort–shape terms. The use of sticks for forelegs creates a technique and choreography that is emblematic. Deer dances that do not use sticks are mimetic, especially with their sharp, jerky head and upper body movements.

Also in the category of walking steps are *antege* with *shushu* (or *suñu*). These are shuffling steps—strong shuffle forward on the right foot and a weaker shuffle back—done by the women in *tunshare* (basket dance).

Another category of steps described by Kurath and Garcia is composed of bounces and hops. The double bounce in the corn dance involves stepping onto the right foot with the knee bent, bouncing again on the right leg, then repeating the same on the left leg. The steps are short and the posture is erect. This double bounce is used as well in the deer dance but here it remains in place and the posture is bent forward because of the sticks. Patting steps are found in many dances including, most notably, the *ba'a* (belt) and the *tseshare* (eagle). In these, the dancer pats the half-toe on the ground, then steps onto that same full foot, alternating sides. This is very common across American Indian dance. The belt dance also has a hopping step in which the dancers hop forward, alternating feet.

Jumping, and the combination of jump and hop, are most common in the dances of clowns, in men's fast dances, in the eagle dance, and in other "show" dances. Women do not jump. In competitions organized by Anglos, there is always the tension between the kind of showy steps preferred by Anglos and the restrained, smaller steps dictated by Tewa aesthetics. One resolution has been the adoption of other dances like the hoop dance and some of the Plains fancy dancing by Tewa in which they may move much more vigorously than in their own dances. These adopted dances also tend to be ones that focus on the individual rather than on a group. Sweet describes the hoop dance of San Ildefonso as showy, exciting, and a crowd-pleaser. She finds no link between this dance and the traditional ritual calendar. In addition to the quick, intricate footwork, the hoop dance differs from other Tewa dance in its costume, usually a breechcloth and feathered headdress, and in its sole reliance on drum rather than drum and song.

The steps used by the clowns and other individuals in dances that burlesque other traditions or in the dance interludes of larger dance suites that serve the same function lie outside the ordinary technical repertoire of Tewa dance. I have described the movements of the white and black *tsaviyo*. Other clowns, categorized as *kosa* (clown of the winter moiety) and *kwirana* (clown of the summer moiety), employ fast, running steps, jumps and hops, and perform outside the group line and circle formations. They also perform during intermissions between plaza circuits. In the rain dance, *antegeshare*, for example, a March 29, 1964, performance recorded by Don Roberts notes that the clowns did a burlesque of the Catholic Church. One, dressed as an archbishop, delivered a sermon in Tewa and English. Aided by his acolyte, he also blessed the congregation with holy water, dipping a long-handled car-washing brush into a bucket of water and waving it over the crowd (Kurath and Garcia 1970:135).

Other burlesques include the Navajo dance, done by women taking both male and female roles and dressed as Navajo. Their movements sometimes imitate Navajo dances. Then there are the "Apache" in the Tewa deer dance, who both dress and move like Apaches. Comanche dances exist in every Tewa pueblo and come from a time when Tewa and Comanche interacted either through trade or raids of each other. The dance style is fast-paced and full of individual display, as are most of the Plains men's dances.

There are enough differences between women's and men's dancing to refer to two techniques. In this regard, Tewa dance is no different from other genres such as classical ballet or Kabuki or *bharata natyam*. The techniques are distinctive across postures, gestures, and steps. Further, some dances are appropriate for women and some are not. Women may never be clowns among the Tewa; they are not allowed to participate in the most sacred line dances; in mixed-gender dances, they never lead; and they are not featured as musicians. In contrast, women dance equal and perhaps more prominent roles in *tunshare* (basket dance), all dances characterized by *wasa* (weaving), all harvest dances, the *konshare* (buffalo dance), *kwitara* (Comanche dance), and all social dances. Their posture is less flexed than men's; they tend to hold their torsos erect. They use a full repertory of gestures—bringing the rain, planting crops, harvesting, and, in the basket dance, accompanying the dance at one point by scraping their baskets with notched sticks. Women engage in wicked parodies as in the *ashare* (bow and arrow dance) and the Navajo dance. As in most societies that are predominantly agricultural but with some hunting and gathering, women play an important role in ceremonial events, including dance.

Performance Outside the Pueblo

The custom of dancing for the non-Indian world is rooted in the discovery of this remarkably beautiful part of the United States by Anglo artists, writers, and tourists. The building of the Atchison, Topeka, and Santa Fe Railway was completed in 1888, and all along its route were restaurants established by Fred Harvey. They were legendary and contributed to the popularity of seeing America by rail. Harvey also had a keen eye for the exotic appeal of Indian art and Indians. In Albuquerque, he built the Alvarado Hotel and between it and the railroad created the Fred Harvey Indian Building. He hired Indian craftspeople to set up work areas where they could weave, make pots, or design jewelry. These were enormously successful. Indians also came to perform, one group of four men captured in a 1905 photograph at the Alvarado Indian Building.

The Harvey enterprises were just one of the many opportunities for paid performance. Anyone interested in attracting the tourist trade, especially in the towns of Albuquerque, Gallup, and Santa Fe, knew that Indian dancers and singers had a strong appeal and hired them to perform in "ceremonials" (Sweet 1985:11). The ceremonial in Gallup is the oldest continuous Anglo-organized event. Sweet documents the participants and their dances for 1923, the first year of Tewa participation: "Tesuque dancers were contracted to perform short segments of the bow and arrow, buffalo, and eagle dances, and a San Juan group performed segments of the buffalo, basket, war, deer, dog, turtle, and butterfly dances" (p. 49). Santa Fe developed a reputation primarily for its arts and crafts fair but dancers are hired to perform short segments of dances in the patio of the Palace of Governors.

The implications of these ceremonials and the more recent arts and crafts fairs for the form of Tewa dance are complex. First and foremost, there is an ongoing dialectic between dances done outside the pueblo context and those done within and for the pueblo. In a fundamental sense, it does not matter whether the outside events are Anglo- or Tewa-organized. The shape of the choreography will be radically altered whenever dance is done outside the pueblo, because one of the most fundamental features, the plaza circuit, cannot be reproduced. The shape of the dance, in terms of performance from beginning to end, will be different because Tewa abbreviate dances, choose segments out of the whole when they perform for non-Tewa or even for Tewa at a fair. Plaza dances are repeated the requisite number of times depending on the number of plazas and the kind of dance. This repetition would simply not work in a nonpueblo setting. The choice of dances usually favors those that are more appealing to Anglos—that is, more colorful in terms of costumes and participants, more flamboyant in terms of movement—and, in general, those that resonate with Anglo stereotypes of Indian dance. This will be the same with both Anglo- and Tewa-organized events, if both anticipate primarily an Anglo audience.

The Tewa have initiated theatrical dance events, too. The first was organized by the Santa Clara Tewa and took place at Puye Cliffs, an ancient site about ten miles from the pueblo. The event was quite popular and was given every year from 1957 to 1981. Anglo elements were kept to a minimum (no prizes, for example) and Tewa prayers were embedded in the structure. The event's first organizer, Juan Chavarria, spoke to its serious nature: "I know for sure that [the ancestors] are out there in spirit among the dancers . . . and I very much believe that they are among us and that we are all taking part in dancing—as well as when we are dancing in the pueblo—the same feeling—you have to put your whole heart and yourself into what dances you are taking part in—no matter where you are dancing" (Sweet 1985:53). The event was dropped after two women were killed by lightning in 1981, a tragedy regarded by many as a supernatural warning.

Nambe Tewa organized the Nambe Falls event in 1961, and, from its inception, it has incorporated Anglo as well as Tewa elements. Originally it was a fundraiser for the Nambe Catholic church. In order to draw the largest crowd, it is held on July 4. Possibly because of this, it opens with a flag-raising ceremony—the U.S., New Mexico, and Nambe pueblo flags.

Then an elder gives an invocation in Tewa after which the dances may begin. Other pueblos may also participate in the dances, although most are performed by Nambe villagers. It has been an important vehicle for inculcating Tewa customs into the younger generation.

One of the most significant events offering an opportunity to dance and to sell artwork is a fair organized by the Eight Northern Indian Pueblo Council, which has been held every July since 1973. The location moves from pueblo to pueblo—the six Tewa pueblos, plus Picuris and Taos. Sweet (1985) commented that the two-day event attracts between ten and twelve thousand people and I can attest to that on the basis of my attendance in 1992. Among the dances I saw in 1992 were the basket dance, the eagle dance, the bow and arrow dance, and the buffalo dance. By far the largest area is devoted to displays of arts and crafts. The dances are performed in a separate area.

Tewa, like most Indian people, travel to intertribal powwows to perform. What dances they do depends upon the hosts and the other participants. With their Comanche dance firmly established in local repertories, they are able to dance in most powwows, even ones hosted by Plains groups.

Basket Dance, Eight Northern Pueblos Arts and Crafts Fair, 1992. Photograph by Anya Peterson Royce.

Basket Dance, Eight Northern Pueblos Arts and Crafts Fair, 1992. Photograph by Anya Peterson Royce.

Finally, the Indian Pueblo Cultural Center in Albuquerque, an Indian-run center with a museum, gift shop, and restaurant, features Indian dance and song performances by Pueblo groups each weekend in the summer months.

As part of an extensive ceremonial calendar, most Tewa pueblos maintain an annual cycle of dances that acknowledges their agricultural and hunting origins. The patronal feast is a major event and Christmas sees versions of the *Matachines* dance in most pueblos. These ceremonies that take place within the boundaries of the pueblos involve most of the people who live there as active singers, dancers, composers, choreographers, or audience members. In addition, Tewa men and women participate in a variety of outside events, some as close as in other pueblos, during the Eight Northern Pueblos Arts and Crafts Fair, at a weekend performance in Albuquerque, or farther away at intertribal powwows or Smithsonian-sponsored festivals in Washington, D.C.

The truth of the matter is that for all of their history the Tewa have been engaged in activities that have brought them into contact with other peoples. Many of these activities have been economic, based on trade of agricultural products for hides, but there were also occasions when aspects of ceremonial life were observed and sometimes borrowed. Tewa interacted with other Indian peoples, the Spanish and later the Mexicans, and finally the Anglos. Some were passing through; others were making their homes there. The *Matachines* dance is probably the most significant single ceremony from the outside that was adopted by the Tewa but their history is one of continuous interaction and selective borrowing.

It is useful to examine further the kinds of changes in Tewa dance and ritual just as we have looked at change in other forms, such as Kabuki, the commedia dell'arte, and classical ballet. The Tewa demonstrate a similar pattern. They have adopted entire new dances, like the *Matachines*; they have created new dances based on their interaction with other groups, like the Comanche dance, the Navajo dance, and the use of Apache figures in the deer dance. They have adjusted the ritual calendar to accommodate to new ways of making a living that constrain people's time in different ways. They have danced more frequently outside the pueblos where the context and purpose are completely different. They have accepted the notion of competition in Anglo-sponsored events even though they do not compete in their own context. What seems not to have changed is the basic technique of both dance and song. I argue in the example of Michel Fokine that technique, once set, changes only rarely. Minor variations, like calibrating a fine machine, are necessary in any genre, a kind of flexibility that allows for continuity.

Tewa dance within the pueblos is part of a web of social and ceremonial relationships that binds all the residents, indeed, that binds those who return for special events. It has been a vital and continuing part of Tewa life. It is vital in that it has incorporated elements that reflect changing and new contexts, continuing in that its fundamental technique and core set of ceremonies have not changed. The basic aesthetic principles by which Tewa have judged themselves and others as dancers and singers hold true today just as they did in the past. The idea of competition is accepted as part of doing business with Anglos but has not changed the fundamental values of communal versus individual, restrained versus extravagant.[2]

The Tewa enjoy a rich and varied ritual life, revolving centrally around dance and song. They recognize individuals whom they designate as excellent performers and those individuals are sought out for participation. They have roles for composers and choreographers, lead singers, and lead dancers. Their music and dance have codified techniques recognized by members of the community. Much of what they do falls toward the ritual end of the ritual–theatre continuum but they have also developed dances and songs that allow them to participate in more theatrical events. The future seems assured for Tewa ritual and dance as it continues to evolve around a solid core of technique and ritual calendar, making accommodations to modern demands of different jobs and pueblo members living outside the pueblo.

Notes

1. Peoples who have successfully endured changes in the larger political and social structure have done so, in large part, because of their flexibility and willingness to accommodate foreign elements into their cultural repertoire. If one examines which elements and how they are incorporated, one finds that they are generally those that either fit within deep cultural values or make life more interesting and comfortable. In the case of competing religions or rituals, usually the former applies and elements are selectively adopted (Royce 1982).

2. A revised and updated edition of Jill Sweet's work on Tewa dance is being published in June 2004 by School of American Research Press. This edition promises to have much material on Tewa aesthetic judgments and criteria as well as on changes that have occurred in both the dances and the dance contexts.

CHAPTER SEVEN
ARTISTIC PERFORMANCES: JANOS STARKER CRAFTS THE INEVITABLE

Disciplined performance strives for purity and simplicity, not for mere effect.

—Janos Starker

In studio 155, in the School of Music, virtuosity and artistry are the order of the day, every day since Janos Starker came to join the faculty of Indiana University forty-four years ago. Excellent young cellists have come to study with Starker, hoping to become better, virtuosos, perhaps even artists. So many have come that he has trained a good percentage of the cellists currently performing, teaching, and recording. And they continue to come. A large part of the attraction must surely be his reputation as a performer. Martin Mayer wrote this about Starker in 1961, one year after Starker's first New York City recital: "Every so often an artist appears who dominates his instrument in the minds of a generation, and usually you spot him young. There was never much doubt about Casals, or Heifetz, or Segovia or Landowska. And there is not much doubt today about the thirty-seven-year-old Hungarian-American Janos Starker."[1]

In the subsequent forty-two years, Starker has continued to dazzle audiences with his impeccable and expressive playing. Moreover, he has recorded virtually the entire cello repertoire, including many works composed for him. His ability to meld virtuosic and artistic elements is reflected in this comment by Raymond Ericson of the *New York Times* included in Martin Mayer's 1961 liner notes: "The technical aspects of Mr. Starker's playing are so wholly merged in the solution to problems of interpretation and style, that the listener tends to forget how much technical mastery the cellist has achieved. The pitch is unerringly right, the

Janos Starker. Photograph by T. Charles Erickson, Yale University.

tone is mellow without being mushy, difficult leaps and runs are manipulated with the easy unobtrusiveness of a magician." Whatever the source of the attraction for students, when they arrive at the university, they find more than the extraordinary performer they know from recordings and performances. They soon realize that Starker is as extraordinary a teacher as he is a performer. Ericson alludes to it in his comment. Starker has thought through virtually every aspect of cello playing and of music making. He knows how they work, technically and artistically, and how the technical and artistic aspects interact with each other to produce interpretations that are inevitable. Perhaps most important, for students and for other musicians, is that he knows how to teach all of this. It is no wonder that his master classes and lecture-demonstrations are legendary.

As a colleague of Starker's at the university, I have been fortunate to sit in lessons and the famous Saturday master classes, to have sat through the recording session of the Popper recording he made with pianist Shigeo Neriki, and to have attended performances and collected recordings. Then there have been the annual Eva Janzer Memorial Cello Center weekends, devoted to honoring cellists and others who have contributed to music making and cello playing. Over the years, I have watched cellists like Tortelier, Rostropovich, Garbusova, Nelsova, Parisot, Eleanor Slatkin, Varga, and many others teach, play, and talk about music during these annual gatherings. There is also the annual concert that Starker presents at Indiana University to raise scholarship money. Imagine a concert of all the Beethoven cello–piano sonatas with Starker and Gyorgy Sebok! On top of all this have been the many conversations he and I have had about music, cello playing (I did study the cello with Starker student Helga Winold, a virtuoso teacher herself), performing arts, virtuosity, and comparisons between music and dance.

It was in one of those conversations that the notion of inevitability was raised. We were talking, I think, about musicality and having a sense of the whole work such that each choice of phrasing, bowing, fingering, and note was made in the context of the whole. The result is an interpretation so harmonious with the piece that it seems inevitable. It made me think of great dance performances and of my own performing experience. Because my most compelling training was with Ludmilla Shollar and her husband Anatol Vilzak, who were products of the Russian school that produced Fokine and the dancers of the Ballets Russes, I was taught the importance of phrasing and variation in weight and emphasis, all in the context of the sense of an entire variation. Moreover, that variation had to be crafted in terms of its place in the larger balletic work. Reading Fokine's works about what he envisioned is provocative because it is so similar to Starker's analysis and to my own training. For Fokine, for example, each of the *Les Sylphides* variations should be danced as if it were one breath. This comes quite close to Starker's own emphasis on sustaining a musical line.

Teaching

To understand Starker's own thorough approach to teaching, it helps to hear what he has to say about his own teacher, Leó Weiner: "Leó Weiner taught us to hear and helped us to learn the tools with which to make music. He taught us that in music every note matters. He taught us discipline which first demands the observation of the composers' intentions, and only then can we enhance it with individual recreative ideas. He made us aware of the direction of beats, rhythmic consistencies, breathing, rubato, agogic, unit changes, and pulse. He increased our inner needs for the ideal legato for lines ascending and descending. He helped us to understand the necessity of building climaxes and anticlimaxes. He demanded purity of sound, simplicity of expression, and balanced structure" (Starker 1999:188).

Starker embodies all of these Weiner attributes in his own teaching. While it has been said, incorrectly and by individuals who know only a fraction of his teaching, that Starker is a master analyst to the exclusion of commentary on broader aspects of music making, he is adamant about the ultimate goal of instrumental music—the technique is simply in the service of singing. As he says frequently, "The score is not little pieces; it is not independent notes. It's music; it's line. Play it that way." It is also true that teachers are shaped by their experiences as students and as performers. Starker has said that he cannot play without teaching and that he cannot teach without playing. He has experienced virtually every situation that can arise in the life of a performing musician—as orchestra player, chamber musician, soloist, recording artist—and, across them all, playing every musical work written for the cello. This unduplicated experience, combined with Weiner's and his own musical principles, makes him a formidable teacher.

Starker, responding to the inevitable questions about which bowings or fingerings to use, makes students think of how different options contribute to where they want to go with the whole piece. He has published editions of much of the repertoire with his own fingerings and bowings, and his students find these. What works for him, he tells them, will not necessarily work for them. He is quite cognizant of the individual gifts of his students. "You can only bring forth what is in a student's nature and enhance the love of music by giving the right information. By nature, some people will be ensemble players and some will be orchestral. A few will be soloists. The teacher's job is to help students learn all the skills and principles of instrumental playing. . . . The teacher's reward . . . comes from making a student's imagination work. I'm far less interested in talent than in a student whose brain allows for continual development. I've concluded that we cannot teach talent. We can only teach talented ones" (Jacobi 1999:240).

Starker analyzes bowings and fingerings, two key aspects of cello playing, in terms of technique and interpretation. So in choosing bowings or fingerings one must consider the abilities and the physical body of the individual, always understanding that there are some choices that are not acceptable under any circumstances, because they produce poor sound—as Starker often says in lessons and classes, "you can have your own bowings and fingerings, just don't play nonmusical sounds"—or because they will lead to physical damage over years of playing. But choice also has to do with interpretation. What is the musical sense that you want to achieve? That these choices make a difference is absolutely clear when you listen to successive interpretations of the same piece, but you can hear and feel the impact in a single performance. Starker's recording of the Schumann Cello Concerto in A Minor has such a moment when, at the beginning of the second movement, continuing the same note, he shifts to a high position. The effect is instantaneous. You hear it but you also feel it physically. It is like the deepest sigh, wistful and melancholic. When you listen to the whole concerto, this apparently singular choice becomes an inevitable part of the whole.

Extra-Technical Elements

Those extra-technical elements I outlined in chapter two are also part of interpretation. They include those elements I subsumed under musicality—dynamic variation, rubato and agogic, and sustaining a phrase, as well as the element of economy. Those elements that compose musicality allow variety, contrast, and shading in a musical work just as they do in dance. While this is not surprising given that dance is rarely performed without music, there are aspects of musicality in dance that are quite different. This has much to do with the limitations on the human body and affects duration more than stress. In music, there are no physical constraints on either dynamic or durational variation. Indeed, strings have more possibilities for the latter than do percussive instruments, where the duration of sound is limited by the instrument itself. In string playing, dynamics can be varied by techniques such as the use of harmonics, which creates a lighter sound, or bowing near the bridge. Both techniques produce less sound but the qualities, and hence, the effects, are different. The normal range of the instrument also offers many possibilities for dynamic variation. On the topic of sounds, Starker has spoken in terms of positive or negative sound, singing versus humming, tension, and release.

Rubato and Agogic

Rubato and agogic are two modes of playing with duration, with phrasing. *Rubato*, translated from Italian, means "robbed," and that is exactly what rubato does—it takes time away from one note and spends it on another. The performer temporarily disregards strict tempo. Used properly, it creates excitement or heightens anticipation. *Agogic* literally means "leading" and refers in music to a kind of accent effected by lengthening the time value of a note. It is important to remember that there are constraints on how much one can change the tempi. Starker's definitions of agogic and rubato are significant: the former means freedom within the bar, the latter, freedom within the phrase. How and why one employs these devices makes the difference between a tasteful performance and an indulgent one. It is something that Starker stresses in his teaching, as he does the whole question of license.

In this whole area of dynamics, duration, and phrasing, the sense is the same as it is in dance. The performer has certain points in any given interpretation that are more important than others and needs to choose phrasing and timing that leads the ear or eye to those points of emphasis. A climax has to be framed. In a long piece, there will be more than one and probably there will also be a hierarchy among them. The performer must set out the larger phrase so that it supports each point along the way. An interpretation in which every step or note has the same value is boring. Starker comments on famed soprano Maria Callas's unerring sense of phrasing and climax: "She had an extraordinary ability to lay low to prepare for what's ahead and make that climax a stunning thing. She somehow produced orchestral sounds in singing" (Starker 2001:42–43).

Sustaining a Phrase

Here it is appropriate to introduce the notion of sustaining a phrase, because in many ways it is related to playing with tempi. In dance (see chapter two), sustaining a phrase means to create a sense of movement without full stops. Some choreography requires this and it is done by the subtle use of breathing and almost imperceptible movement that continues the line of the body. In music, it has to do with continuing the sound past the point of silence. It has everything to do with anticipation, meaning that the listener, in anticipating the next phrase, sustains the previous one. Of course, the question is how does the musician create that anticipation in the first place? Starker once defined for me his idea of virtuosity—the largest number of notes a musician can play with one impulse, in a sense, sustaining the sound as if it were one breath, a breath the listener continues to hear even when it is no longer audible. When he first said it, I imagined the exercise of trying to divide one bow stroke into as many of the same notes as you could. This may be part of it, but I think that sustaining a phrase requires, in addition to great technical mastery, elements of playing with tempi and constructing an interpretation such that the listener is led to hear these kinds of phrases because they are the right ones for that moment. I also think that impulse has much to do with phrase length—feeling the beat between the beats. And just as dancers can sustain the sense of movement, making the audience see pauses rather than full stops, so musicians can sustain sound into silence so that the audience continues to hear sound. The line of the music functions very much like the line of the body.

Economy

Economy means selection and discrimination. It also means focus. In music as in dance, focus has to do with selecting those elements that further the interpretation that you have chosen and eliminating all the rest, which can only distract. This is why economy is a crucial component of artistry. To use it well implies that you have studied a piece profoundly enough that you can create an appropriate interpretation. You must choose those elements that are harmonious with that interpretation and discard the others. Economy requires restraint. It does not mean that there is only one interpretation possible; Starker's recordings of Bach ought to be proof enough of that. It does mean that you cannot use all the possible phrasings, dynamics, and so forth in one performance. Even cadenzas, where musicians have the luxury of playing without the orchestra and, theoretically, may embellish as they wish, require economy and sensitivity to the musical whole. That Starker embodies that kind of sensitivity has been noted by critics since quite early in his career. Here is one such note about a 1969 concert in Prague, which appeared in the magazine *Hudebni rozhledy*: "What is important is that while playing, he seems to remain in the shade, simply a servant of music: and one gets the impression that playing the cello is so easy. And this evidently unaffected naturalness is always a feature of perfection. What one will remember about this kind of concert is just the music—beautiful, quiet, emotional" (Jacobi 1999:227).

Impulse

I have already spoken of one of the important aspects of style, namely, impulse. Starker often teaches the importance of this to students, quite literally, by standing behind them and marking the beat between the beats by pushing down on their shoulders. They can then feel it in their bodies and, hopefully, transfer it into their playing. He also pays a lot of attention to beginnings, again getting students to embody that impulse in the first note so that it does not appear to come out of nowhere. The gesture precedes the sound. When you listen to Starker play, he is immediately recognizable by the crispness of his attack, which is a result of impulse. Impulse is what gives music drive and force. Just as it gives movements in dance shape and definition, so does it define the musical phrase. Without it, everything has the sameness of pabulum. Not only is the audience lost or bored without impulse, the musician who cannot recognize it is lost as well, not able to define or shape an interpretation.

Density

Density plays a significant role in dance. It may play an equally important but different role in music. Certainly in music, composers use a kind of closeness of texture or consistency, both in terms of music for single performers as well as in orchestration. One can create a thick sound through compacted instrumentation. It is likely related to musical dynamics in which *sul ponticello*[2] and the use of harmonics (in string playing) create a very thin sound. A denser sound can be produced by the use of double-stops.[3] Vibrato can also be used to vary the thickness of the sound. In piano, the pedal can give weight to the notes. These are two examples but all musical instruments have the capacity to create more and less dense sound. It is interesting to note changing audience preferences for bright, airy music, on the one hand, and heavy, dense music, on the other.

In thinking about the humor of unexpected weight in dance, I realize that there are parallels in musical compositions as, for example, in the second movement of the Prokofiev Cello Sonata. There are subtle humorous passages in many compositions, and then there are also the blatant and obvious interjections of humor provided by such "heavy" instruments as the tuba or any of the bass wind instruments.

Centeredness

Centeredness is present in music in many of the same ways that one finds it in dance. In a very physical sense, the cellist has to be centered in relation to the cello in order to have the freedom of movement necessary for truly fine playing. The tension is in the center, freeing the arms and legs to move. The curves and circles that make up the way the bow arm functions or how the left hand gets around the fingerboard are all related to a notion of center and the understanding that everything in nature is curved. Starker pays a lot of attention to posture with his students. Some come having learned to play remarkably well, but with a posture that is totally wrong and will eventually shorten their careers as musicians. Sometimes the solution is as simple as the length of the end-pin or the height of the chair; sometimes it requires much more diagnosis and prescription. Starker spends as much time as it takes to correct because posture is one of the most critical aspects of being a cellist.

In addition to posture, other aspects of relation to a center have to do with the technical aspects of playing. These may be specific to string playing, though there may be similar technical issues for other instrumentalists. How one divides the bow stroke is critical. Certain effects are created by playing at the tip or, conversely, close to the frog. But one has to know that these are effects and they should be used sparingly in any composition. In a similar manner, playing close to the bridge or far back on the fingerboard can be used occasionally for effect but most playing requires consistent bowing at neither extreme.

Starker raises another way in which one may speak of centeredness. In response to an interviewer's question about how he would describe his sound, he said, "Focused. Centered. The focused sound goes very far in one direction, but it doesn't necessarily cover the left and the right side of the hall. That's in comparison with other kinds of sound production, with the wide vibrato and so on, which doesn't carry very far but sounds luscious nearby. It [focused sound] was primarily influenced by Jascha Heifetz, and at one point Emanuel Feuermann, who was the first cellist to produce sounds that were not necessarily cello sounds. When I was principal cellist of the Metropolitan Opera, I played with the greatest singers. The influence of those singers was primarily from Jussi Bjoerling, who had the purest, cleanest tenor I ever heard" (Starker 2001:42–43).

With the exception of these physical and technical aspects, centeredness in music may have as much to do with the composition as it does with the performance. Of course, the performer has to understand the center–periphery components of any piece or the interpretation will not capture the intent of the composer.

The contrast in significance in dance and mime may well be related to the embodied nature of those forms. The body is both the instrument and the performer. As in music, the simple physical demands require the performer to have a real sense of place, of being centered; otherwise one is always off-balance in a literal sense. But in dance and mime, that placement is also used in a metaphorical way, as the point of balance, the point of tension, and the stable center from which one goes out and to which one returns. In music, this metaphorical function lies in the musical composition, especially if one believes, as does Starker, that enriching the music is the purpose of any re-creative artist.

Simplicity

I spoke about simplicity in chapter three but it is worth extending that discussion here. There are two possible sources of elaborate ornamentation, the opposite of simplicity: one is in the work, the other in the interpretation. A faithful interpretation of a highly ornamented piece will retain that style. I would not argue for simplifying music or choreography that has its own integrity. The interpreter has the choice, however, of whether to impose further elaboration or not. There are places for that elaboration—cadenzas for instrumental music, the whole *bel canto* style of singing, melisma (prolonging one syllable over a number of notes) in certain genres of vocal music, and changes allowed for dancers in solo variations. Otherwise, I would argue that the less performer ornamentation there is, the more artistic the performance will be. Calling attention to oneself as a performer is the kind of virtuosity that may be appropriate for those genres in which the goal is to create tension in the public. In all other performance, such behavior insures that the public sees only the performer and not the work. This is not to say that virtuosity, in the technical sense in which I have described it, is bad or unnecessary. Audiences deserve to see music, dance, and theatre executed well by performers who have mastered the technique of the genre.

Interpretation

If the point of art is to move its audience beyond itself, beyond its everyday concerns, to a place where it can glimpse a beauty and a truth beyond time, then we must have artists who can take us there. Those rare performers who do this create interpretations that are ineluctable, inevitable. Some, even more rare, evoke a quality of transparency so that the audience sees the work in all its perfection without the intrusion of the performer who created that perfection. In performance, the personality and personal tastes of the performer have no place. As Starker has said so often, "It is the music that matters, not me."

Timothy Mangan of the *Orange County Register* caught this sense of Starker's approach in his review of a 1999 performance of the Dvořák Cello Concerto with the Pacific Symphony: "There didn't seem to be a wasted notion in it. . . . Starker gave the music plenty of room to breathe. Most cellists, even the good ones, jump all over this concerto and ride it for all it's worth—exploring every cranny, milking every nuance, exulting every peak, juicing up the vibrato to full power. . . . Starker remained calm and poised, allowing the music to do its own storytelling. That's called trusting your material" (Jacobi 1999:221).

Inevitability of interpretation is not at all the same thing as predictability. The latter would lead to an uninteresting, if not boring, evening for the audience. The not predictable but nonetheless inevitable quality has to lie in the interpretation because the work remains the work. The nature of performance itself ensures that each performance is unique. Even if the work is the same and the performer has not changed the major outlines of the interpretation, the context is not the same. It is a different audience. It may be a different venue. The virtuosity of even great performers varies from performance to performance, affecting the details of the interpretation. Above all, the audience and the performer are joined in the nightly process of creation, which creates unique experiences each time.

Beyond all that, a great performer regards every interpretation as a work in progress. There can be an infinite number of interpretations that have that quality of inevitability. Performers use all those elements of which I have spoken to craft an interpretation that is in accord with the sense of the work and that will produce in audiences a sense of rightness, of resolution. They will not necessarily know where they are being taken in the performance, but at the end, they will feel that it was the only possible endpoint. I think here of the recording of the Brahms sonatas for cello and piano by Starker and Sebok. The listener is lulled, on the one hand, by the rhythmic pace of the music, and startled, on the other hand, by the hesitations in the conversation between piano and cello. It is like old friends talking, silences that are filled with fragments of conversations, one finishing the thought of the other—you are never sure where it is going, but you are confident that, when you arrive, it will be the right place.

Even though there are many possibilities for inevitable interpretations, one wrong choice can create doubt and leave the audience with a vague sense that something was not quite right. Having sat in master classes over many years, especially those in which students were playing the competition piece for that year, has given me much comparative material about interpretations. Hearing the same work played by two or more cellists in a short span of time attunes your ears to all the possibilities and choices. As an educated listener, I can sort out those that are "successful" from those that are not. Sometimes, I can even explain the reasons in terms of style elements. There are always a few wrong notes but those are not what I am talking about in this analysis. The quotation marks around "successful" point to what I mean about the process of interpretation. The ones that sound right are those that are consonant with the composer's body of work. The listener has a sense that the performer knows all the work of that particular composer, and has crafted an interpretation on the basis of that understanding. A piece may, in fact, be aberrant but you only know that by knowing it in the context of everything else.

Even having crafted an interpretation that is at the highest artistic level, an artistic whole with each component leading to the next, the performer still has the public with which to contend. And there will always be audience members who prefer someone else's interpretation over the one they have just heard. Often, these are the most musically educated individuals who, like commedia dell'arte or Kabuki audiences, have favorites. This is one of the aspects of performance that makes a performer's life difficult. They are, in fact, in between the work and the audience. Part of the creative process occurs in the moment of performance, which means that the performer does not have total control of the work. Performers like Marceau have talked about the changes he makes during performances if he feels the audience is not where he wants it to be. However much discipline performers have undergone in the studio and in rehearsal, however much thought they have given to a particular interpretation, they must present themselves to the public whether they feel ready or well. It may be the first and only time many audience members will see them, and they will have an opinion, whether fairly based or not. Starker's distinction between the professional and the dilettante rests on the notion of consistency. "I cannot allow myself the luxury of playing badly if I don't feel well. Every time I am on stage and people come and make the effort to hear me, they should be given their money's worth. Their being there honors me. In return, I must deliver. Discipline is the key. It explains everything. I feel that a professional always must be able to perform at 85 percent of his capacity on any given night. The remaining 15 percent should be a matter of inspiration" (Jacobi 1999:215). So the professional, even on a bad night, plays at a certain level and does so consistently.

This is quite different from the experience of the creators, both of performed arts and of visual or literary arts. Those individuals can polish a piece, set it aside, and come back to it; they do not have to let it be seen or heard until they are satisfied. I speak here of the ideal; the marketplace or need to earn a living are factors that can disrupt this generally positive state.

In a postpresentation conversation with a composer at the Liguria Study Center in Bogliasco, Italy, someone asked if he had a work's trajectory and end in mind when he sat down to compose. He said no, and was immediately seconded by the poets, novelists, and visual artists present who said that the not-knowing was an integral part of their creative process; that the work simply takes them where it wants, and in many directions that lead to dead ends. He said this was part of the excitement. As a writer, even writing nonfiction, I find this familiar because it is the way I work, too, although only in the first drafts. Revision becomes much more like what a performer does in readying an interpretation. The performer, or re-creative artist as Starker calls himself, creates an interpretation in a calculated manner. The entire work has to be laid out and analyzed, and decisions have to be made about phrasing, dynamic variation, emphasis, high points, meaning, and a hundred other things. The interpretation is tested, changed perhaps, polished. By the time it is performed, it is known intimately. The surprise, the not-knowing—this comes in the performance.

Recording

Perhaps the closest a performer comes to the experience of the creator lies in the area of making a permanent record of a performance. Dance, mime, and theatre are now being filmed but films of these genres still are not perceived as adequate alternatives to live performances. Musical recording has a longer history, and, for some, recordings are preferable because they are "perfect" in a way live performances are not. This is not my opinion, by the way. I like recordings; indeed, I hear different things in them and I like being able to compare recordings by the same artists from different times. For me, however, there is an immediacy and excitement about a live performance that is simply not there in a recording.

Both Starker and Marceau have spoken about the peculiar requirements of recording and filming. The presentation is not the same as it for a live performance in either case. For Marceau, the first films made of his mimes were very disappointing because neither he nor the filmmakers realized that they could not simply film a mime as if it were being presented on a stage to a live audience. Those early films are flat, almost two-dimensional, and have none of the qualities that make Marceau such an exciting performer. Subsequent films, however, are quite another story. He changes the mimes and uses close-ups, fade-outs, and other filmmaking techniques. They are full of interest. Some might quibble and say that they are not the same mime; that is true, they are not, but they are good theatre, and they are Marceau.

In a similar manner, Starker changes works when he is going to record them. He thinks through the interpretation; he practices differently from how he practices for a live performance; in short, the work he performs for a recording is not the same as the one he would perform for a live audience. He offers a succinct commentary on recording versus live performances: "The recording is supposed to represent an artist's view of a piece under perfect circumstances. If there's something you don't like, you can do it again. If there is a wrong note, you can correct it. You're supposed to make a statement or a testament in some sense. . . . The conditions are basically perfect. It's supposed to represent your maximum view and ability through a given piece. But it's a different art. It's cinema versus theater" (Starker 2001:44).

The recording sessions I watched for the Starker and Neriki Popper pieces were very instructive as far as the actual recording was concerned. The recording was made in the Musical Arts Center at Indiana University, which has excellent acoustic properties, and it can be miked properly for recording. Starker and Neriki are frequent partners, both in performance and on recordings. They had played a number of these pieces in performance. The idea was to record all of the Popper pieces, something that had not ever been done. One of the crucial questions, which arose all throughout the sessions, was that of balance between piano and cello. In a performance, initial decisions are made and pretty much remain through the performance. In a recording session, the medium itself introduces different sound qualities. You also have the reality of constant playback which makes change almost impossible to resist. Finally, when there are two artists, it is virtually never the case that both are wholly satisfied with their individual performance on any given take. In performance, of course, you cannot go back and play a piece again but recording is something else. They played every piece as many times as necessary to reach a performance satisfying to both. Starker has referred to these as partnerships in which it is a matter of knowing the strengths and tendencies of the partner, and then experimenting your way into an integrated interpretation. One difficulty in this kind of recording is maintaining the same sound or the same approach or the sense of the interpretation over many, many hours.

One of the most notable differences between a live performance and a recording, according to Starker, deals with the use of silence. You cannot use it at all the same way. In a live performance, you can extend periods of silence much longer than you can in a recording. If you were to allot the same time to silence in a recording, it would fall flat; it would be dead. Performance allows you to build up the intensity, the anticipation, because you are there as a physical presence. You generate energy between yourself and the audience that fills the silence and gives it meaning. None of that holds true in a recording so your interpretation, or that part of it that uses silence in particular ways, has to change, perhaps to use other elements to create the same feeling. As a matter of fact, Starker makes silence one of the defining features of a live performance: "When you're playing on stage, you interact with the audience, either by silence or by making noise. The major objective of the musician is to create silences. When you play a phrase and wait, that's one of the most beautiful things, when the hall is completely silent" (Starker 2001:44). This is what Nijinsky created so compellingly in his choreography for *Afternoon of a Faun*, a stillness that obliged the audience to participate actively in its performance.

Transparency

Transparency is the ultimate characteristic of great performers, including ethnographers. It is that requisite state of detachment from a process that has consumed you all your career. It requires you to hand over to a public a work that you have fashioned out of all your intelligence, body, and passion, and to disappear. You must care with all your being for your art and care nothing for yourself.

Paul Valéry, in his essays on aesthetics, makes a similar point about the importance of the work, not the creator, and I think he would have extended this to the person of the interpreter: "Art as a *value* depends on the indeterminacy of the act of communication. It is essential that between the producer and the consumer there should be something 'irreducible'; that the work, the medium, should not give the person it affects anything that can be reduced to an idea of the author's person and thinking" (1964:xiii). And, if this were not clear enough, he writes, "A creator is one who makes others create."

Artists often speak in metaphors that suggest that they are vessels. Film director Ang Lee says, for example, "I believe that all we create is sent from somewhere. It is as if our ideas already exist, and pass through us in order to be seen" (Laufer and Lewis 1998:104). Poet Mark Doty remarks in much the same way: "The poem is more something we find than something we make. . . . I need to move into a state of quiet so that I can experience that connection and so that I can be receptive to inspiration" (Laufer and Lewis 1998:105).

The *griots*, or traditional storytellers and bards of West Africa, think of themselves in similar and poignant ways. Stoller said, "The words of history are much too powerful to be 'owned' by any one person or group of people; rather, they are possessed by the forces of the past. Put another way, the *griots* don't 'own' the 'old words' they put to memory; the 'old words' own them. By decentering themselves from 'old words' and the forces of history, these *griots* are infused with great dignity" (Bochner and Ellis 2002:299).

Letting the light pass through you, being open to being changed, being ready with a disciplined body, heart, and mind—this is what it requires to mediate between a work and an audience. We might take a lesson from many Native American peoples in whose conception shamans and curers, through fasting and visions, become a hole through which the power could come. Black Elk, the Oglala Sioux medicine man, described it thus: "Many I cured with the power that came through me. Of course, it was not I who cured. It was the power from the outer world, and the visions and ceremonies had only made me like a hole through which the power could come to the two-leggeds. If I thought I was doing it myself, the hole would close up and no power could come through" (Neihardt 1972:173–74).

But, it is very hard to resist being lionized and, therefore, begin to believe that it is you and not the work that matters. Why not? You are the active force in the relationship between work, performer, and audience. Its only existence is in you. Of course, in many cultures, people do not lionize performers. For the Tewa, for example, it is an obligation to the community to perform. As we saw, for some large communal dances, the ritual clowns go around the village gathering up individuals who have not yet come out to dance. It would be embarrassing to a Tewa dancer to be singled out for praise for a particular performance even though aesthetic judgments are routinely made. Interestingly, it may be in these kinds of communally expected performances that transparency on everyone's part is the norm, desired by performers and spectators alike.

In our own Western societies, however, where performance is a particular, marked-off category given over to specialists, those specialists—the performers—are people set apart. In some respects, this situation has many parallels with religious specialists, a set-apart people with extraordinary gifts and extraordinary responsibilities. Often, throughout history, performers as varied as dancers, actors, and bullfighters have talked about what they do and about themselves in quasi-religious terms, not only as vessels but also seeing themselves as dedicated to one passion, to mediating between the object of that passion and a public, to making sacrifices for it, and even to associating chastity and purity with what they do (see Royce 1987b). Religious specialists share many of these same characteristics. They mediate between a higher being and people and this requires sacrifices of them that ordinary people do not have to make. It is not surprising that transparency is a concept frequently discussed in homiletics classes nor that it characterizes particularly fine preachers. Create a space where the people and that higher being can come together without another presence; that is what transparency means.

Clearly, it is not given to every performer to achieve that state of transparency. Wonderful performances happen all the time in its absence. But if you are lucky enough to witness it, you will know it, and it will stay with you always as a touchstone. It is there, too, for the performer, an elusive state devoutly desired and tirelessly pursued.

Notes

1. Martin Mayer wrote the liner notes for the Mercury recording of the Dvořák Cello Concerto, including the material of *New York Times* reviewer Raymond Ericson.

2. This refers to a nasal, somewhat brittle sound produced by bowing near the bridge of the instrument.

3. *Double-stop* refers to playing two or more tones at the same time, which gives a denser sound.

CHAPTER EIGHT
SILENCE AND STILLNESS IN MUSIC AND DANCE

Silence is all of the sound we don't intend. There is no such thing as absolute silence.

—John Cage

We choreograph our breathing by mimicking rhythms of silence.

—Narciso Jaramillo

While there is breath, there is sound and there is movement. Virtually every culture recognizes the signal importance of breath. In speaking about poetry, Peter Davison recalls what poet Robert Pinsky called the "technology of the breath." "The breath is the most intimate aspect of our existence. . . . Time may be able to teach us new ways of using our minds, but I very much doubt whether it can teach us anything new about ways of breathing—or even about what happens to our being when we can no longer breathe. To learn poetry, we need to take poems into our breath and blood and that requires us to hear them as we read them, to learn to read with all the senses, especially with the ear" (Davison 2000:ix).

It is too elemental for us to think about. It is our alpha and omega. The last stanza of Davison's poem *Escape* tantalizes us: "We attain fulfillment only if we carry/the breath of the world/without surrender/or escape" (2000:3). Marcel Marceau, the master poet of mime, gives a fundamental importance to breath and breathing: "Breathing carries energy, carries the silence and makes the silence musical. Breathing is like a light you switch on. It's a force, an energy force. The energy comes from our breathing. . . . Without the artistic breathing, the lyrical appeal is gone. It's like a symphony without space between movements. All the other music is paced between silence and sound" (interview, April 5, 1981).

There are no full stops in nature; neither is there absolute silence. The world and everything in it would have to stop breathing. Musicians and dancers know perhaps better than anyone else about this subconscious hum that accompanies us in ordinary and extraordinary life. Composer Carl Nielsen spoke to this when he said, "For what is . . . a rest? It is a continuation of the music; a cloth draped over a plastic figure, concealing part of it. We cannot see the figure under the draping, but we know . . . that it is there; and we feel the organic connection between what we see and what we do not. . . . The rests, then, are just as important as the notes. Often, they are far more expressive and appealing to the imagination" (Fisk and Nicholas 1997:216). Dancers and musicians are constantly playing with pauses, creating the illusion of stillness or silence, balancing interpretations between moments of overpowering sound and movement and those illusory moments in which there appears to be nothing. This is art. This is why recordings of performances will never replace performance itself. While technology allows us to make them virtually flawless, they do not have the play of breathe that an artist can offer in performance.

Time and Space

Time and space are elements that delimit both music and dance. Time is clearly more fundamental in music. It exists for dance because dance is behavior and must occur in time and because most dance is accompanied by music. Space is the arena dance commands. Its use is limited only by the limits of human ability or by the deliberate choices of particular genres. Music can create space in the imagination of the listener, but it is not constrained by physical space. Poetry, as a written narrative form, plays with images of time and space even as we breath it and make it our own.

Dance forms that play with both time and space in unusual ways, creating all possible permutations on silence and stillness, are perhaps overly represented by those that originate in Japan. The oldest traditional Noh and Kabuki contrast slow-motion movements with moments of speed. The acting techniques of Kabuki put much emphasis on *ma*, defined by

Masakatsu Gunji as "the slight dramatic pause left between a particular moment in the narrative as expressed in the music or dialogue, and the bodily movements and facial expressions that correspond to that moment in the acting" (1985:18). And certainly the technique known as "cutting a *mie*," referring to the arrested poses, heavily but not exclusively focused on the face, that are liberally scattered throughout any Kabuki play serve a similar purpose of drawing the audience's attention and heightening the tension.

Edwin Denby, one of the great dance critics of our time, wrote an essay about a performance in 1960 of an ensemble from Tokyo Kabuki. Not only does it illustrate the crucial importance of time, but it provides an insightful glimpse of three great Kabuki actors, Kanzaburo XVII, Utaemon VI, and Shoroku II. The dramatic scene of which Denby wrote was one of several that the ensemble presented from *The Forty-seven Ronin.* In it, Kanzaburo XVII plays the hero, a young nobleman, who is forced to commit suicide by an evil provincial governor. His death will mean that all his wealth will be seized by the governor, and his wife and children will be paupers. Alone, but for two government witnesses, in a room of his mansion, the young noble has made all the ritual preparations for his suicide and sits on the floor center stage, facing the audience. His eyes are half-closed: "He is steeling himself. No one moves. A pause. His face unchanged, he flicks one shoulder and his kimono slips from it. A pause. He flicks the other shoulder, the silk kimono drops, a swift gesture of his hands tucks it back. His position has not changed, his eyes have not moved. A pause. He is wearing a second kimono. Again he flicks a shoulder, and pauses; flicks the other, tucks the fallen silk back, and pauses. . . . Horrifying though the heroism of the ritual was, I noticed by this time that the recurrent pauses had each been a trifle too long. I was sorry that so great an actor should overplay so great a scene. . . . In any case his gleaming half-closed eyes held us. Without moving them, he picked up the disemboweling knife, plunged it to the hilt, deep into the far left side of his belly; and, screwing up his face, pulled it slowly with both hands in a straight line toward the right. As he reached his middle, a commotion occurred at the back of the audience. Keeping his face screwed tight, he stopped and held the knife firmly where it was. A retainer ran toward him across the *hanamichi* and prostrated himself, wailing and sucking in his breath. The hero, in a thin clear voice, asked him a commonplace question. The terrified retainer answered yes. . . . The hero was past hearing him. Both hands gripping the hilt, he steadily pulled the knife to the far right of his belly, eased it out, raised it to slit his jugular, and dropped awkwardly forward" (Denby 1986:400). The next day, Denby was remembering the performance when he realized that the pauses were part of the story. The nobleman was waiting for his retainer so that he could pledge him to vengeance. He could not wait too long because of the witnesses. His question of the retainer was meaningless to the witnesses but it bound the retainer to avenge him. "So the listening look in his eyes, and the slightly overlong pauses, which spoiled the perfection of form, were decisive to understanding the scene and the character of the hero. They were not stylized effects, they were realistic ones" (p. 401).

Butoh

The forms of dance categorized as *Butoh* (from *ankoko butoh,* meaning "dance of utter darkness"), which emerged in post–World War II Japan—some say in resistance to Westernization after the war, others that it was a way of speaking about the devastation of Hiroshima and Nagasaki—are the clearest examples today of a radical use of time and space. They, in all their many forms, negate the expected use of space for dance; in some ways, they condense both space and time in a manner similar to mime.

Examining the performance style of two founders of Butoh, Ushio Amagatsu, founder of the Sankai Juku (School of Mountain and Sea) company, and Kazuo Ohno, still a solo performer at ninety-four, we find movement stripped down to its minimal state. Jennifer Dunning writes of Ohno's solo performance at the Japan Society of New York: "Mr. Ohno seemed simply to stand still and take a few crabbed steps about the stage, his arms jutting out and back and his long fingers furled. But he blooms onstage." She continues with what is a perfect description of the power of this performer, speaking of it as "the flamelike intensity of his movement and presence" ("So Hobbled and Yet Serenely Certain," *New York Times*, December 11, 1999). I have seen Ohno's solo *Admiring La Argentina*, an homage to the great Spanish dancer. With a few gestures, he conjures up that wonderful dancer. He scarcely moves away from his own center yet manages to create a sense of vibrancy and movement.

Ohno's philosophy of dance is exemplified in the dance itself. He speaks about a "dead" body as the basis for being able to convey truth and deep emotion through gesture and dance. Expression put into the "living" body becomes distorted by that body's social experience. In the same way, an intellectual decision about what and how to express something takes away its purity. Ohno explains with this analogy: "If you wish to dance a flower, you can mime it and it will be everyone's flower, banal and uninteresting; but if you place the beauty of that flower and the emotions which are evoked by it into your dead body, then the flower you create will be true and unique and the audience will be moved" (Viala and Masson-Sekine 1988:22–23). Although he himself has worked in a number of techniques, Ohno does not teach a technique in the usual sense, seeing the teaching of technique as a violation of his profound feelings about the dance and its foundation in each individual body. What his philosophy engenders is a kind of stripped-down dance, not always economical in its use of space or gesture, but always freed of gestures that are imposed from the outside, which have aesthetic but not emotional content. In chapter two, I discuss a performance of Sankai Juku. Ushio Amagatsu was the soloist in that performance. Here he is reviewed by Anna Kisselgoff (*New York Times*, November 14, 1996), in his *Yuragi: In a Space of Perpetual Motion*. She writes: "As the protagonist, Mr. Amagatsu alternates with the other dancers . . . beginning and ending his eternal trek in the same place. Yet there is no escaping the paradoxical sense of movement within near stillness that defines the choreography."

These dancers and the genres in which they work are intentional about the way they use space, time, stillness, and silence. While a company of dancers may use the entire stage, each individual dancer may choose to use only the space around the axis of his body. In moving from one point to another, the walk is more often than not slowed down to almost stillness. Gathered energy, bodies taut and disciplined, the overall sense of restraint marked by the occasional burst of movement—these are characteristics of all of Sankai Juku's choreography. What keeps the movement alive is the intense energy in the dancer, a vibrancy, as Dunning writes about Ohno. What happens to one's perception of time, given the use of space and stillness, defies the actual passage of time. The Sankai Juku performance to which I have referred was actually ninety minutes long with no intermission. It felt as though it were perhaps twenty minutes. Intuitively, one might think just the opposite would be the case.

Perhaps it is not surprising that a philosophical approach to silence and sound, similar to what these new Japanese genres are doing with stillness and silence should come from Toru Takemitsu, a twentieth-century composer born in Japan but seeking a fusion of Eastern and Western music. As Fisk wrote, Takemitsu once said that his goal was "to achieve a sound as intense as silence" (Fisk and Nicholas 1997:455). Takemitsu elaborated on what he saw as the critical role of silence: "Confronting silence by uttering a sound is nothing but verifying one's existence. It is only that singling out of one's self from the caverns of silence that can really be called 'singing.' . . . It is in silence that the artist singles out the truth to sing or sketch. And it is then that he realizes his truth exists prior to everything. This is the love of art, and at the same time is something that could be called 'the world.' These days too many arts have left the meaning of silence behind" (p. 455).

L'Après-midi d'un Faune

Coming from quite another context, Nijinsky filled the eleven minutes of Debussy's prelude to *L'Après-midi d'un Faune* with a whole world of imagining using the barest suggestions of movements. The power of the work, as Nijinsky conceived it but as we have rarely seen it performed, lies in its stillness, its unhurried pace, its economy. To achieve this required 120 rehearsals, and the total crafting of every bit of the choreography. As Marie Rambert, Nijinsky's rehearsal assistant, commented, while the choreography went against everything the dancers knew from their Imperial Russian training, to do it successfully required that kind of disciplined training. The unheard-of number of rehearsals was due, in part, to the unfamiliar movements and gestures Nijinsky demanded but also came from his inability to explain what it was he wanted from the dancers. He could demonstrate it so clearly that there could be no mistake about what the movement should look like, but explain it he could not. Dancer Lydia Sokolova tells of her frustration and exhilaration working with Nijinsky. "One day he came up to me during rehearsal and said, with Mim [Marie Rambert] interpreting, 'You must try to walk between the bars of the music and sense the rhythm which is implied.' . . . To be allowed to take part in the *Faune* was an honor. The dancers had to be musical as well as rhythmical and it was necessary to relax and hear the music as a whole: it had to trickle through your consciousness, and the sensation approached the divine. One walked and moved quite gently in a rhythm that crossed over the beats given by the conductor. . . . For every lift of the hand or head there was a corresponding sound in the score. It was most ingeniously thought out. . . . In order to preserve the patterns of the frieze, you had to keep your hands and arms flat in profile: to do this it was necessary to relax the hand and arm, for if you tightened or forced the gesture, the wrist fell back and the straight line from elbows to fingers was lost" (de Meyer 1983:24–25).

What Sokolova describes is the genius of this choreography—less is more, less tension, fewer gestures, an almost complete dependence on the horizontal use of space, and, underlying all of that, stillness. Edwin Denby commented on the deliberate simplicity of *Faune* when he wrote a brief commentary about the de Basil Ballets Russes performance of it twenty-three years after its premiere: "From the point of view of visual rhythm, the repetition of the Nymph's gesture of dismay is the perfection of timing. It is, of course, because so few gesture motives are used that one can recognize each so plainly, but there is no feeling of poverty in this simplification. The rhythmic pattern in relation to the stage and to the music is so subtly graded that instead of monotony we get a steady increase in suspense, an increase in the eyes' perceptiveness, and a feeling of heroic style at the climax" (Denby 1986:39).

Jill Beck, the first to stage the ballet on the basis of the reconstructed Nijinsky notation, comments similarly on the stillness and absence of attractive or eye-catching steps. She notes that "when little is happening on stage, what is happening acquires enormous significance. . . . Movements do not rush by us; they linger in view, permitting the soft stroke of our imaginations" (1991:70–72). The appropriate audience attitude must be one of paying close attention and viewing the piece actively not passively. The audience must become part of the Faun's reverie. This was just as difficult for the audience of the 1912 premiere as it is for today's public. In 1912, Nijinsky was the Faun and the choreography was as he wished it. Today we have no Nijinsky and, until the reconstruction in 1987, we did not have the original choreography.

Dance and Space

Dance genres vary considerably in the extent to which they "use" space. Classical ballet is extravagant in its use of both horizontal and vertical space; the only limits are those of the human body. Other forms, for example, the classical Indian dance *bharata natyam*, use only a small space around the dancer's body and vertical use is limited to the distance between deep squats and some half-toe gestures. Arms extend the vertical space as well. There are some small jumps, but they are more a lifting of the feet off the floor while the body remains essentially at the same level. Kapila Vatsyayan, the most respected of India's dance scholars, speaks about it this way: "The Indian dancer's preoccupation is not so much with space as with time, and the dancer is constantly trying to achieve the perfect pose which will convey a sense of timelessness" (Jonas 1992:60). One of the confounding variables in other classical Indian dances, as is true of their incarnations across the diaspora of Hindu peoples and cultures, is that male dancers use a much wider stance than do females.

Dancers who were the predecessors of tap dancers used a small rectangle of wood as a portable floor on which they could tap whenever there was the possibility of an audience. We have drawings from the nineteenth century showing small boys entertaining people along the Mississippi while barges were loaded and unloaded. This, too, has earlier antecedents in European traveling performers, who carried not only their costumes and props with them but also their stage. Our word "saltimbanque" comes from the Italian *salta-im-banco*, meaning literally jumping on the bench or trestle. What one could do in the way of performance was limited by the size of the stage, and that was limited by the troupe's ability to carry it with them.

Flamenco is an interesting case. Vertical space is not used extensively at all; horizontal space may be used in group dances, rather more than in solo performances. Women's movements, simply in terms of space occupied, tend to be more extensive than men's—an exception to a general pattern. But even within these general stylistic parameters, dancers play with space for effect. Anyone who has seen Cristina Hoyos in Antonio Gades's film *Carmen* understands the impact of understatement. In the film, she has agreed to teach Gades's protégé, and there follows a scene in which nothing moves but her hands. The power in that small scene is extraordinary. It is paired in a later scene in which Gades dances a *farruca*—more silence than sound, more stillness than movement. How effective this introspection and stillness can be is illustrated by the recent performance of dancer Pilar Rioja in New York. Of one piece, Jack Anderson wrote in the *New York Times*, August 2, 2002: "She began *Soleá* by sitting still, her face averted from the audience and her focus entirely on her musicians. Then she slowly rose and danced, proudly and stormily, as if carried away by the music." That combination of self-containment and abandon is more powerful than either one alone.

An example from film that shows the same power of economy is Anthony Hopkins's portrayal of Hannibal Lecter in *The Silence of the Lambs*. His stillness and silence create extraordinary tension. It is that tension and the need to do something to break it, in fact, that leads Clarice Starling, the young FBI agent, to approach him again and again.

Mime

Perhaps the most economical genre in terms of both movement and sound is mime, especially the classical mime tradition created by Marcel Marceau. "Dance is the art of movement and mime is the art of attitude" (Marceau, interview, April 5, 1981). Mime consciously slows movements and gestures and condenses time. First, it slows time in both movement and gesture because gestures done at their normal speed are lost on an audience. The slowing down is a way of limning, allowing the gesture to be seen and comprehended. If you imagine all the ordinary activities in which we engage every day—walking, sitting down, opening a door, picking a flower, buttoning a jacket—and think of portraying them on a stage so that an audience can see and comprehend them, you will understand that each of these activities has to be *shown*, outlined, held up, slowed down. Marceau's classes are full of exercises that help students master this fundamental aspect of the art. So fundamental is it that every street mime uses it as the basis of performances. The second way in which time is manipulated focuses on the passage of time in the narrative the mime is telling. Marceau's *Creation of the World* tells the whole story of creation in fewer than three minutes.

Mime also condenses space, living really in stillness while giving the illusion of movement. Vincent Angotti and Judie Herr write, "Translational movement, which transfers a body from one point to another, does not concern the mime as it does the traditional actor or dancer. The mime is concerned instead with *concentrated* movement, which condenses space as it condenses idea and time. Such concentrated movement denies translation movement without sacrificing either quality or quantity of expression. . . . The mime—who walks, runs, climbs, swims, or flies *sur place* (in place)—obtains these effects through technically controlled concentration in each of his movements" (Angotti and Herr 1974:4). The paradox of mime is that it portrays the ordinary through extraordinary, contrived, and conventional means. It can tell the most complicated and extravagant story with the utmost economy.

Shamans and Healers

The performance of shamans and healers in their altered states, the subject of chapter eleven, relies on the alternation between silence and sound, stillness and movement. For many, going into a trance state requires that they sit immobile even while a powerful musical rhythm surrounds them. Some describe that stillness as being present and open for whatever the spirits wish to do. This is particularly true of shamanic traditions that involve flying somewhere in one's altered state: to the underworld to consult with the dead, to the world of the spirits to enlist their aid, to another village to spy on a shaman who may be practicing bad medicine. The body that is left behind is empty of the shaman's soul—the source of its vulnerability, and a dangerous time for the shaman. I have watched these transformations with Isthmus Zapotec healers in southern Mexico. When they are elsewhere, their bodies appear vacated. When they return, you can see the reanimation. When they are present, they are vital, and their stillness can be overwhelming. Possession trance works with a similar kind of transformation. It begins in quiet and stillness; the body gradually awakens with the presence of the spirit or god and moves and speaks as that animating spirit. These descriptions of trance are very reminiscent of what his contemporaries said about Nijinsky. When the god leaves, the body seems to retreat to a limp state as if it were waiting for its original inhabitant to return. In Bali, the return is brought about by "smoking" trancers with incense and sprinkling them with water blessed by the priests. For the Ju/'hoansi of South Africa, the full state of trance is a very violent one, again contrasting with the stage preceding it as the trance takes hold of the healer.

Other Genres

Even in those genres that choose silence over sound and that constrain movement, there are moments of contrast. Antonio Gades standing utterly immobile at the beginning of a *farruca,* then exploding into movement that is all angles and sharp twists, followed by long moments of immobility—that is dance that holds the viewer captive and convinces that there is some place of truth which we have just glimpsed. Gades's notion of dance springs from simplicity, purity, and a classical line. It is uncluttered and does not seek out virtuosity; rather, as Gades has said, he searches for the essence of dance.

Such contrast keeps the audience in a state of anticipation and uncertainty. African-derived dance and movement was a source of unease to most of white America. Katrina Hazzard-Gordon explains why that is. First, there is the power implicit in movement qua movement. Then, these genres coming from African roots are characterized by the alternation of contrasting qualities such as coolness and energy, order and disorder, coupled with asymmetry and a kind of containment of the unpredictable. Those qualities made them more disturbing in their unpredictability than they would have been had the movement been consistently wild and uncontained (see Hazzard-Gordon 1990).

Contrast and the metaphorical use of movement and sound are woven throughout Dante's *Inferno.* Dante was writing in the context of medieval notions such as the Great Chain of Being, but I think he touched on very deep associations about movement and sound that remain salient today. The circle of the Inferno reserved for the greatest sinners, Lucifer and Judas, was a landscape of souls frozen in ice, immobile, unable to communicate, surrounded by silence and darkness. These sinners are deprived of the basic qualities of humankind—speech and movement. They are removed forever from joining the souls in Paradise whom Dante depicts as moving, dancing, singing for eternity around God, who is shown as a point of light in constant movement. In contrast is Dante's evocation of those souls who abandoned themselves to their passions while alive. They occupy the second circle, punished by being blown about forever in the darkness of a raging storm, which Dante describes as bellowing like a storm-wracked sea.

Immobility and uncontrolled movement represent states that are frightening, and people look for a middle ground. Similarly, we have negative associations with unrelieved silence or the inability to make sound, as well as the constant roar of unregulated sound. Moving and speaking, just like breathing, are fundamental ways in which we know we are alive.[1]

Paolo et Francesca, *1905, Musée Rodin, Paris. Photograph by Ronald R. Royce.*

Artistry in music, dance, and theatre is defined by the interest a performance generates. Part of that interest has to do with balance and contrast. A performance with no variation of movement or of sound is not interesting unless the goal is to create some kind of altered state. Stillness and silence create intensity, but they must be alive. Fine artists have that intensity even when nominally at rest. Some contemporary genres, especially in the West, seem to feel compelled to fill every silence with sound and every pause with movement. Admittedly, it is difficult to be still or to know how long a silence to maintain. There is the risk of vulnerability. We should follow the example of shamans who, for as long as there have been human communities, have practiced the art of being present in silence and stillness, understanding its power to illuminate and bind worlds that we keep separate.

Note

1. For a more extended discussion of these notions and associations, read "Movement as Visual Metaphor," in *Movement and Meaning: Creativity and Interpretation in Ballet and Mime* (Royce 1984).

CHAPTER NINE
THE AUDIENCE AS CREATOR AND INTERPRETER

"A creator is one who makes others create" (Valéry 1964:xiii). Paul Valéry, in his essays on aesthetics, took the position, contrary to many of his contemporaries, that art is, above all else, a process. This stance resulted in the important shift of focus from the product, the created work, to the process, the creation of it. The process of creation, moreover, was without a fixed endpoint. The creator fashions a work. In the performing arts, the work is then given over to the performer-interpreter, who creates another iteration of the original. In performance, the interpretation is presented to an audience who then generates its own interpretation. Finally, there is that specialized audience member, the critic, who suggests yet another definition. Performance and reception may prompt a dialectical call and response leading to revised interpretations. The process is truncated in the case of the visual or literary arts. In these cases, the work is made available for an audience without the intermediate step. Viewing or reading the work, individuals imagine a story that is theirs and different from that of the creator. Criticism plays a role in these arts, too, and may influence the interpretations that individuals reach.

In this process of art, the numbers are not balanced in terms of creators and interpreters. Creators are few, performers are more numerous, but audiences potentially are limitless. Here, I explore the ramifications of this state of the creative process—reception—focusing on audiences and their interaction with performers. The previous eight chapters are about virtuosity, artistry, and interpretation, largely from the point of view of performers, those persons in the middle. But much as the original work is on the minds of performers, so is the audience and its perceptions. How much knowledge do they have? What is the balance on any given night between connoisseurs, claques, and persons simply interested in the genre? What are they bringing to this particular performance? What is the feel of that mass beyond the footlights? The answers to these questions are important to performers in terms of their success and the appropriateness of their interpretation, and also in terms of their interaction with the audience and their sense of the audience's own creation.

Performers on Performance and Audiences

Performers vary greatly in terms of what matters to them in performance. For some, the strongest relationship is always that between them and the work. Here is the beginning of a review by *New York Times* critic James Oestreich (February 27, 1999) of a concert by Janos Starker and Shigeo Neriki: "The veteran cellist Janos Starker is given to making big statements these days, but in the unshowiest of manners. Last season he played a program at the 92nd Street Y consisting entirely of three Bach cello suites, in which he seemed to be communing with the composer rather than performing in public." It is not that Starker is unaware of the audience, it is that his first obligation is to the music. If he is true to that, then the performance will be meaningful for the public.

At the other end, we have performers for whom the work is only a medium through which they can exert their own personality. I have spoken to the temptations posed by some of the public eager for superstars. And today, with the possibilities for performances multiplied by the speed and ease of travel, it is tempting to gather more and more audiences and then, gradually, to give them what they want. Often what they want, at least the majority who know very little about the art, is what is exciting, so dancers replace *entrechat six* (jumping beats at the ankle) with *entrechat dix* (jumping beats with additional beats) or they add more and more turns. For musicians so inclined, cadenzas become showstoppers. In these situations, audiences are entertained rather than inspired or educated. And, contrary to Valéry's dictum, they have created nothing themselves except, perhaps, a frisson.

In the hands of artists who care for the work more than for their own renown, performances can create an environment for audiences in which they can become more educated consumers, creators of an experience that takes them out of themselves. Here lies perhaps the challenge. There will always be, among the public, those who count the number of *fouettés* (whipping turns) the ballerina does in the *Black Swan pas de deux*, and those who come to performances desiring to be transported, if not transformed. In the middle are those who do not necessarily realize the possibilities but who are open to experiencing something new, something they recognize but cannot explain.

Marcel Marceau, the father of modern mime, understands the public—old, young, sophisticated, unformed, of all nationalities and cultures. He has performed all around the globe for more than sixty years. He is generally optimistic about the public's ability to understand, and works hard to construct his programs so that they include concrete as well as more abstract mimes. In our interview of April 5, 1981, he commented on the topic of audience: "People have to use their own imagination . . . the less a person is exposed to good theater, the more difficult it is for him to get excited about imagination or stylization. . . . In the composition of a program, I have to be careful not to lose my public. I have to build it up to a rhythm which keeps the attention. . . . Also I have to alternate funny numbers with tragic numbers. It's very important how you put one number beside another because a show is a whole, not just one number. . . . A public that does not concentrate would not get anything. They would just understand *The Lion Tamer*; they would just understand if I am seasick; they would not understand complexity. But people are trained with symbols and they are trained to use their brain and their imagination." Later, in the same interview, he says, speaking of the mime *Remembrances of a Past Love*, "I think the public slowly enters into the atmosphere. I love for the public to dream with its own imagination about the theme. I leave it completely open to the public sometimes" (Royce 1984:104–5).

In a recent conversation in Bloomington, Indiana, Marceau talked about the new mime-drama he is working on, *Fight with an Angel*. I will not reveal any more about it because it has not yet been premiered, but it will be one of the more abstract, complicated solo mimes that he has in his repertoire. When I asked him if he thought the audience would understand it, he said that he has great faith in the ability of audiences to understand what are fundamental human emotions. Their understanding, of course, has to do with the economy and clarity of his portrayal. In all the many audiences in which I have sat for Marceau's performances, I have never encountered a single person who could not understand and appreciate any of it. National character is sometimes a factor. American audiences, for example, want to know what is happening at very short intervals, while French audiences can let almost an entire number be presented before they need to have some closure.

The two case studies in this chapter include the seventeenth-century commedia dell'arte, an effervescent, improvised, popular theatrical genre that vanished with the advent of scripted comedy, and the highly stylized Kabuki theatre that has spanned almost six centuries and is one of the four most important performing arts of Japan. The two forms, widely separated in space, if not in time, share many characteristics. Both have standardized plots; both arose out of popular street theatre, which then migrated to the courts and back again; both emphasize the importance of the performer; both use masked characters whose personalities and behavior are fixed and well known to the public; finally, in both, the plots or stories sustain the status quo. The one important difference, especially for our discussion, is that the commedia was a highly improvised form while Kabuki and the roles within it are scripted and very formal.

Commedia dell'Arte

Seventeenth-Century Modena Troupe

Between 1688 and 1704 in the northern duchies of Italy, with tours that ranged from Modena to Venice, there was an extraordinary company of commedia dell'arte players who were under contract to the Duke of Modena. Their repertoire consisted primarily of the fifty-one three-act *scenari*[1] collected and eventually recorded by Francesco Melchiori da Oderzo in the 1744 catalogue of the Soranzo collection, housed in the Biblioteca Marciana of Venice. Those *scenari* were discovered by Vittorio Rossi in 1895 in the collections of the nearby Museo Correr, where they were archived as Correr Codex 1040.

On the basis of a reconstruction of the likely players associated with the particular masque names in the Codex 1040 (names that are quite unusual), I was able to link the group and the repertoire with the Duke of Modena's company as it existed at the end of the seventeenth century. Reinforcing the connection are all the letters and contracts in the archives in Modena that attest to the existence of a company with these masque names (see Royce 1986,

1990). Earlier writers had dismissed the *scenari*, having assumed a date in the early part of the seventeenth century, as not very good examples of golden age comedy. I see them, rather, as iconic of a silver age of comedy that flourished in the last quarter of the seventeenth century, before Goldoni introduced scripted comedy. That period has been thought to be of no consequence, characterized by bowdlerized versions of golden age plays and poor translations of Spanish plays. Yet, in this collection we find the devices of *maschere* (consistent characterizations) and *lazzi* (bits of acrobatic action) fully formed, giving these plays psychologically sophisticated characters and a recognizable and consistent structure not developed in golden age comedies.

Using the Modena company as an example, let us examine the performing venues and the players. Individual players were under contract to the duke and performed at his pleasure. These included women as well as men. The commedia was the first dramatic form in Europe to allow women on the stage. The duke sent his actors around to other courts as well. Early in the seventeenth century, entertainment took place primarily in private homes and palaces. Francesco I, who became duke of Modena in 1629, was passionately fond of the theatre, especially the commedia dell'arte. In his reign, there were two theatres built. The Teatro Valentini was opened in 1643, and, until it passed into the hands of the Fontanelli family, it was devoted exclusively to commedia dell'arte. On the site of the old Spelta granary in the main piazza, Francesco reconstructed the Teatro Ducale della Piazza (or Spelta, as it was sometimes called). The architect was Gaspare Vigarani, and his design became the model for modern theatres. The Teatro Ducale had every imaginable provision for stage machinery and its auditorium could accommodate three thousand people. Vigarani went on to build an identical theatre in Paris for Louis XIV. In both stage and theatre design and opportunities for actors, the duchies that made up what became Italy led the rest of Europe.

Francesco, unlike some of his royal counterparts who had companies and painters and singers because that was what great princes did, was a real fan of the commedia and its actors. He attended performances in both theatres, the Valentini and the Ducale, and, in addition, sponsored performances in the palace for very select audiences. In these intimate performances, Francesco and one of his courtiers would join the other actors, playing the roles of witty and stupid *zanni* (masked clown characters). In the frequent absence of his actors (even though it is likely that he had two companies), who were borrowed by dukes and rulers as far away as France and England, Francesco satisfied his need for commedia by hiring Spanish companies who were traveling through Italy.

Francesco was not the only fan of the commedia. It was wildly popular among all social ranks. The Spelta theatre, with its three thousand seats, made money so we may assume that it attracted large audiences. Let us spend a little time now examining the structure of the commedia dell'arte to see what made it exciting, on the one hand, and comprehensible, on the other.

Structure of the Commedia dell'Arte

The commedia dell'arte, at this time, was an improvised form of theatre. We must ask then what allowed players to anticipate each other's actions and what allowed audiences to understand what they saw. Several conventions provided the framework for anticipation and interpretation: masques, *lazzi*, standard plots, commentary outside the performance frame, and overall play structure. The ways in which these devices were shaped gave a distinctive style to a company even though the conventions were common to all commedia.

Masques

Masques, or more properly, *maschere*, were the coherent, consistent, psychologically developed characters of the commedia. They were divided into high and low, serious and comic, not masked and masked. The masked characters, all comic, included at a minimum one *zanni*, the male comic servant (common names, which number in the hundreds, include Arlecchino, Fritellino, Truffaldino, Trivellino, Bagolino, and so forth); one *serva*, the female comic servant, who was not actually masked, but filled the same position as the other masked characters (common names include Colombina, Argentina, and Zerbinetta); an old male, father or warder, usually Pantalone or Magnifico; another old male, Il Dottore, to whom the daughter or ward is to be married; and the swaggering military figure, Il Capitano (first Turk, then Spanish). The high characters, again at a minimum, include the first high female lover (e.g., Isabella, Flaminia), the second high female lover (Rosaura), the first high male lover (Orazio, Mario, Leandro), and the second high male lover (Flaminio, Francesco).

Arlequin, *Théâtre du Séraphin, eighteenth century, Musée Carnavalet, Paris. Photograph by Ronald R. Royce.*

Brighella, *Théâtre du Séraphin, eighteenth century, Musée Carnavalet, Paris. Photograph by Ronald R. Royce.*

Pantalon, *Théâtre du Séraphin, eighteenth century, Musée Carnavalet, Paris. Photograph by Ronald R. Royce.*

Le Docteur Bolognais, *Théâtre du Séraphin, eighteenth century, Musée Carnavalet, Paris. Photograph by Ronald R. Royce.*

Each of these *maschere* were taken from figures that one might see across Italy; indeed, as stock characters, they resonate with humanity in general. Pantalone, or, in his original manifestation, Magnifico, was taken from the wealthy Venetian merchant, always looking to get more money as well as to get a young girl. Dottore was a caricature of an academic, usually from Bologna, a bit pompous, and looking for a young wife. The Captain was a bit of a boaster but was, in fact, afraid of everything. He stood for whatever foreign soldiers were currently threatening Italy. The servants represented the lower classes, conniving against their masters or mistresses, sometimes helping the course of true love, or falling in love themselves. The *serva* was level headed and gave advice to her mistress about ways to get the man she wanted, but she also played tricks on the mistress and on her fellow servants. *Zanni* came in a variety of characters. Originally based on the rustic from Bergamo, they further divided into the shrewd rustic from upper Bergamo (often Brighella) and the dumb victim of his appetites from lower Bergamo (Arlecchino). Both were trickster figures.

The lovers, of both sexes, represented the upper classes. They were played by young, handsome company members who had to memorize long passages in upper-class Italian (then the Florentine dialect). Their love affairs and friendships were the pivot points of most plays.

Lazzi

Lazzi were bits of comic action—American comics on the borscht-belt would refer to the equivalent as schtick and used it in much the same way. They functioned to advance the action, to comment on what was happening, and to focus audience attention. Many of the *lazzi* were named and always used in the same way or at the same point in a play. The commedia treatise writers of the day, Perrucci and Andreini, describe many of these: the *lazzi di paura* (*lazzi* of fear), *di correre* (of running), *di spiritati* (of ghosts), the *lazzi di mostrar la lettera* (*lazzi* of showing the letter), and the longer, more elaborate *lazzi di notte* (the famous night scene) and the *lazzi di ammazarsi* (suicide). There are many others whose names suggest that there were *lazzi* that could fit almost every situation in the play.

It is not surprising, then, that there were conventions about how the *lazzi* should fit into the general structure of the play. Those of the Correr Codex 1040, for example, fall into four categories: (1) *lazzi* of bargaining, often between *zanni* and *Magnifico* but also between the senior males and between the servants, are part of the plot and serve to delay and complicate the play; (2) *lazzi* of affectionate coaxing or bantering, most often occurring between the male and female servants, providing a parody of the love scenes of the high lovers; (3) *lazzi* to focus attention, the importance of which is supported by the fact that they occur so frequently, ensuring that the audience does not miss something crucial because of wandering attention, for example, the *lazzi* of showing the letter—usually a love letter that is supposed to go from the high female to her male counterpart but the servants see that it takes many turns and is read by many for whom it was not intended—was one of the most often used; and (4) *lazzi* that make fun of someone, usually one of the comic high characters like *Pantalone*, the *Dottore*, or the Captain. In fact, only the underdogs of the commedia, the servants, are granted this license to poke fun at anyone or anything, except the Church.

Lazzi were especially important in the polyglot context of the commedia. Comic roles were spoken in regional dialect so that, even within Italy, not everyone could understand all the spoken dialogue. Outside the borders of Italy, it became even more problematic. *Lazzi* provided the nonverbal amplification and clarification of what was being said. They did so in bold, unmistakable ways, not only providing an additional explanation but also enlivening the performance in their own right.

In most companies, it was the comic characters who made *lazzi* an essential part of their role. Many of the *lazzi* occurred during the night scenes (usually in the second act). Night scenes served the structural purpose of allowing the lovers to realize their desires under the protective guise of dark. They were, of course, also magnificent opportunities for all manner of jokes and burlesques—ladders placed against the wrong windows, characters disguised, packages given to an unintended party, *zanni* taking advantage of the dark to beat his master.

The basic plots were simple and few. The father or guardian (*Pantalone*) wishes to marry his young and beautiful charge to whoever can bring the biggest dowry, usually his old friend, the *Dottore*.

Scène de la Comedie Italienne, I Gelosi, *sixteenth century, Musée Carnavalet, Paris. Photograph by Ronald R. Royce.*

She, of course, wishes to marry for love—usually to a handsome young man with apparently no prospects. The servants connive to bring the young lovers together after some instances of deliberate misrepresentation. It turns out that the young man actually is the long-lost son of a wealthy prince and so, in the last act, they are married with *Pantalone*'s blessing. Servant pairs may also marry, as well as the second set of lovers. There are variations on this theme—best friends who are rivals for the same woman; women who are rivals for the same man; twins separated in their youth, usually captured by pirates.

One very interesting device, especially for our purposes here, was the commentary outside the performance frame. Perhaps stemming from the earlier practice of individual performers in settings other than the traditional theatre of the seventeenth century, the comic masques were free to step out of the performance frame and address the audience. As a structural device, its uses were several. It made audience members active participants and conspirators, an important consideration given the brevity of attention spans and the number of distractions, like wandering in and out of the theatre, buying food and drink, gossiping, and catching the attention of the opposite sex. This commentary was used as a means of explaining complicated bits of plot and action. Sometimes it was a way for a character to carry on an internal monologue. The practice continued down through the scripted plays of Goldoni, in which what had always been at the discretion of the actor became part of the stage directions. A number of years ago, I witnessed precisely this in a performance of a Goldoni play done by a Venetian troupe using dialect and all the traditional conventions. The Arlecchino who came downstage to talk to the audience about what was happening neatly upstaged his fellows.

All of these devices were set into a structure, which itself followed a number of conventions. Looking again at the Codex 1040 *scenari*, we note that all of them are divided into three acts. We can characterize these as the three stages of exposition, reversal or confusion, and resolution. This is not a structure unique to the commedia, but it is certainly more straightforward and unrelenting there than elsewhere in the theatre. The night scene, the most frequent mechanism for confusion and reversal, occurs most often in the second act or the beginning of the third. Act three invariably ends with the assembling of all the characters, usually in the context of a wedding or weddings.

Within the framework of each act, characters advanced the plot with dialogue. Normally, the dialogue involved just two characters at a time, although there may have been more on the stage. The pairs of actors entered and exited the two houses that made up the typical commedia set (one on either side of the stage, with a street or piazza in the middle), or they would exit stage right and stage left along the streets in front of the set. Changes of set, other than from day to night, were virtually nonexistent. Music and dance provided breaks from the dialogue–*lazzi* pattern. These interludes were most common when a lover set about to serenade his lady, or at the end when the marriages were celebrated.

The actors themselves provided some consistency that helped audiences understand plays that rivaled those of Shakespeare (whose comedies were, in fact, modeled on the commedia dell'arte) in complexity—twins, pairs of twins, men dressed as women, women dressed as men, mistaken identities, and so forth. Masques tended to be passed down along family lines, usually with no more than one player in a generation using the same masque name. Players tweaked the masque in order to make it fit their own mode of playing; they developed a personality and a consistent character. The costumes and masks were specific to each character as well. The comic characters invented or altered *lazzi*, creating a unique repertoire. The high characters had long passages of dialogue to memorize, and different players would add it to their repertoire or use it in different ways. The dialogue was bits of unconnected text. It was used in performance when the situation called for it. For example, if the love scene were one of leave-taking, each of the participants would have memorized dozens of lines appropriate to leave-taking. They could choose whichever they thought best for that particular performance or whichever happened to be favorites of that pair of lovers. Players each kept a little book of their particular *lazzi* or dialogue (*zibaldone*). Unfortunately, almost none of these have survived.

The technique and rules of the genre were clear but left much space for individual choice and elaboration; so, at once, you have the anticipation of originality and freshness combined with a familiar structure. You know the persona by their costumes, *lazzi*, and position within the overall structure. You also know them because they sprang from types in the society as a whole. Clearly, performances were smoother and more interesting when they were done by players who knew each other well. Some troupes were well known across continents and were in constant demand.

Audiences

What of the audiences for the commedia dell'arte? In this section, I speak only of performances given in public settings. Those in the court had courtiers for audiences. The theme was often dictated by the royal patron; the patron himself often took part. In the theatres like the Spelta and Fontanelli in Modena or the San Samuele in Venice, audiences came from all social stations.

During Carnival in the Venetian theatres, upper-class patrons would come masked, with black cloaks, so that they could be incognito. This was a way to pursue a love affair in a fashion blessed by custom. The central floor, what we call the orchestra today, had no seats and was the least expensive. All around the hall and raised above it were the loges, which had upholstered chairs and curtains for privacy.

Each theatre had different regulations about food and drink. We know from material in the Modena archives that at the Fontanelli theatre during Carnival season card games and the selling of food and wine was allowed (Archivio di Stato, spettacoli pubblici, busta 8/a, Modena).[2] Performances

Teatro San Samuele, Venice, *from* Bolletino per L'Ingresso nel Teatro appresso S. Samuele introdotto l'anno 1758 in tempo di Carnovale, *in Nicola Mangini, I Teatri di Venezia (Milan: U. Mursia, Editore, 1974). Photograph by Ronald R. Royce.*

were drastically curtailed during Lent in all the cities so the specification referring to food during Carnival season is not surprising. In the Venetian theatres devoted to commedia, hot chocolate was sold. Again, we know this from archival materials documenting the argument over who owned the rights to the chocolate concessions. In any case, some of the wealthier patrons had their servants bring whole baskets of food and carafes of wine. Eating was part of attending a performance—people would wander in and out, perhaps take in a card game, and vendors would sell food inside the theatre itself.

Much socializing took place in the theatre as well—business was conducted, affairs were begun or continued, and feuds sometimes interrupted the constant flow of chatter. What one can assume is that no one sat through a performance the way our modern audiences do, rooted to the seats, paying attention. People at that time watched a performance as one of the many kinds of entertainment available at the same time and place—talking, eating, drinking, fighting, playing cards, making love, all competed with the performance for attention. The structure and devices of the commedia, which could attract the public's wandering attention at important moments, make perfect sense within the context of the times. The outsized caricatures and physical comedy of the *lazzi* made people laugh. The Arlecchino came downstage and spoke to the audience, people listened and responded. The intervals of music and dance were lively enough to compete with everything else. And individual audience members also had their favorite performers whose playing they knew intimately. They knew when a *lazzi* was coming or a particularly good piece of dialogue, and they would fix their attention on those moments. The same descriptions have been offered of Shakespeare's theatre, much of which derived from the commedia.

Sometimes audiences would fight over the relative merits of different performers. And sometimes performers did not want to play in a city if they knew that a rival was a favorite there. We have a wonderful example of the complications that arose from rivalries and temperaments of and between players. In 1651, Francesco d'Este, duke of Modena, sent his players to perform at the Obizzi theatre in Padova. The first problem arose when actress Angiola Nelli told the duke she could not go to Padova because she was already engaged for Milan. In fact, she was reluctant to go to Padova because her rival Armellina had many fans in that city. Following on the heels of Nelli's excuse, the duke received a letter from his players then in Bologna. The letter informed him that they had received three letters from gentlemen of Padova urging them not to come to that city because of the division between supporters of their company and the supporters of Armellina. They take pains to assure the duke that these letters are not an invention on their part, nor on the part of the Signora Angiola and her husband, the company's Dottore (Archivio di

Stato, comici, busta unica, Modena). Francesco suspected that all this was a caprice on the part of his restless actress Angiola, and he ordered the troupe to meet their obligations in Padova.

It may have been a caprice on her part, but it is equally likely that the rivalry was true. Fans were notorious in the lengths to which they would go to promote their favorites and to tear down any rivals. This became especially tragic when it happened with respect to an aging actress who was still playing the high lover roles. Audiences, and fellow players, could be quite cruel. Witness the following story of Marzia Fiala (née Narici) who joined the Modena troupe in 1651 playing the high lover Flaminia. Her husband, Giuseppe Fiala, entered the duke's players at the same time, in the role of Il Capitano Sbranaleone. Bernardo Narici, her brother, was also in the troupe as one of the high lovers, Orazio. There are seven letters in the Modena archives between Fiala and the duke (six from her to the duke and one response) and they tell a sad tale. She was aging, thus inciting the scorn of her fellow players (whose livelihood depended on the popularity of the troupe as a whole), and losing the good will of the duke. Women who play one of the lovers have a particularly difficult time because there are no other roles for them to take on as they age.

Her letter of November 6, 1677, to the Duke is especially eloquent. She found herself in competition with Agata Calderoni, Flaminia, who had been brought temporarily into the service of the duke. The reason for this had to do with her husband, Francesco Calderoni, who, as Silvio, was one of the most desired actors of the time. Enhancing his own reputation by signing the Calderones, the duke made Marzia Fiala's position unbearable.

Her letter begins by telling that duke that she has tried to be obedient to his wishes but that Silvio (Calderoni) does not want her to study even one line, that his wife will play Flaminia. "Hence I do not see how I can continue in my good service to your Serenissimo and that torments me and wounds me to the heart. Worse, Mezzetino and Finocchio are saying that they do not need me either on stage or in the piazza, that I should leave the theatre because I am so old and incapable of acting that the public does not come to performances. Such is their influence that the noble theatre owner has forbidden me to play. All this has caused me to weep tears of blood. . . . Prostrate at the feet of your Serenissimo, I humbly beg you, to give me a contract because I have served you well. . . . I find myself in such a ruined and oppressed state that I will be grateful for whatever you can do to help me earn my bread and support my children" (Archivio di Stato, Modena, comici, busta unica, my translation).

Dukes were notoriously hard hearted. They were always looking for the best, new talent to hire away from their rivals. If a player was not attracting audiences, even if the player had been in service all his life, there was no pity or thought of accommodating him in some way. And audiences then, like today, also wanted to be entertained by the best. They did have favorites but their allegiance was fickle, lasting only until the next interesting player came along.

In every generation, there were stars, acknowledged by fellow actors, by their royal patrons, and by audiences. Their lives were enviable, for the most part, until they were replaced by the next star. Tristano Martinelli (1553–1630) was one the of the great *Arlecchinos* but his was not a modest personality. His sense of his own importance led him early in his career to sign himself *Arlechinus* and sometimes as *Dominus Arlechinorum*. He served for a time as a political advisor and ambassador both for the French court and for the duke of Mantua. In return, he was not at all shy about asking for favors for everything, from release from his contract (which he did not get), to having the French king and queen baptize his children, to having a constant supply of his favorite delicacies (the latter two he did get). In his interactions with royalty and patrons, he was swaggering and arrogant, but because he was a star, he got what he wanted rather than being thrown in a dungeon. Even stars, however, if they were too importunate, would be thrown in prison. The duke of Mantua, for example, was quite fond of trying to steal the really good players from his fellow dukes. He would lure them on the pretext of performing for his court, and then throw them into the dungeon while he negotiated with their patron. They remained in the dungeon with absolutely no recourse, dependent upon the whims and wills of the royal patrons.

In the great shift from improvised commedia under royal patronage to scripted commedia performed in theatres, the lives of players, the nature of the genre, and the audiences all changed drastically. Although Luigi Riccoboni, high lover of the Modena troupe and playing under the masque name *Lelio*, tried to control commedia performances by scripting them, he was miserably unsuccessful. His plays took a didactic, moralistic tone that did not appeal to fun-loving Venetians. It remained for Carlo

Goldoni to bring about this change. Even with the unpredictability of royal patrons, players' lives were more stable and more independent than when they were playing as a company in a theatre under the often dictatorial direction of the playwright and the theatre manager. In the older style, the most important person was the performer. Under Goldoni and those who followed, the playwright was the star.

Plays were published, almost never in dialect, so people could buy them to read in advance of a performance. The excitement of an improvised performance in which no one, neither performer nor audience, knew what twists and turns it might take, was replaced by actors reading a script. Many of the actors trained in the old style left the theatre, unable to adapt. Judging from the many pay receipts and contracts signed with Xs, a high percentage of players could neither read nor write. It was a new world for everyone. The themes of many of the comedies under Goldoni became middle-class family dramas in which family tensions replaced those between rich and poor, urban and rural, and learned and unlettered. This kind of theme attracted a different kind of audience, a primarily middle-class one rather than one in which the rich and the nobility rubbed elbows with the tradespeople and the workers. Italian society was changing, and the comedy changed with it.

Kabuki

I have mentioned some of the similarities between commedia dell'arte and Kabuki theatre. Their histories and origins are strikingly similar. Kabuki began as street theatre in the 1600s. It was performed in the countryside outside of Kyoto, mainly for merchants and frequenters of the taverns, and its performers included female prostitutes. The content of the "plays" was sensual if not lewd; indeed, the word Kabuki means "unconventional behavior that meets with disapproval." Kabuki became extremely popular—people flocked to the performances, ate and drank, and made propositions to the women performers. The theatres, very similar to commedia theatres, supported these kinds of behaviors. Kabuki theatres were divided into two basic sections whose names also described two kinds of theatre patrons: the *doma*, or floor in front of the raised stage, sometimes known as the *oikomiba*, or "place to pack them in" (Gunji 1985:60), and the *sajiki*, or raised section on either side of the *doma*. *Sajiki* patrons paid premium prices and comprised merchants, real connoisseurs of Kabuki, and the occasional samurai and high-born courtesan. Even cheaper seats existed at the far left side of the stage itself on a raised platform called the saint's pedestal, where the view was of the actors' backs, and at the very back of the *doma*, which was known as the *omuko* or great beyond. Critics, called *hyobanki*, were contemptuous of actors who played to the *doma*. One remarked, "He must have been aiming at the *doma* audience; certainly the servants and apprentices on their annual outing went home greatly contented" (Gunji 1985:63).

In the early years, there were frequent riots, causing the government in 1629 to forbid women to appear in the plays. The women were replaced by young men, who introduced a kind of acrobatics known as *hoka* (throwing), an aspect of Kabuki that still characterizes contemporary performance. Even the all-male Kabuki continued to inspire scandalous behavior, leading to the banning of Kabuki in 1652. It was so popular, however, with all classes of society, from rulers down to street sweepers, that the ban was eventually lifted. For a time, Kabuki was assigned a different name, *monomane kyogen zukushi*, signifying that it was now a kind of dialogue drama with mimed sequences and gestures. As part of this transformation, plots and performance devices were taken from Noh and Kyogen. Kabuki continued to be performed by all-male casts. It was at this juncture that the *onnagata* (woman-person) as a significant role in Kabuki began to be developed. In order to assure the government that there were no women in the cast, only female impersonators, the actors playing *onnagata,* had to be registered with the local magistrates. This registering of *onnagata* was probably the beginning of the division in Kabuki of the standard kinds of roles, a structure very much like that of the commedia dell'arte. Like other roles, the *onnagata* tradition was passed down along family lines; sometimes talented performers were added to the family by adoption. With Nakamura Utaemon growing older, Bando Tamasaburo is probably the most well known and idolized *onnagata*.

Tamasaburo did not belong to a Kabuki lineage; rather, he took classes in classical dance to strengthen his body after a mild case of polio. Evidently, his talent was obvious even at an early age since he was adopted into a Kabuki family at the age of six. In addition to his studies of technique, he also studied the performances of the great *onnagata* such as Nakamura Utaemon VI. He watched the films of Greta Garbo, Katharine

Hepburn, and Marilyn Monroe. Tamasaburo, now in his forties, certainly has a coterie of admirers every bit as loyal and vocal as those of any of the great *onnagata* of the past. He is without doubt known more widely because, in addition to his performance in classical Kabuki theatre, he also appears in Western drama, playing both male and female roles, and he has collaborated with other superstars, Yo-Yo Ma and Baryshnikov among them, in performances that cut across genres.

Although the Kabuki genre was less remote than Noh, it was still highly stylized, its technique composed of gestures *(kata)*, poses (*mie*), and kinds of movement. Within these broad categories, selections of gestures, poses, and movements belonged to particular characters. Colors also signaled the identity of a character. It became more stylized and formal when it began being performed for the emperor. There was a brief period at the end of the nineteenth and beginning of the twentieth centuries when Kabuki theatre tried to be more relevant, with contemporary themes and Western costumes. This was a failure, and it returned to its traditional form, if anything, becoming more removed from the public's experience.

Today, Kabuki is performed in a variety of venues: the most informal represents a kind of return to the original tent theatres. Kankuro Nakamura, a young star of Kabuki, created these performances, called Nakamura-za, for a tent set up on the banks of the Sumida River in the heart of Tokyo. He performed one of the more ancient plays, and people flocked to it.

One can also see Kabuki at the traditional Kabuki-za in Tokyo, where performances are often selections of well-known scenes interspersed with dance numbers. Tamasaburo, along with other venerated actors, performs here frequently.

Finally, there is the annual December Kabuki in Kyoto, which is the most traditional. Kabuki, unlike Noh or Bunraku, is not supported by the government, forcing it to rely on audience support. This may explain why there have been more changes and more experimentation in Kabuki than in either of the other two government-subsidized forms.

The kinds of experiments that Kankuro has initiated have involved a freer kind of theatre with audience members feeling like they can speak to the actors in performance. Here is one audience member's comment about a performance she saw of Kankuro's *Hokaibo*: "I've watched many a Kabuki play, but I've never felt so excited," Mrs. Matsumoto said. "I could feel the actors so close to me that I could even talk to them. They moved my heart" (in Strom, "Arts Abroad: Actor's Goal: To Make Kabuki Nothing to Snooze At," *New York Times* review, December 12, 2000). The actors and stage hands come out into the audience during intermissions to explain what is going on in the play, further enhancing the feeling of interaction.

As was the case with the commedia dell'arte, the performer is the attraction of Kabuki. Most performers come from a long lineage of Kabuki actors. It is only when a lineage has too few young members to continue that it "adopts" a talented outsider. Although composed of *kata*, codified movements and gestures, Kabuki expects that individual performers will interpret those building blocks according to their own gifts and inclinations. As contemporary Kabuki actors say, a role will look quite different when performed by different actors. In this way, the genre changes and grows with the times, maintaining its connection to a popular audience. Balancing what might be unchecked innovation is the system of schools, called *iemoto* (headmaster), whose heads are descendants of famous actors and acclaimed themselves for their performance style and skill. The schools tend to preserve the traditional style of Kabuki and so prevent it from deteriorating into a kind of circus. Because the heads have been great performers, they understand the role of individual innovation. The balance has been an effective one, judging from the long history and ongoing popularity of the genre.

Kabuki Conventions

Kabuki has many other conventions similar to those of the commedia dell'arte that facilitate audience comprehension. The stylized body movements, or *kata*, number in the hundreds and are the stock of performers and audiences alike. They fall into different classes: those involving props, those revolving around particular gestures, and those in the category called *roppo*, meaning the attention-getting entrances and exits down the runways of the theatre. *Mie*, or frozen poses, help focus the audience's attention. "Cutting a *mie*" means that "the character is in the grip of an overpowering emotion like anger or defiance, or is struggling for equilibrium" (Jonas 1992:148). These are used to build tension. "Kataoka Takao . . . likens the *mie* to a movie closeup: 'It's an enlarged vision shown in frozen motion that reveals heightened emotion'" (p. 149).

Costume, including wigs, masks, and makeup, also helps the audience understand the story, differentiating between high and low characters, comic and serious, warriors and merchants, characters from the spirit world, male and female. By costume alone, one already knows a great deal about the character and the character's place in the story. Loosened hair (*obakege*), for example, indicates that the character is supernatural or a ghost. Movements and gestures are also highly stylized to make these contrasts. Posture and walk are two that signal quite clearly into what category a character fits. *Aragoto* and *wagoto*, for example, are two different kinds of males: the first the strong male, the second the soft. There is also a small repertoire of plays on which Kabuki is based so audiences may easily be familiar with all of them. The plots, like those of the commedia, are few—a heroic commoner beats a bad samurai; a respectable woman sold into prostitution falls in love with a customer who cannot buy her freedom, so they both commit suicide; a "good" outlaw holds off the bad constables of the rich. The language, like the language of the commedia, is not readily understandable. The commedia resolved the problem by using many nonverbal cues to the action. Costumes, symbolic use of colors, standard characters, and plots in Kabuki conveyed meaning, but today's audiences feel somewhat alienated by the archaic language. Kabuki theatres have resolved the problem by renting headsets that provide explanations of the action and the dialogue in more contemporary Japanese.

Onnagata

One of the most interesting roles in Kabuki, in terms of conventions, technique, stylization, and audience understanding, is that of the *onnagata*. These are males who play female roles, and it is an inherited tradition. There is a curious play of gender roles across many of Japan's theatrical forms. *Onnagata*, as we have seen, developed as a response to the ban on women in Kabuki. From remaining documents, what we can say about the early style of men playing women is that it was fairly rough. Most of what indicated female came from the costume and makeup rather than movement and gesture, so icons of women—kimonos, hair dress, fans—stood for woman. Gradually, however, there developed a whole subtechnique of gesture and movement, very stylized, that came to mean female. Kabuki actors and audiences alike maintain that a woman could not play the female roles as well as the male *onnagata,* who develop their images of femininity over lifetimes of observation and practice of stylized gesture and movement. For better or for worse, the *onnagata* portrayal of women is what stands for woman.

As a convention, the *onnagata* has been borrowed by other actors and directors. In an inspired bit of choreography, Lindsay Kemp incorporated the figure of the *onnagata* in his production of *Flowers*, based on Genet's *Nôtre-Dame des Fleurs*. Genet's play was an homage to Divine, one of the most stunning, bold, and tragic of the transvestites. Genet himself lamented having to tell Divine's saga in words "that are weighed down with precise ideas" (Royce 1984:15). *Flowers* began as a spoken drama, but on tour it transformed itself into theatre without words. Kemp, playing Divine, enters on a balcony, then descends the stairs to the stage. He is dressed in a white, close-fitting, long gown and his steps are *onnagata* steps, sliding the foot forward, pointing toes up, then down, sliding the other foot forward. It was totally mesmerizing, this excruciatingly slow progress from one side of the stage to the other, then equally slowly down the stairs. The use of Kabuki *onnagata* conventions sent the unmistakable message that this character was female and, as an audience member, you were totally oblivious to Kemp's maleness.

The movements and gestures of the *onnagata* are not those of a woman going about her everyday life. They are not casual gestures but rather are stylized movements like those taught to geishas, slow, sculpted, deliberate. The posture itself—hips tucked under and forward, knees slightly bent and together, turned-in toes—is a convention that signals femaleness. All these, as well as the conventions of standing and sitting in a kimono, sleeve etiquette, and using a fan, have been incorporated into the codified technique of the *onnagata* role.

Twentieth-Century Genres

Nihon Buyo, a form of dance that originated toward the beginning of the twentieth century, is performed almost exclusively by women. The style of movement derives from the *onnagata* tradition, that being the only theatrical representation of women other than Noh drama. Other dance forms like *gagaku* have only male roles and techniques. Finally, as an obvious development, Japan has seen a new entertainment come into being, *Takarazuka*, in which all the roles, male and female, are played by women.

Accommodations have been made in the more stylized forms, like Kabuki, so that audiences can understand the story and the action—program notes, headphones, or the more innovative examples in which audience and performers actually interact. Nihon Buyo, as a genre, does not need this kind of explanation because it is dance that can be enjoyed for the movement alone, whether or not there is a narrative. Noh, Bunraku, and *gagaku* (the oldest form of court dance) have government subsidies, and therefore do not have to worry about ticket sales.

Other new forms arise in response to the society in which they are set. Butoh, a contemporary dance that developed in the 1960s as a reaction to the traditional, unchanging forms of Kabuki and Noh, created a new audience for its own kind of social commentary, both in Japan and abroad. More recently, producer Mayumi Nagatoshi showcases new Japanese dancers and choreographers. Takarazuka was certainly a response to audience demand for entertainment. Each genre has established its own dialectic with the public, accommodating more in the case of nonsubsidized forms.

The relationship of audience and performer in performances of set-apart genres such as the commedia dell'arte, Kabuki, and classical ballet requires knowledge on the part of the audience beyond what they would have as a typical member of a society, although anyone could attend and derive some enjoyment at a superficial level. Further, audience and performer agree to certain conventions of the genre and both parties must honor those terms for the genre to succeed. Tewa ritual performance, on the other hand, is accessible to all Tewa because everyone ultimately will be a participant. The cosmologies and beliefs that underlay these performances are known by every member of Tewa culture, although some details may be known only to ritual specialists.

Whatever the situation, whether communally embedded or professionally performed, genres are governed by aesthetic codes and conventions of form and story known to both performers and audiences. And whether it is a performance by Tamasaburo, a commedia troupe, or a Tewa ritual society, performances are evaluated, implicitly or explicitly, within the context of that governing aesthetic. Audiences are more and less sophisticated in their ability to articulate the terms of the aesthetic, but they do recognize it.

Notes

1. *Scenari*, or scenarios, did not approach anything like a script as we think of it. For a three- or five-act play, the scenario would be perhaps four pages. At the top of the first pages would be the title and the cast of characters (not the actors), a list of props, and the setting. The rest was limited to what we might call stage directions: *zanni* enters; Magnifico enters; Mag gives letter to *zanni* with instructions and exits: *zanni* does *lazzi* of the letter and exits. Even more abbreviated versions of these were posted backstage so that players would know what was the fare for the evening. Since many players were illiterate, extensive scripts and directions would have been useless. In any case, they knew their craft, each other, and the repertory.

2. The manuscripts that are the basis for the discussion of the commedia dell'arte in Modena and in Venice include the following:

Museo Correr, Correr Codex 1040, 51 scenari, Venice.
Archivio di Stato, spettacoli pubblici, busta 8/a, Modena.
Archivio di Stato, comici, busta unica, Modena.

CHAPTER TEN
PERFORMERS AND GENRES: THE FORM AND MEANING OF INNOVATION

Yo-Yo Ma, solitary, sits on a chair, cradling his cello, beginning the prelude of the fifth of Bach's solo suites. The stage is dark. Far off in a corner, you notice a figure in white. It comes closer, circling, long white sleeves making patterns that repeat the curve of the skirt. Now the figure is almost upon you, a flash of sleeves, white hands, and, stage front, a bank of candles lights itself. Tamasaburo Bando, the world's best-known *onnagata*, spirals away to ignite another bank of candles as the notes of the prelude sparkle and dance with him.

Inspired by Bach is one of the many collaborations prompted by Yo-Yo Ma's curiosity and willingness to stretch the limits of traditional genres. In this instance, he says that the impetus came from Albert Schweitzer's description of Bach as a "painterly" or "pictorial" composer. He wanted to explore that aspect and not through the music alone. The six suites involve collaborations with others of the same caliber as Ma himself, from garden designer Julie Moir Messervy, film director François Girard, choreographer Mark Morris, film director Atom Egoyan, ice dancers Jayne Torvill and Christopher Dean, to Tamasaburo Bando. All our traditional expectations are challenged. The medium, first of all, is film—and film that loops around in a decidedly nonlinear fashion. Bach's unaccompanied suites suddenly are the companions to genres as widely distant as dance, gardening, the visual art of Piranesi, ice dancing, and film. And the dance genres that are paired with the suites are not those that Bach envisioned when he composed what are essentially dance suites—*sarabandes*, *gigues*, and *minuets*.

While I have no doubt that what we think of as traditional genres of performing arts will continue, with the kinds of stylistic changes that we saw, for example, with Fokine, I am also certain that collaborations across the arts will push us into areas we can now only imagine. I want to use this chapter, first, to examine some of these collaborations in more detail in order to understand the processes of genre formation and change, the role of performers versus creators, and the new rules of interpretation in these cross-genre performances. Then, I turn to what we might call essays into new genres, exploring the relative importance of technique as opposed to the artistry or charisma of the performer and asking the question, what does this balance mean for the viability of the genre or for its relationship to an audience?[1]

Collaborations

Yo-Yo Ma and Tamasaburo Bando

When Yo-Yo Ma asked Tamasaburo which of the Bach suites he might consider choreographing, he immediately responded, "the fifth suite." Both he and Yo-Yo Ma regard it as the most melancholic of the suites. The title of this collaboration is *The Struggle for Hope,* and reflects the emotional connections between Tamasaburo and the music. By listening to the emotional palette of the suite and letting it wash over his own experiences, Tamasaburo created a work faithful to both a Japanese aesthetic and to the fundamental passions in the music itself. "You enter a world beyond the sound of the cello," he says in the liner notes for the video. The entire collaboration was a melding of opposites: male/female; Eastern/Western; classical/modern; classical genres/modern presentation. The two performers were separated by language, by distance, and by genre. They worked through interpreters; they worked through exchanges of videotaped presentations of ideas as the work progressed; Yo-Yo Ma found time in his performing schedule to visit Tamasaburo in Japan. When, after some three years, the work had come together, director and filmmaker Niv Fichman came to Japan to direct the filming. Fichman deliberately did not bring his own artistic collaborators, choosing instead to use a Japanese film crew in order to open the filming up to the "Japanese way," as he called it. In the process of filming, every detail engendered discussion, since no common ground existed. The result is a rich, stylized, simple performance of stunning visual force.

Tamasaburo's ability to stay fundamentally within the Kabuki *onnagata* tradition while creating a choreography and a persona totally outside that tradition is uncanny. He could have chosen to portray a male dancer—in his life outside the theatre, he is male—but he did not; rather, he captures the qualities of woman with none of the aids that Kabuki provides its *onnagata*. His costumes are loose-fitting, flowing, long draperies, not kimonos. His makeup is subtle in contrast to the highly stylized Kabuki face. His hair is loose, not covered by the *onnagata* wig except as it is undone, in a long braid or loose. The small movements close to the floor so characteristic of *onnagata* are replaced by rapid, large, sweeping movements. These are still close to the floor; as Tamasaburo has said about *onnagata*, "physically we are on the ground but in our imagination, we fly."

The arms are freed to move expansively. Emotions, however, as in Kabuki, are conveyed primarily through the body rather than the face. Tamasaburo uses a fan in two of the movements—cutting crisp swathes in the third movement, titled *Denial*, and encompassing the cellist, the light, and hope with it in the sixth, titled *Reconciliation*. In the fifth movement he dances with a small two-headed drum attached around his waist. The collaboration becomes a fine-grained performance that takes the viewer through hope, catharsis, defiance, prayer, and reconciliation. The viewer comes to the performance with expectations of Kabuki, *onnagata*, and Bach, and sees a blend unlike whatever might have been imagined. Tamasaburo, great artist that he is, has created a performance that is totally unexpected and totally inevitable.

In this particular collaboration, Tamasaburo is very much a performer, but he is also the creative force behind the piece. His interpretive work lies in drawing out the sentiments in Bach's music and giving them a corporeal existence. That the resulting collaborative performance is of such coherence supports the argument for a corpus of aesthetic principles that cut across time and cultural traditions.

Yo-Yo Ma and Mark Morris

The other dance collaboration in *Inspired by Bach* is that between Ma and Mark Morris and his dancers to the third solo suite, a collaboration titled *Falling Down Stairs*. Morris is musically sophisticated, composing with a score in hand because, as he says, "When you're just listening, you can't hear every part. Also, there are subtle things, mathematical things: harmonic progressions, phrase lengths. You'd end up having to make a chart, and there is already a chart—the score" (Acocella 1995:172). He is fondest of Baroque music because of its structure and clarity. So this collaboration, if not inevitable, is certainly a happy one. When Yo-Yo Ma asked Morris which came first by way of inspiration—the idea, the movement, or the music—Morris replied, the music, always the music. The music of Bach has such structural clarity that it lends clarity to the dance, which is always a bit imprecise because it must rely on the dancers' bodies (p. 163). Both artists wanted to create something that would add to a piece of music already superbly made.

Morris has been accused of mirroring the music in too simplistic a way but, in fact, while he does this, he also plays with time values and uses rhythm and duration for dramatic effect (Acocella 1995:166). He does all of this in this third suite. In the opening prelude, he gives each dancer five bars of different movement, which they do sequentially and simultaneously, in patterns across the large space between the raised platform where cellist Yo-Yo Ma sits and the stairs where the dancers begin and to which they return. The *Allemande* strikes a very different tone with its two lines of dancers and their mechanical motions, forming, reforming. The *Courante* is full of wavelike movements passed back and forth between three groups. The *Sarabande* is befittingly solemn with a long line of twining bodies dressed in long velvet costumes. The *Bourrée* is a fascinating play of hands, arms, and heads in a canon structure. The concluding *Gigue* uses different groups of dancers and different motifs to bring out the themes of the movement. That the music and the dance are in dialogue with each other is clear. In the liner notes for the video of *Falling Down Stairs*, Yo-Yo Ma says: "Bodies have to follow the natural laws of gravity and so if somebody launches themselves up in the air, you know the timing and the feel it takes before they land again, and that gives me a sense of what I have to do." Morris, for his part, plays with the music but plays within the rule of the musical structure. He described this collaboration as a "transcendent, transparent, transmogrifying kind of situation," and I think he is right.

Tamasaburo Bando has undertaken other collaborative works. In 1999, he created a piece, *Dance with Three Drums and Flute*, for Baryshnikov, to a score by Rosen Tousha. The two artists had known each other for many years. Indeed, the first performance of a piece to Tousha's score was a duet for the two men choreographed by Dana Rietz. The work, *Cantata for Two*, blended Japanese traditional dance and music with modern, Western music and dance. Jennifer Dunning had this to say in her August 19, 1999, review in the *New York Times* of the solo piece: "Mr. Baryshnikov's strong, stern gaze is at times unnervingly unchanging. He shifts abruptly from an almost mystical stillness to tumult and back again with astonishing clarity. As clear are the sudden shifts in direction in the geometric paths Mr. Baryshnikov takes. . . . One audience member saw in the repeated angular folding of his arm a metaphor of sorts, an invitation to follow Mr. Baryshnikov."

Baryshnikov himself had the following reactions in an article by Jennifer Dunning (*New York Times*, January 12, 1999): "There is no context or story. Some of the movements mean something in Kabuki theater, like dancing with a fan or a hop on one leg. . . . But in this dance they just mean movement. And, from my point of view it is close to modern dance, or mime, in the purity of the movement. . . . There is a certain stillness, a sculptural quality—that deadness or shell that burns from the inside—that is very Japanese and is projected in her [Martha Graham's] work so much."

Mikhail Baryshnikov

Baryshnikov, of course, has had more experience than most in breaking with old traditions and creating new ones, trying everything. It was one of the reasons that he left Russia and the Kirov. If one sorts the world, as did Isaiah Berlin, following the Greek poet Archilochus, into hedgehogs and foxes, then Baryshnikov, together with Yo-Yo Ma, Tamasaburo, and perhaps Mark Morris, is a fox among foxes. What Berlin said in his classic essay on Tolstoy was that hedgehogs relate everything to a single, central vision while foxes move on many levels, seizing upon the essence of a vast variety of experiences and objects for what they are in themselves . . . without trying to fit them into . . . a unitary inner vision (Berlin 1993:3).

Artists the stature of Baryshnikov may be foxes, but they are foxes who have mastered their particular craft to a level that goes far beyond most practitioners. This gives them the status, the confidence, and the knowledge to venture beyond the confines of their art. It is that mastery, I think, that also makes it possible for them to work collaboratively. While the techniques of their respective arts may be quite different, the elements that define great artistic creations are common to all. I have named and examined these in previous chapters but raise them again here in the context of how these stars in their own fields work in and with each other's art. The elements include simplicity above all, an economy of effort whether it is movement or sound, an economy of visual cues. Centeredness is another—the self-knowledge that allows a performer to go out from and return to a center so that movement and sound are not random, external phenomena, but are generated by a center of balance and of quiet. They are motivated by that center, and emerge from it. Impulse is what lets the audience share the motivation, see the shape of the sound and movement, feel it before it arrives. Density outlines and calls attention to the performer. It provides drama. It makes the movement and the sound hum with life. Phrasing comes from some internal pulse, the ability to feel a continuous flow even in silence or stillness. Watching Tamasaburo and Yo-Yo Ma, one can see the connection between the music and the movement, and it is phrasing that links them, not a slavish following of the musical beat or even line. This is true as well of the Ma–Morris collaboration where each artist is cognizant of the inner pulse and the dialogue necessary to create a harmonious whole. It is that same embodied sense of peaks and valleys and how they ought to be in that particular performance. And, finally, transparency. Each of these performers puts his art first, far ahead of any claim to personal achievement. Their collaborations are not exhibitions of egos but a working toward an artistic performance which is greater than each or than all collectively.

Genres and Innovation

These collaborations do not create new genres but they do expand our notion of what each component genre is. We often think of genres as classificatory devices and, to be useful for this task, we assume that genres are defined by shared characteristics. But Kallberg, reviewing the philosophies of Wittgenstein and others, argues that shared characteristics are only partially relevant. "They provide factual information about a term; they classify it. But they do not explain its meaning. The meaning of a term instead is connected to the willingness of a particular community to use that word and not another. . . . Meaning . . . must emerge from the context of the term" (Kallberg 1996:4–5). Genres, in fact, are negotiated in the contract between the creator-performer and the public-audience. There have to be enough of the characteristics that all have agreed define the genre so that audience expectations are met. Similarly, there may be shared ideas about what is not permissible in a particular genre. While genres tend to take on the immutable properties of a Platonic idea, there is also a great deal of flexibility and give in them, as well as a degree of tolerance on the part of audiences. A performance of Shakespeare's *Richard III* done in Kabuki costumes and style performed at the Folger Library Theatre in Washington, D.C., was warmly received by an intrigued audience despite the fact that its conventions were far from those of Shakespeare's time.

There are limits, however, on the kinds and number of changes that an audience will accept. The opening night reception of Nijinsky's *Sacre du Printemps,* at which the audience booed and hissed so loudly that the dancers could not hear the music, is an excellent example of expectations being dashed. The Parisian public were used to the new and distinctive, but still quite balletic, style of Fokine's works. They came to the theatre expecting something in the same genre, and were outraged by what they saw.

Audience expectation and preparation are crucial in determining how innovative a work can be. Some members of a Midwestern audience were confused and then offended by Twyla Tharp's *As Time Goes By*, a ballet to the last two movements of Haydn's Forty-fifth Symphony first performed in 1973. Although classical in its fundamentals, this piece turns the traditional gender roles in ballet around so that the ballerina is the assertive one while her partner is passive and vulnerable. Tharp also plays with time, making many steps into parodies of themselves because they are held too long or done too slowly. Unsuspecting audience members came prepared for an evening of "serious" entertainment because that is what traditional ballet is expected to be. It was inconceivable to some that this might be a deliberate parody.

A similar theatrical event was the Paris production of *Flowers* by Lindsay Kemp's company. The posters advertising it depicted a white-faced mime holding a flower. In very small print at the bottom, it announced that this was based on Jean Genet's *Nôtre-Dame des Fleurs*. One was led to think that this was going to be an evening of mime–drama. The half hour of pre-curtain music—sweet, late-nineteenth-century vocal music—reinforced that notion. The performance was anything but a touching, romantic mime-drama. It was the Genet piece, full of gender reversals, nudity, and brutality accompanied by ear-splitting music by the Chrome Circus. It was a spectacular evening of theatre; one that left half the audience on its feet booing and the other half yelling bravos.

What Tamasaburo has said about Kabuki is a very clear analysis of why theatre works. "When the make-believe is believed on both sides," he says, "it appears to be true." There has to be a complicity in attributing truth, in the sense of coherence, to a work of art. Artist and audience both have to suspend all normal critical faculties and expectations of reality during those moments in a darkened theatre in order for this elevated, more transparent reality to take form. This is one of the bases for the effectiveness of Tewa ritual. The community understands both the form and the meaning of the performances that are part of the yearly cycle. The performers belong to the community, and, while some performers are acknowledged to have special gifts, everyone participates. Outsiders who may come to see the ritual are irrelevant to its success, and community-based rituals are not altered to accommodate non-Tewa guests.

Given the implicit contract between audience and performer about the nature of the genre, how does innovation occur and how and when is it manifested in technique? What shape does interpretation take in "new" forms of performing arts?

Opera

One of our most enduring musical forms resulted from a conjoining of two genres—music and dramatic text. *Opera* is, in fact, defined as drama that is primarily sung. The text is conveyed through arias, duets, ensembles, and recitatives. Orazio Vecchi (1550–1605) was the choirmaster of the cathedral in Modena for most of his life. It was his combination of madrigals and commedia dell'arte, titled *L'Amfiparnaso*, that premiered in 1594 and proved an early antecedent to opera. The honor of being the first major work in what was to become opera goes to Monteverdi's *La Favola di Orfeo*, performed first in Mantua in 1607. While Florence and Rome were important sites of operatic development, it was in Venice that the first opera house was constructed, thereby moving opera from entertainment for the courts to public spectacle. With its own theatre, especially like those in the Veneto with immense capacity for staging and grand set designs, opera became a genre that brought together music, drama, singing, dancing, and theatre. It also created a whole cadre of virtuosos—the singers. First to appear were the castrati such as Farinelli (Carlo Broschi), Gasparo Pacchierotti, and Caffarelli (Gaetano Majorano). Among the greatest singers of all time, these men were paid enormous salaries, were pursued by royalty as well as huge coteries of fans, were the recipients of fabulous gifts, and lived lives that kept them always in the adoring gaze of their public. Women were not to be outdone. Francesca Cuzzoni (1698–1770) and Faustine Bordoni (1700–1781), whose stage name was Faustina, were superstars and rivals, both singing in Handel's opera company.

With all the subsequent changes of style and school in opera—*opera buffa*, *opera seria*, *bel canto*, *tragédie lyrique* (Lully and his successor Rameau), the *Gesamtkunstwerk* or music drama of Richard Wagner, and all the contemporary variations—the role of the interpreter remains supreme. And, perhaps more important, there are conventions agreed upon by composers, performers, and audiences that define the genre, although there are always individual works that challenge the conventions.

Pilobolus

Pilobolus provides a rich contemporary example of innovation in the dance genre.

Pilobolus is a dance company founded in 1971 by students at Dartmouth College, primary among them, Moses Pendleton and Jonathan Wolken. Neither had any previous dance training, but were expected in their modern dance class to choreograph a piece. Moses Pendleton describes the origin of that first work, called *Pilobolus* after a fungus: "I felt very paranoid about getting up and doing a dance. We felt that maybe we couldn't dance, so why try to? When we began, we didn't really feel free, moving in space individually. We literally *had* to hang onto each other. We all figured we could at least do that much, and it was something larger than any one body could make. It wasn't so difficult if you did create this shape, a thing that moved. We began to play around combining bodies" (Brown 1979:154).

Pilobolus. Photograph by John Kane.

From the beginning, the company departed from the usual definitions of dance. The geometric shapes that formed and metamorphosed into other shapes moved in a slow-motion, wavelike manner, lacking that kinetic energy that is one of the defining features of dance. Its pace and weight were much more those of mime. It did not have that constant

Pilobolus. Photograph by John Kane.

rhythm that can be translated into movement energy (Royce 1987a:272). In the early works, even after the addition of two women, Alison Chase and Martha Clarke, the bodies of the dancers were simply building blocks for the architecture of space. The shapes they created had no recognizably human element; the intrigue came from seeing how one might use the human body to make patterns that were totally abstract, indeed, patterns that made you forget that they were created by human dancers. The absence of a kinetic energy and any human quality either in form or in narrative meant that, after the initial interest of seeing something totally new, there was little to make an audience wanting to see dance keep coming back. It was then that the company began to change. Pendleton remarked about this: "We're using music more . . . sometimes in the old Pilobolus, we were much more visually oriented—we approached choreography as if it were painting or sculpture. But we're in great need of the musical phrasing, the delicacy and balance you find in ballet. I think Pilobolus now has the potential to become a dance company" (Brubach 1982:63).

Pilobolus has, indeed, become a dance company. It has achieved this gradual metamorphosis while still maintaining two fundamental characteristics that distinguish it from other companies. One is the sculpting of space with their bodies, supporting each other and playing off each other's bodies. The second is the fact that the troupe is guided by the vision of four dancer-personalities rather than the usual case where there is one dominant choreographic voice. Those two characteristics are intimately related. The first is simply the visual working out of the second. The piece by Alison Chase, *Ben's Admonition*, introduced for the 2002 season, may stand as a metaphor for the troupe and its philosophy. Chase and her collaborators manage to maintain the signature architecture of space built by bodies working off each other while launching the dancers into the weightlessness of movement liberated from the ground. In that weightlessness, the two dancers begin a swinging odyssey that carries them through quiet harmony, friendship, dependence, anger, and, finally, isolation and solitary deaths. The musical score by Paul Sullivan adds the energy that makes this dance rather than gymnastic formalism.

Two other works are also illustrative of the continuing evolution of the company. *The Brass Ring* was choreographed by Michael Tracy for the 2002 Cultural Olympiad and owes much of its shape to the music, a primarily all-American selection (Fauré is the one foreign composer) that begins with Copland's *Fanfare for the Common Man*. The dancers slide through tight circles of bodies, make a solemn group of two-person-high sentinels, flow into slow-motion gymnastics, give us subtle impersonations of midway shows, and become a carousel, all with their trademark shifts from wackiness to gentle intimations of a world gone awry, one emotion melting into another like molasses. It builds a steady pulse to an ending where all the dancers fly slowly through a darkening sky, becoming constellations just as the curtain comes down. While Dunning describes the experience of watching it as similar to "watching the final rounds in an Olympics gymnastic competition" (*New York Times*, July 1, 2002), it has a steady kinesthetic pulse that marks it as dance rather than sport. *The Four Humours*, choreographed by Robby Barnett and Jonathan Wolken, takes the dancers through the humors of the blood in ancient Greek medicine. There is much independent, in-the-air movement here, such as one expects in a dance company. Anna Kisselgoff refers to the surprising illusion of weightlessness since the company style has focused on leveraged support (*New York Times*, June 11, 2002). This piece, more than others, defies that signature gravity.

Pilobolus began as a class exercise, created by amateur gymnast-dancers. As they continued, it became clear that they would have to do more than simply create more pieces like the original ones if they were to continue having an audience. The early works were interesting intellectual explorations into the kinds of shapes human bodies could create. But performance that is based on the human body must have some human element about it that appeals to the public once the novelty ceases to attract (Royce 1987a:269). Further, Pilobolus was neither gymnastics nor dance as they were then defined as genres. The four original members took the company in the direction of dance once they began using music and building from its kinesthetic rhythm. In the process, they created a movement style and a technique that made them recognizable, and, importantly, which made it possible to recruit new dancers. In the original small company, the dancers were both creators and interpreters; with the addition of more dancers, the company is moving toward a pattern in which there are separate categories of choreographers, on the one hand, and performers, on the other.

Two of Pilobolus's founders, Moses Pendleton and Alison Chase, also founded Momix in 1980. Named after a brand of cattle feed, this company is composed of "dancer-illusionists" who combine gymnastics, modern dance, circus, acrobatics, and visual theatre. It may well represent the kind of company Pilobolus might have become had it not chosen to emphasize the more dancelike aspects of its work.

Butoh

Butoh is another innovative twentieth-century genre. I mention it in chapter four as an example of the evolution toward simplicity. There is a more extended discussion of it in chapter eight; I use it as an example of radical and different uses of time and space. Here, the question has more to do with how it came into being, its techniques, its evolution, and its practitioners—solo performers or members of companies. We know that is was pioneered in the late 1950s by Kazuo Ohno, Kasai Akira, and Tatsumi Hijikata. One of the striking characteristics of Butoh is its aversion to organized companies, standard repertoire, or technique.[2] All of its three founders have been almost exclusively solo performers. Tatsumi Hijikata framed this aversion quite bluntly: "I dislike the idea, let alone the creation of a 'regular' dance or theater troupe. . . . I'm not in search of such superficiality between people. . . . I'm convinced that a pre-made dance, a dance made to be shown, is of no interest. . . . In other forms of dance, such as flamenco or classical dance, the movements are derived from a fixed technique: they are imposed from the outside and are conventional in form. In my case, it's the contrary: my dance is far removed from conventions and techniques . . . it is the unveiling of my inner life" (Viala and Masson-Sekine 1988:85). Hijikata had a following of students whose lessons were more philosophy than dance. Kazuo Ohno also had a following and a studio. He would tell potential students that it would take five years for them to learn dance. In those years, the student would be taught "to analyze and organize his own body gestures, while deepening his consciousness of life" (Viala and Masson-Sekine 1988:176). Ohno was trained in gymnastics and, in addition to self-knowledge, his students were trained in what he called elementary movement.

Butoh was born out of revolt. It was a protest against the traditional theatrical forms of Japan and as a statement against what the world had become. It is difficult to maintain that sense of revolt, particularly since a part of the original rebellion was against codified genres of performance. This is why the "schools" that the founders gathered were more akin to the followers that Socrates gathered around him than they were like dance schools. In fact, they were very much in the tradition of the *iemoto* (headmaster) system that was the basis of Kabuki.

Two reviews of the 2002 season help us see the contrast between Butoh in its original manifestation and what Butoh artists are doing today. Akira Kasai, one of Butoh's three founders, appeared in a solo performance at the beginning of the New York season. Jennifer Dunning describes a disappointing seventy-minute solo titled *Pollen Revolution*: "The familiar decay and fey humor of old-style Butoh were evoked. But Mr. Kasai brought nothing of his own to them, in performing what was a superficial and blandly repetitious flow of mugging facial expression and tottering grafted onto an otherwise inexpressive body." She continues with this important comment: "Whether or not one likes the worlds created by Mr. Ohno, . . . there is an urgent core and unity to the old master's performing that was missing here" (*New York Times*, April 30, 2002). Those who choose the solo performer route in Butoh must have all the qualities of virtuosity and artistry in themselves as individuals. They cannot rely upon a recognized technique whose mastery would bring them the interest and attention of audiences. I would also argue that those successful soloists like Kazuo Ohno display the elements of artistic style common to performances of all genres at that level.

The other series of performances this season are by a troupe, Dairakudakan (The Great Camel Battleship), which had its inception thirty years ago. When it first began, its founder, Akaji Maro, was also its sole choreographer. At that time, he belonged to the shock category of Butoh; indeed, he earned the title "visual terrorist." Over the years, he has been nurturing a new generation of dancer-choreographers and it is their work that is being shown in this New York season. The major piece is *2001 Paradise in a Jar Odyssey*, by Kumotaro Mukai. It harkens back to Butoh's early days with the white-powdered bodies clad only in cloth dance belts. The two touches of color, black and red at the eyes and mouth, seem startling against the monochrome of the bodies and recall the red fingernails of Sankai Juku's *The Egg Stands out of Curiosity*. Children, ghosts, emissaries from hell capering about the stage, forming sculptures with their bodies, talking to themselves—these are some of Dunning's descriptions of a piece that has dark moments that were the hallmark of the original genre at the same time that it is bawdy and humorous. She says that it works because of the immense skill of the performers, their timing, their unselfconsciousness, and their individuality (*New York Times*, July 18, 2002). Dairakudakan has evolved from being the creation of one performer to being more of a repertory company with some stability and continuity. Founder Akaji Maro still maintains a presence. At the North Carolina Dance Festival in July 2003, the company performed his *Ryuba*. Maro

Dairakudakan in Ryuba, *2003. Photograph by Bruce Feeley.*

made brief but riveting appearances in *Ryuba* as the old woman. With or without Maro, and with the addition of other choreographers, Dairakudakan may be the less-sanitized complement to Sankai Juku. Both companies are fortunate in having brilliantly imaginative choreographers and dancers who, whatever their training, are disciplined, masterful performers. Because the genre has little of the virtuosic about it, the appeal relies on the form and meaning of the pieces, and so its continued survival depends on those creative individuals who compose works that have meaning and interest for audiences.

Commedia dell'Arte

The commedia dell'arte, the subject of chapter nine, provides another way of looking at new forms and how they evolve. What we understand as the fullest manifestation of Italian improvised commedia dell'arte was preceded in the fifteenth and sixteenth centuries by private performances for the amusement of young Venetian noblemen who organized themselves into clubs called *compagnie della calza* (stocking societies), after the distinctive hose that each group chose. For the masses, there were open-air performances put on by traveling players. Those small troupes, mostly families, also followed the cycle of fairs, which were excellent opportunities for adding to their usually meager earnings. Lastly, there was the custom of giving betrothed couples a little homily about proper married life on the eve of their wedding. These skits, humorous, bawdy, and sexually quite explicit, were called *mariazi*, and involved at least two of the subsequent commedia characters—Magnifico (Pantalone) and *zanni* (clown).

The seeds of the genre were there, but it took changes in the larger context and in the form before it flowered into what we know from later accounts. Royal patronage provided the actors with more stability than their predecessors, although patrons treated even very great actors quite badly (see chapter nine). Troupes were able to work together over longer periods of time, formalizing the repertory, and developing a performance style based on intimate knowledge of each other's acting. Children grew up in the company, learning through apprenticeship. Patrons built theatres exclusively for the commedia, and with them, scenery, props, and sometimes costumes, though the latter were considered more properly the responsibility of the actors. Plays could be, and were, more complex with the resources provided by a stable venue. The literate among the actors kept their speeches and acrobatic bit of business in prompt books called *zibaldone* (lit. miscellany). Some, like Andrea Perrucci, wrote treatises describing the structure, characters, speeches, and *lazzi* that functioned like handbooks for the genre (1699). Others, such as Luigi Riccoboni, actor, playwright, historian of the theatre, wrote massive histories complete with drawings of commedia masques.

At that point, we could say with certainty that the genre was established. It thrived for two centuries; was exported all over Europe, even into Poland and Russia; and it survived the shift from royal patronage to performances in theatres before a public. While possessed of rules for form and aesthetic judgments about good and bad performers, it still maintained the effervescence of a basically improvised form. Actors could anticipate lines and situations but they were not scripted. Actors could choose among a number of possibilities for each situation. In this incarnation, it was very much an actor's theatre. Audiences came to see their favorites and the plots mattered little.

The genre changed radically when scripted comedies began to dominate the productions. Actors had to follow the script. Audiences now went to the theatre, not to see outstanding performers, but rather to see a particular play.

Habit d'Arlequin Moderne, *from Luigi Riccoboni,* Histoire du Théâtre Italien, II, *Paris, 1731. Courtesy of the Lilly Library, Indiana University, Bloomington.*

Lazzi, used more infrequently, were also determined in advance by the text. This occurred over a period of time and coincided with the aging and death of the great actors who were masters of improvisation. The new actors were literate and without background in the kind of slapstick, rollicking comedy of the older troupes. They could be tamed, and were, by playwrights such as Carlo Goldoni, who shared the contempt of many authors for the actors they

Habit de Pierrot, *from Luigi Riccoboni,* Histoire du Théâtre Italien, II, *Paris, 1731. Courtesy of the Lilly Library, Indiana University, Bloomington.*

had to rely upon to bring their creations to life.[3] The new plays used almost no dialect, and became dramas of the middle class. Gradually the commedia dell'arte became comedy, ceasing to exist except in revivals and as exotic museum pieces.

Twentieth-Century Genres

We can see similar patterns in both Western arts and Eastern arts in the twentieth century. Frustration with the perceived limitation of old forms led, in some cases, to radically new styles while retaining the basic structure of the technique. Examples here would include Michel Fokine's new Ballets Russes and Nijinsky's incomplete revolution of technique and style. Sometimes, new genres were created by jettisoning everything about the old genre, including the technique. Here, we might place Pilobolus and Butoh. The commedia dell'arte survived centuries of change only to fall victim to literacy and the rising middle class. Then there are all the collaborations that have created exciting and thought-provoking performances without creating new genres—Yo-Yo Ma and Tamasaburo Bando, Yo-Yo Ma and Mark Morris, Tamasaburo Bando and Mikhail Baryhsnikov, Baryhsnikov and Mark Morris.

Nihon Buyo

Nihon Buyo, the classical dance of modern Japan, provides us with a final example of a classical form created at the beginning of this century that drew from Kabuki and Noh and is now undergoing yet another metamorphosis. It is a particularly interesting example because of the shifts in gender roles and portrayal in both the technique and the subject matter, and because it is a form that looks backward to past traditions and forward to what might be. And, like Pilobolus, it may well prove to be a form which is moving toward the codification of a technique.

Masakatsu Gunji speaks in terms of the new dance movement that began in Japan during the Taisho era (1912–1926). It was a movement propelled by the ideas and determination of Fujima Shizue. Born in 1880, Shizue studied Japanese classical dance with a local teacher. When she was nineteen, she went to Tokyo to study with Ichikawa Kumehachi after seeing the actress in a performance of *Musume Dojo-ji*. Unsuccessful in this plan, she returned home to return to Tokyo to study under Fujima Kan'emon, taking her professional dancer's name. In 1917, she organized her own dance troupe, Fujikage-kai, at first led with a fellow student but then on her own, creating original works. She came to the attention of the public, critics, and Kabuki actors in 1921 when she staged *Shibon*. It guaranteed the continued interest of a wide public and, in 1931, she founded the Fujikage school of dance, changing her name to Fujikage Shizuki.

All of the innovative dance being done in this period was done by women. Other pioneers included Tamami Gojô and Sumi Hanayagi. In Japan at that time, dance, divorced from drama and theatre as in Kabuki and Noh, was considered the domain of women. The two dramatic forms had become highly formalized and difficult to change. As Gunji suggests, it was not only the rigidity of the forms themselves that prevented change but also the headmaster (*iemoto*) system that demanded conformity to a conservative status quo from its disciples. The power of this system was demonstrated in the response to the women who had been granted the right to become choreographers by headmaster Hanayagi Jusuku II. They were denied the privilege of using the professional names of the established schools (Gunji 1970:178). It was difficult for any of the heads of schools to break with tradition because the system was so powerful a force. Even the greatest of them had to bow to tradition. So it was the women, who were not encumbered by the constraints of a system in which they were not allowed to take part, who were the primary creative impetus. What they envisioned was a classical dance that was poetical, in which movement had its own significance apart from a narrative.

But what about form and genre? Gunji criticizes the tendency of many of the master dancers: "To present new themes in old forms of expression or to use new forms of expression unsupported by themes, is to display a lack of faith in a coherent form of dance" (1970:180). Because of the hereditary claim to teach and perform certain genres, all but those with family ties or who are "adopted" into a family are excluded from the tradition. So it was women from nontheatrical families who studied Japanese dance and they did so with no prospect of becoming professionals. The training was not then as rigorous as it was for those destined to carry on the great family traditions. Gunji criticizes the ever escalating numbers of dancers who acquire technical prowess without any idea of artistry and who set themselves up as masters.

The basis for the new dance comes from dance on the Kabuki stage. All of the characteristic movements and gestures of that genre were incorporated in dance that stood by itself and was performed almost exclusively by women. It is a curious unfolding for gender symbolism. All roles in the forerunner of Kabuki were danced and played by women. They were replaced in a moment of reform by young boys and men whose playing of female roles was as caricature, *en travestie*. Finally, another reform brought all-adult male casts. The *onnagata* became one of the major roles in this new Kabuki. Men who were more feminine than women; men who presented the essence of woman. Some lived as women offstage, some as men, but on stage, they came to stand for woman. Now, ironically, it was the movements and gestures of the *onnagata* that provided the basis for women creating Nihon Buyo. The women instrumental in Nihon Buyo as performers, choreographers, and teachers founded their own schools, thus perpetuating the *iemoto* system.

As this dance genre continues to evolve, it has taken the direction of a broader use of space for choreographic patterns; more movement, particularly replacing the slow, small steps with very rapid ones that cover more ground, a less restrictive kimono, a change from the stark white face to a more natural one, and less of the traditional female head tilt that signals demureness and subordinate status (Yamazaki, personal communication). In a performance of the New Nihon Buyo (*sôsaku*), the work *Shiki no Hana* (*Flowers of the Four Seasons*), illustrates all these changes. The eight women dancers cover a large stage in expansive patterns, with choreography that emphasizes unison steps and poses. The theme is clear not so much from the movement as it is from the changing scenery and music. The music itself is new, by composer Yamato Gaku, but uses a combination of traditional instruments (*samisen*) and scales with women's voices and harmony.

More interesting perhaps is the entrance of men into what has been a genre exclusive to women. The men are mostly sons of Nihon Buyo dancers who want to continue the line, perhaps another effect of the old headmaster system. In the work *Ombashira* (*A Sacred Pillar*), based on a Nagano folk ritual in which the men cut down a tree and slide it down the mountain to make a new pillar for the shrine, all the dancers are male. The genre itself has taken the same directions as the female dances—more movement, broader patterns, moving rapidly in and out of formations, and using shouts and foot stamps to punctuate the movement. The concept of gender here is intriguing. Kazuko Yamazaki comments that male roles in Kabuki were meant to portray a larger-than-life masculinity in the same way that the *onnagata* exemplified femininity. "But watching these newly emerging men dancers perform, I think their intent is not so much about creating new masculinity. They are a lot more interested in moving and movement" (Yamazaki, personal communication).

Perhaps then we have reached a point in this twentieth-century creation where movement and technical accomplishment are the focus, as is the case with so many performing genres, and narrative is simply a backdrop or a pretext for performance. Until very recently, in Nihon Buyo, "the body [has been] trained as a result of dancing rather than as a foundation for dancing. . . . To separate the body from dance and to work on, exercise and prepare it as an instrument may be more specific to theatrical dance forms where the body is meant to be presented for others to see" (Yamazaki 2001:21).[4]

If form becomes foregrounded, and the body with it, then virtuosity becomes an issue as well, and a satisfying performance does not hinge upon a charismatic solo performer whose artistry holds the attention of the public. There is, further, more likelihood of the persistence of a genre that is based on technique rather than single performers relying exclusively on charisma. Were this to happen, then Nihon Buyo might join the great enduring classical dance genres like ballet or classical Indian dance.

Other chapters examine virtuosity and artistry, interpretation and audience, ritual embedded within a changed but persistent cultural context, style and metaphor. In this chapter, I turn the lens to those same concepts as they appear, support, and are negotiated in the ferment of innovation. Today's audiences are bigger and broader-based than earlier ones, ones that characterized the societies when most of the forms I talk about were created. Performances are not necessarily live anymore. We have media to bring us music, dance, and theatre almost on demand. Cross-genre collaborations seem to have exploded in the last twenty years. Virtuosity in competitive sports such as gymnastics and ice skating has touched the classical genres, raising audience expectations of all performance. We continue to recognize and respond to great artistic performances whether we can articulate the reasons or not. Those arts that have persisted have been able to balance audience demands with the integrity of the art; they have been those with foundations in technique and standards for judging performance. They have also all produced great artists from time to time who remind us of the importance of those imaginary worlds they create. Some arts have anonymous audiences; others spring out of face-to-face communities. It is perhaps easier to see the need in those small, known communities but the need also exists in the world where performer and audience are strangers. Perhaps it is even greater.

Notes

1. The number of examples—of collaborations, of shifts in style, of new genres, of genres that cease to be—is almost limitless. With a few exceptions, I have focused in this chapter on genres that fall primarily within dance and theatre. Clearly, the evolution of musical forms through time has much to teach us, but it is beyond the scope of this discussion.

2. The big exception to this generalization is Sankai Juku, a troupe that some have described as having "sanitized" Butoh for a wider international audience. Even in its sanitized form, it evidently is still too foreign for some audiences. In the performance I described that took place here in Bloomington, there were people who eventually left the auditorium after first fidgeting, then saying to their dates "they aren't moving; nothing is happening," then finally variants on "this is ridiculous: it isn't dance." I had been given the task of reviewing the performance for the local paper and I came early in order to write down my usual outline, a kind of frame for taking notes. I realized not long into the performance that what I had constructed was purely Western and that it had nothing to do with what I was seeing. Those who left did so, I think, because they were expecting to see "dance." Sankai Juku did not fit any of their categories and was too slow to engage or keep their interest.

3. Playwrights, directors, and critics have all written about the disadvantages of having to rely on humans in order to realize their work. Certain themes appear again and again, beginning with von Kleist's 1810 essay *Über das Marionettentheater*. Control and self-awareness were problems that von Kleist thought could be resolved by having puppets instead of human actors or dancers. Gordon Craig offered the idea of the *über-marionette*, which was to replace the actor. For Craig, theatre should be controlled: performances should be like ceremonies. With their self-awareness and temperament, actors are incapable of the necessary discipline. The only appropriate emotions, Craig felt, should be those of the audience. Antonin Artaud dehumanized his actors by turning them into puppets through the mechanical gestures of Balinese-like dance.

Polish director Tadeuszc Kantor thought the idea of puppets replacing humans was naive, but he does exert virtually total control over his actors. He frequently appears on stage, literally directing the actors' movements. In his play *The Dead Class*, he flicks his wrist and the hitherto dead class comes to life. When he uses puppets, they stand for death. Finally, Jonas Barish discusses the antihumanism of the new theatre: "The theater seems to be committing itself to a science-fiction-like attempt to reinvent the human, as if we were all suddenly to awake on a new planet, and had to recommence the history of the race anew, with no reference to the past other than that of repudiation" (1981:459). (See discussion in chapter one.)

4. My student, Dr. Kazuko Yamazaki, has written what is the definitive study of Nihon Buyo to date. Yamazaki examines this new classical dance from the dual perspectives of practitioner and anthropologist, seeing its historical roots, exploring the deeply embedded notions of gender and body, providing a thorough description of how it is taught and recreated, and giving a firsthand account of a major new production.

CHAPTER ELEVEN
ARTISTRY AND ALTERED STATES

"I was taken to a beautiful palace with many rooms. There were flowers everywhere of every kind and every color. Their perfume filled the soft breezes. I could see my body lying on the mat, but I did not want to go back to it. I met a beautiful young girl—she was our Virgin María. We walked through many of the rooms and came to a place where I could see a dark current racing by. As we came closer, I could see that it was blood. I could not smell the perfume anymore, only the darkness of the blood. The Virgin told me that the blood was the shame of humans. They had sinned so much that her son had to die. The river of blood disappeared, and we were in a bright room. She took my hand and told me that I was not going to die. Our Father has given you the power to heal; that is what you must do. When she said that, I felt myself back on my mat. Now my skin was cool, and my family were filled with happiness."

This is the first vision of Ta Feli, Felix López Jimenez, one of the most senior and respected healers in the southern Isthmus Zapotec city of Juchitán. He was fourteen when he was struck by a high fever that left him delirious and at the point of death. When his beautiful Lady took his hand, the fever left, and he sat up very hungry.

Ta Feli is a *espiritista* and a *binni guendabianni* (a wise person). An espiritista is one of the categories of healers while a binni guendabianni is a person who is wise, willing to be transformed, and who helps others achieve transformation. Like the West African *griots*, Ta Feli is a vehicle for light and power, both of which pass through him.

Ta Feli has had many visions, many of which he has shared with me in the course of a healing or a conversation. But this one, his first, is the one that announced to his family, and to his healer uncle, that he was

Ta Feli—Felix López Jimenez. Photograph by Anya Peterson Royce.

Temple of Ta Feli. Photograph by Anya Peterson Royce.

destined to be a healer. Delirium, high fever, a seemingly miraculous recovery—all these are elements of a life-changing event. His first transformation, it opened the path to many more.

In his early apprenticeship to his uncle, Ta Feli was sent to work with Mayan healers in Guatemala. Such study is a tradition that goes back at least to the great Classic civilizations of Mesoamerica (a forerunner, perhaps, of residencies and postdoctoral fellowships in our own culture). Since he established himself in his own *templo* in 1970, he has not traveled in the way we normally think of travel; rather, he ranges widely in an altered state in order to meet his obligations.

For the most part, those are meetings with other *espiritistas* and *curanderos* for prayer that will keep the world from destroying itself. In the reality that most of us recognize, Ta Feli holds prayer services three days a week in his temple. The prayers are a blend of Roman Catholicism, traditional Zapotec belief, and myths deriving from both Eastern and Western beliefs. Feli is adamant that this work must be done to keep the world alive, and urges followers to help him. The prayer services usually have from six to eighteen people. Most of the time, Ta Feli sees individuals who come to him for all manner of illness, diagnosing them by "pulsing" and feeling the state of the body as he massages limbs, head, and neck. Patient and healer sit facing each other on wooden chairs, knees nearly touching. He uses big bunches of a small-leaved basil (*albahaca*) or a room-temperature egg or white onion brought to him by people seeking his help. He holds one hand by the wrist and beats that hand and arm lightly with the basil. He changes arms, moves to the back of the neck, head, and face. On the face, he gently passes the basil across the forehead, cheeks, and chin. Then he might move on to the legs. While he is doing this, he may pray, tell about the visions he has had, recount some of the myths about the end of the world, or ask you questions about things that may have happened to you. After half an hour or so, he sits back in his chair, closes his eyes, and holds one of his hands, palm open, in front of his face. For those moments, he goes somewhere else, seeing why the patient is ill. When he returns, he picks up the massaging once more, telling you why you feel unwell and what you need to do. He may ask more questions. The end of the healing is marked by Ta Feli running his hands down your arms or legs, bringing them cupped to his mouth and blowing. Done, he says, having blown away all the badness.

The healing comes through prayers that he prays for the patient while he massages them; through the coolness of the basil or sometimes mescal sprayed on the legs that counteracts the heat of the illness; sometimes through "prescriptions" that he gives. These latter may be combinations of herbs or particular foods or they may be actions you have to do. A large part of the healing, I am convinced, comes from the caring, gentle attention that he gives to each person who comes. An hour or so is not unusual and, for that time, you are the sole focus of his healing gift. The massage is extraordinarily relaxing, taking away all tension by the time he finishes. And, in a climate where temperatures are routinely in the high nineties, the cool, moist basil refreshes.

Ta Feli has had a number of apprentices. One, José Manuel, studied with him for many years, then opened his own temple in 1997. When I went to visit him, he asked immediately if I had worked with Ta Feli. He went on to acknowledge Feli's gifts and how much he had learned from him. His style is quite different from Feli's, emphasizing visions and using followers who are adepts in the course of the temple services. He and they work through group mediation as a way of supporting someone who has come for a cleansing. That individual comes forward to one of the adepts, who uses basil over the whole body, beating lightly. The person then stands barefoot on the basil while being blessed by the adept, who tells the individual a vision that he or she had while using the basil. In my case, the adept (an older woman who has worked with José Manuel since he opened his temple) said that she had seen a white flower dropped into a large glass of deep purple liquid; the flower rose immediately to the surface. This, she interpreted, symbolized my gift, the gift of light that was the white flower. Sometimes, I was tired and sad and the purple liquid represented the envy of others who tried to keep me down. "Too bad you are leaving," she said. "You could work with us and develop your gift."

Both Ta Feli and José Manuel are artists and performers of healing and spiritual guidance. They differ in their style—Feli commands attention by the sheer force of his will, with few props. His temple has the standard six-stepped altar set with candles, images, flowers. While the images include Christ, Catholic saints, and Masonic symbols, the flowers are the ones that the Zapotec regard as having healing powers, like the frangipani (*guie' chaachi*), or that are associated with liminal states, like the white gladiolas.

Altar in the temple of Ta Feli. Photograph by Anya Peterson Royce.

In one corner, there is a white, draped chair flanked by two wooden chairs where the calling of the spirits of the dead takes place. Then there are rows of benches for those who come to participate. On feast days, there are more candles and flowers, usually white gladiolas and frangipani, but also several of the many varieties of jasmine. Ta Feli sometimes has an apprentice, currently his fourteen-year-old nephew, but otherwise he works alone.

José Manuel holds his services in a much more elaborate temple, although the basic floor plan is the same. Women and men sit segregated, behind the chairs for the adepts and apprentices who wear white robes. At his services, you are expected to participate by meditating with your eyes closed at certain points, by responding to questions, and by being willing to be called forward for a cleansing. The healing with José Manuel is much more communal and less individually focused than with Ta Feli.

All Zapotec healers are responsible for an extensive repertoire of knowledge unknown to the average Zapotec. The Zapotec beliefs about wellness and illness are based on two fundamental dichotomies: that between wet and dry, and that between hot and cold. These concepts cut across all domains of life and are related in complex, dialectical ways. Most Zapotec have some general notions about them, but none have the specialized knowledge that the healers must have. Then there is the wealth of information about ethnobotany and herbal medicine that healers must command in order to treat patients. Diagnoses frequently are based on traditional Zapotec beliefs about states of being—fright, anger, and melancholy—that, when out of balance, cause illness or the arrival of harmful beings like the *bidxaa*, a person who turns himself into an animal and causes illness or death. Cosmology looms large, too, in the prayers and explanations of healers. Healers must also develop the skills of reading the body by pulsing, by seeing problem areas in posture and body tone; in other words, they must, like any Western practitioner, be able to diagnose on the basis of the patient's responses and the patient's body.[1]

All of this knowledge, plus the ability to weave Roman Catholic and Zapotec prayers together, comprise the core of what I would call the technique or craft of healing; this is what you need to know simply to function as an ordinary healer. Each kind of healing (and there are some seven categories) has its technique that everyone in that category has to master. While most people will not know the details of this technique, they know enough to tell healers who know it from ones who do not. The years of apprenticeship impart the technique to those who have been singled out by a vision.

Beyond that level of knowledge comes the artistry of those who slip in and out of altered states to bring healing to those who seek them out. The Zapotec of Juchitán recognize healers who go beyond the level of craft. These are the *binni guendabianni* (wise ones, people of light). What seems to define them is their ability to let themselves be transformed, on the one hand, and their gift for being present, on the other. The letting go of self that transformation demands is common across healers, shamans, and trancers of many cultures. At a psychological level, letting go of self characterizes that self-knowledge and confidence that allows an individual to step out or be lifted out of the known. It facilitates trance and visions; it allows the spirits to possess the person. Ta Feli is recognized for this ability. He slides in and out of a trance state while working with a patient; he does the same in the gatherings for prayers. He also acts as a medium for the spirits of the departed who speak through him to their loved ones; not all healers in Juchitán have this ability. The other quality that marks some healers off from others is the presence they exude. Ta Feli is neither striking nor imposing. His usual attire is a white T-shirt and too-big pants gathered up around his waist; he is barefoot and slight of frame. He looks like any other old man until you sit across from him and he takes your hand. Then you feel the power flow between you.

Shamans and Healers

Feli and healers of his stature know their patients. They select from the huge range of diagnoses, spirits, myths, and remedies exactly the right combination for each person. I have watched Ta Feli work with a number of people, and I have been treated by him many times during the last eight years. Each time and with each person, he tailors what he does and what he prescribes. As a result, he has a loyal following and is regarded as one of the most adept healers in Juchitán.

The roles of healer, medium for the spirit world, and shaman have great antiquity and a worldwide distribution. There is great variation in their recruitment, training, and style, but fundamental to the roles is the acquisition of supernatural powers that enable the person to heal or to cause illness. Our word *shaman* comes originally from the Tungus *shaman*, from the Sanskrit *sramana* (ascetic). In the case of Siberian shamans, their power comes from communion with a spirit, ghost, animal, or inanimate object, and is exhibited when the individual is in a self-induced trance state. The traditional Tungus shaman was someone with a powerful personality and great intellectual capacity who believed absolutely in his identification with supernatural beings. In those characteristics lay his ability to heal body and soul (Kurath 1950:1004). Descriptions of Siberian shamans document the magical feats and sleight-of-hand that were the essence of their performances—ventriloquism, self-mutilation, handling of fire, sword swallowing, extraction of "illness" from people's bodies, manifestations of particular spirits, and battles with rival shamans carried out in the spirit world.[2] Their trance state was induced by the rhythm of the shaman's drum, sometimes played by the shaman and at other times by the apprentice. It is in the person of the Siberian shaman that we see the most spectacular and intentional performances. Schechner is speaking primarily of this type when he offers the following summary: "Shamanism is the oldest technique of theatrical performing. Primary shamanism probably originated in Paleolithic times in central Asia. . . . The techniques . . . are singing, dancing, chanting, costuming, storytelling. The shaman goes on a journey, or is transformed into other beings, or represents the struggle among beings. . . . Like the actor in the Western tradition, the shaman is both himself and others at the same time. The audience is engaged at a very deep level; participation is a necessary condition for the shaman's feats" (Schecher and Schuman 1976:123).

The distribution of roles that are based on altered states of consciousness includes cultures in Central Asia, Russia, Japan, Fiji, Bali, the Americas, Haiti, India, and Africa. It is a deeply embedded alternative reality that is a fact of life for many people. Can we consider this kind of performance in the same way that we have examined other performative genres? Trance, possession, healing—these, like Tewa ritual, have an outcome that is desired and sought, so they are not "entertainment," pure and simple. On the other hand, these traditions, again like Tewa ritual, obey a series of conventions and their performance is highly stylized. Moreover, audiences, recipients, and community members make judgments about how good individual healers or shamans are and those judgments are not framed exclusively or even primarily in terms of success in bringing about the desired outcome.

Possession Trance

Anthropologist Melville Herskovits commented on the conventional nature of possession trance, in particular: "In some cultures the patterns underlying the forms of possession are difficult to discern because of the seemingly idiosyncratic nature of those possessed. However, on closer acquaintance, the patterned regularities which underlie the individual expression of the phenomenon as found among a given group become apparent and make it possible to subsume variant behavior in terms of the overall tradition" (1950:881).

I would argue that the patterned regularities result from the codification of a body of knowledge and prescriptions for conduct that I call technique. The idiosyncrasies come about through individual style, the way in which personal experience and preference translate into a unique approach to the craft. Technique and style, these are the same distinctions that underlie all the performing arts.

Balinese Trance

One of the most well-known and documented traditions of possession trance comes from Bali. Early work includes a remarkable film, *Trance and Dance in Bali*, made by Gregory Bateson, Jane Belo, and Margaret Mead, between 1937 and 1939, and Jane Belo's thorough analysis, *Trance in Bali* (1960). All trance is attributed to being chosen by a god. Some individuals are never chosen; others are chosen in ways that they do not expect. The vocabulary for speaking about trance provides a clearer picture of what it means and how it happens. In an article for the August 2002 issue of *Latitudes* magazine (Bali), writer Degung Santikarma offers the following: "Common Balinese words for trance include *nadi*, meaning 'becoming,' *kerangsukan*, meaning 'to enter,' *kerauhan*, meaning 'to arrive,' and *tedun*, meaning 'to go down,' all of which refer to the gods' descent to earth to animate the bodies of their worshipers. Trance is also called *ngayah*, meaning 'to serve a god or king.' It is a form of collective devotion, as well as an intense personal experience."

Belo identified seven kinds of trance associated with different cultural contexts. They range from the little girls who act as trancers for a brief time but cease when they grow up; to "folk" trancers who portray animals and objects; to the male and female *kris* dancers who participate in major temple festivals, stabbing themselves while in trance; to those who represent major figures, such as *Rangda* (the Witch) and *Barong* (the Dragon), in ritual dramas; and finally to the trance doctors and mediums who diagnose and divine (1960:2–4). These represent the varying degrees of commitment possible for the Balinese to serve the gods in this particular way. As Degung Santikarma says in the article mentioned above, there is a populist quality about trance, "human social hierarchies are set aside and the choice of the gods prevails" (2002). If chosen, a person can serve in any number of capacities.

Two *sadeg* (pillars of the gods), or trance mediums, from Intaran district help us understand better the commonalities and the differences among individuals in the same role. As Belo notes, Intaran district was an intellectual center because of the disproportionate number of high priests and scholars who lived there. The people of the district paid a lot of attention to religious observances. Their many temples were sites of frequent festivals and, because of their relative prosperity, they were able to mount exquisite and elaborate rituals to honor the gods. At the time of Belo's fieldwork, the district had fourteen major and minor temples in addition to all the household temples that were part of every house court.

The *sadeg* in that district were both men and women, belonging to all four castes. Among them were some of the most fantastic types, the kind people would turn around to stare at if they passed them in the road (Belo 1960:18). Their first trance may have come about as a result of illness or, in rare cases, not. After the sign of the god having chosen them, there was an initiation ceremony, *mesakapan ke déwa* (same term as for marriage ceremony). The relationship between *sadeg* and temple priest was a complicated one—many *sadegs* were also priests of the temple whose god they represented in trance. Not all were also priests, and many priests were not *sadegs*. In the one case of someone being chosen without an illness, Mémèn Gentir, *sadeg Poera Iboe Samping* (*sadeg* of one of the Mother Temples), was already serving as the *pemangkoe* (priest) for the temple. She was there as part of one of the major festivals when she went into trance for the first time: "First my head got suddenly heavy, and my feet burned. . . . My body was suddenly burning from the earth straight up to the sky" (Belo 1960:26). Her relatives realized what had happened, and lifted her to the platform where all the *sadeg* sat. When asked to speak, she said that it was the god of that temple who had entered her body.

Mémèn Gentir was past sixty when Belo knew her. She had been dancing at all the temple rituals since her first trance when she was a new mother. She went into trance at every ritual, no matter what the temple was. She sat at the back, nearest the priest, her legs folded beneath her and to one side, hands clasped, and eyes closed. When the god approached, she began to shake, then finally raised her hands above her head, a sign that the god was there. When she fell back, the assistants helped her to dress in the special costume. When she spoke, it was in a tiny, childish voice, or she might utter little cries. But her pronouncements were not why she was so highly respected; it was her dancing, delicate, at an angle even to the normal angled Balinese dance. Belo describes it, remarking that it seems as though she has been possessed by a small, delicate, feminine god (Belo 1960:27). Mémèn Gentir had not been trained as a dancer; after her first trance, she simply began to dance, recognizably within the Balinese tradition but with her own decidedly fluid, brisk, oblique style. She was tireless in her dancing even though, at home doing her ordinary activities, she walked with a limp and never very far.

About as different as one can get and still be in the same category of *sadeg* is Djero Plasa, also a *balian* (trance doctor). Belo describes Plasa's attitude toward her work and her public: "Like the perfect old actress that she is, she does not fail to play up to her audience. She takes, and holds, the center of the stage" (1960:23). She was in her seventies when Belo was in Bali but appeared much younger when in her element, in the temple or healing. Originally from a distant province, she was taken by one of the princes of Peliatan as a concubine. She escaped and her family walked with her as far as they could go. They settled in Intaran and she married a trance doctor, keeping her title of Djero (high-born) that she had as a result of her relationship with the prince. She contracted an illness whose symptoms were sores that covered her body. They would not heal until one day she had a "message" that she should go to the sea. She and her husband went, and she saw a spring with pumice stones. She scoured her body with the pumice and in the morning her sores were gone. Shortly after that, she was at the shore with friends. Many of the canoes they were in turned over, but she went into trance and stood up in the canoe speaking in the words of the god. When she came to the shore again, she was completely dry, a sign that she was possessed by a god. As people tried to help her home, she felt that she was high up above them in a coconut palm.

When she came out of the trance, she slid down the palm frond and the people carried her home. The god who possessed her was Ratoe Agoeng Madé Kajangan, the god of the temple of Kajangan. She was then initiated, and began to serve the temple as well as be sought out by people who wanted her to diagnose and heal them.

While her friend Mémèn Gentir was possessed by a delicate, feminine god, Djero Plasa took on a male aspect. She sat cross-legged like a man and, in trance, she spoke in a deep male voice. In movement, she assumed "an intense forceful expression," making a "compelling, highly dramatic performance . . . never to be forgotten" (Belo 1960:25). Unlike her friend, she talked constantly, answering questions put to her, talking to the other gods possessing her *sadeg* colleagues, humming to herself, or scolding the assistants who tried to dress her. Like all the *sadeg*, when she came out of trance, she raised her hands, palms together, to her forehead and reverenced three times. She concluded by smoking her hands and face over the brazier of fire and incense.

Both women, indeed, all who were called to serve the gods, had mastered a complicated set of prescriptions and behaviors. These include knowing the ritual calendar of the various temples and the observances that marked every ritual occasion as well as rituals for secular events (naming, tooth-filing, healing, and so forth), the dress for each occasion, the kinds of offerings of flowers and food for each, the ways of keeping oneself purified for service, expectations for going into and coming out of trance, the characteristics of the particular god who possessed you, and dancing. Even in nontemple dancing or healing, certain rituals were always observed. Belo, on two occasions, asked Mémèn Gentir to dance so that she could photograph her. The first time, Gentir had everyone wait while she bathed and changed her clothes. She then made offerings to a shrine in the center of her courtyard, lighting the incense brazier and making offering gestures with it. Finally, she took the brazier and began to dance with it in the courtyard. The second time, she had been cooking, and in response to Belo's request, raised her hands to her forehead and made three reverences before she began to dance.

Djero Plasa, in her role as a trance doctor, received clients at her house. They came to her bringing offerings, which she received. Then she went to the water spout and bathed her face and hands, letting the water spray on her torso. She combed her hair and put a red flower, usually a hibiscus, in it. She put on a coat and scarf, wearing the scarf in the male fashion—high up around the torso. Finally, she took part of the offering and put it in the shrine of her house-temple. After reverencing the god, she sat down cross-legged and went into trance.

While there is a goal in all this activity, no one takes the straightest path to it. There is a fine sense of aesthetic choice in all of the ritual that cannot be attenuated or eliminated. The ritual takes the time and the shape it takes. Perhaps because trance implies possession by a particular god, individuals develop their own styles beyond the requirements of the craft. Erika Bourguignon makes the important distinction between possession and the kind of impersonation of gods that uses masks. In the former, the body itself becomes the god, an internal transformation. In the latter, the person is hidden and the god is represented by the mask. It is uncommon for both types of impersonation to occur at the same time but this is precisely what we see in Bali, especially in the big dance-dramas centering around Rangda (the Witch) and Barong (the Dragon), both of which are masked. They are usually played by more than one person if the ceremony is a long one and during the performance the masked dancers may be in and out of trance.

Possession remains very much part of contemporary Balinese life. Degung Santikarma looks at one of the most popular ceremonies, the anniversary ceremony of the *pura dalem* temple of Pengerebongan, just outside of the city of Denpasar, through the eyes of eighteen-year-old Agus. He is a normal teenager who listens to punk and heavy metal, smokes cigarettes, hangs out, and watches girls, but he has been a *keris* (or kris) dancer since he first went into trance at the age of thirteen. Although some of his classmates tease him about it, they and he both regard it as a sign of the god's favor and an obligation that must be met. Explaining what going into trance feels like for him, Agus says, "My head suddenly feels really heavy and my body feels incredibly strong, just ready to jump. It feels like this intense energy is flowing through my body and pushing me to act. It's almost as if I was chained before and I have to break free, or like I'm carrying something really heavy on my shoulders and I have to throw it off. . . . I feel invincible, like I'm so powerful nothing can hurt me. I feel like I'll rage unless I have the *keris*. After I *ngurek* [the action of thrusting the point of the *keris* into the chest and twisting it up and down] I'm calmer again" (Santikarma 2002).

Those who trance with the *keris* do so as part of the larger temple festivals that include the masked figures of Rangda and Barong. This battle drama is one of the most well-known and documented. Both Gregory Bateson and Jane Belo recorded it in various districts and temples. Belo provides an example of the drama from the village of Dendjalan, offering it as a contrast to other villages where the festival performances are preoccupied with the religious aspects of bringing down the gods. The Dendjalan performances were organized by a group of young men who wanted to have the best play of all the villages so that everyone would speak of the excellence of the Dendjalan Barong. All of the ritual was observed, down to the smallest detail. The wood for the Barong mask came from a tree at the temple Poera Dalem and he (the Barong) lived in a small temple all his own. The rest the younger men left up to the priests. When it came time for the dancers to go into trance, they all did. By all accounts the Denjalan Barong was one of the finest, drawing large crowds of foreigners. Clearly, artistry characterizes these performances. In order to have the best possible performance, dancers known for their abilities were recruited from great distances. At the same time, the fundamental purpose for the ceremony, an invitation to the gods to come into their people and an offering of the best that humans can give, was not forgotten. This nonnegotiable aspect can be seen in the issue of creativity. How do festivals, ceremonies, and performances change?

The Barong of Dendjalan underwent a rather radical change in which parts of another play, *Tjalonarang* (the story of the Witch) were interpolated into the middle of Rangda and Barong. This took place in 1936 and Belo asked about how that happened, having been told that such innovations have to come at the direction of the gods. The gods' wishes were communicated by someone in trance, called *saking pekajoenan widi* (at the desire of the gods). One of the group's leaders answered her by saying "It was at the desire of the gods and also at the desire of the club" (Belo 1960). Going against the gods' wishes or not observing the proper ritual can bring disaster, but there are ways to accommodate everyone's wishes, whether human or god.

Ju/'hoansi Trance

The power of the gods or spirits, as well as their capriciousness, is well known to those among the Ju/'hoansi or !Kung of Namibia and Botswana[3] who are chosen by the gods to trance and to be healers. *Num*, or the energy that comes from the gods, is the most powerful force in the !Kung universe. It lives in the pit of the stomach and the base of the spine, and, in healers, it is activated by dancing, which warms them to the point of sweat. Then the *num* boils up to a vapor, rising to the base of the skull, at which point *kia* happens. *Kia* is an enhanced state of consciousness that comes from the boiling up of the *num* (Katz 1982:41). All those who have chosen to activate their *num* and work as healers (called *num kausi* or owners of *num*) describe the physical sensation as being very painful and frightening. "Your heart stops. You're dead. Your thoughts are nothing. You breathe with difficulty. You see things, *num* things; you see spirits killing people. You smell burning, rotten flesh. Then you heal, you pull sickness out. You heal, heal, heal. Then you live." This is a vivid description by Wi, an older healer (p. 45).

Women and men both understand the central role that healing plays in their small communities, and most men and about a third of the women give some serious effort to becoming healers. Children play at it, imitating the dance steps and falling into trance. In fact, most children have models of healers in their immediate family or a very close relative. But to be successful requires more intentional behavior. Young men begin to attend dances for the purpose of "seeking *num*." With women, the age varies because of childbearing. The seekers find healers who are willing to help them. Part of this help takes the form of putting *num* into the novices during the dances. Healers "shoot arrows" of *num* (*num tchisi*) into the student, and rub them with their own sweat; they support them when *kia* approaches; and they are afraid, sometimes making them stop dancing to "cool" them down. Richard Katz lets a younger !Kung tell of this experience: "In *kia*, around your neck and around your belly you feel tiny needles and thorns which prick you. Then your front spine and your back spine are pricked with these thorns. Your *gebesi* [an area centered at the waist, sides, and stomach] tightens into a balled fist. Your breathing stops. Then someone rubs your belly and the pricking stops and you start to breathe again" (1982:46).

If a person manages to achieve this ability, he or she still must learn to heal, to pull the sickness from people and then expel it from him or herself, a process referred to as *kowhedili* and a time when the healer is in great pain and danger. At this point in the healing ritual, the healer goes from person to person in the circle, laying hands—one on the chest, the other on the back—in order to pull out the sickness. This is a struggle between the spirits who have caused the sickness and who want to keep the person, and the healer who is trying to get the person back. The drama is expressed in shrieks and howls and shouts directed at the spirits to get them to let go.

The intensity lies in the performance rather than in any props or costumes. The dances take place at night, with most of a community participating. A single camp, for example, might have fifteen or twenty people at a dance, seven to ten women singing and four or five men dancing. One-quarter of the singers and two-thirds of the dancers might be healers (Katz 1982:38). Sometimes several camps join together for a dance when, for example, a large animal like a giraffe is killed and people gather to share the meat.

No special clothes are worn; there are no musical instruments except for leg rattles made of dried cocoons filled with pieces of ostrich eggshells, and occasionally a drum. Not all the dancers may have them but they accent the steps, as do the walking sticks that most dancers bring with them. Healers may use plants ground and mixed with fat, which they heat in a kind of turtle-shell brazier, letting the smoke drift toward those who are to be healed.

Marjorie Shostak began her work with the !Kung in 1969. She stayed for two years, followed by a return in 1975. That work, especially her collaboration with a !Kung woman, resulted in the book *Nisa: The Life and Words of a !Kung Woman*, a book that has become a classic. Her last trip was in 1989 after she had been diagnosed with cancer, had a mastectomy, and knew that this return to Africa was one thing she could not afford to put off. She describes a healing dance done for her on that last trip. It was after the sun had set when the women began to sing and clap. The drum joined the voices and the *num* began to rise. "Nisa seemed quick to feel the change in her thought patterns, and focused her gaze into the darkness. She sang and clapped, swaying slightly. Sweat glistened on her forehead; her body trembled; her upper torso shimmied; then she was on the ground, sitting slumped to one side beside the fire, eyes closed" (Shostak 2000:216). Nisa and another woman began to go around the circle laying hands on people. They came often to Shostak. "Nisa came to me often, sometimes with Chuko. They worked on me together—rubbing my sides, pulling out whatever sickness they could 'see'—and they worked on me separately. I loved the touch and the attention, and visualized the seeds of disease flying out of me as they laid on hands" (p. 216).

The dance lasted for two hours; it might have gone on longer but for the bitter cold. Nisa summarized the healing for Shostak: "We saw a little sickness in your chest. We took it out and now it is gone. We also fired your insides with *num*. It should keep you well until you come back" (p. 217). Sadly, that was not to be—Marjorie Shostak died on October 6, 1996, without returning.

The power of the healing, the laying on of hands, the absolute belief of healers in what they do, clearly communicates itself to those who go to them for help. When I was leaving Juchitán after I had met Ta Feli for the first time, he wanted to make me a potion that would keep me safe until I returned. I explained that U.S. customs officials would probably question a mysterious liquid in an old mayonnaise jar. He did not even pause before replying that he would then make me an invisible one. He did, and I like to think that it kept me safe.

There are always a few among the !Kung healers who have a charisma beyond the rest; they are called *ama ama* (the real ones, the biggest). These are healers who travel more often to where the gods live, who are called for the most desperate illnesses, who transform themselves into lions. They do not need the rhythm of singers and dancer to activate their *num* and they heal themselves more easily than others (Katz 1982:230). Katz was curious about what might distinguish healers from nonhealers in terms of their psychology and he concluded three things: healers are emotionally more expressive; they have a self-image that has more to do with inner states than with external anatomy; and they have a richer fantasy life. The *ama ama* healers have all these qualities in abundance. And, while !Kung society is egalitarian, both the great healers and the members of their bands acknowledge that they are special. Two of those special healers with whom Katz worked, Wa Na and Kau Dwa, commanded everyone's awe. Of Wa Na, another healer said, "She's fantastic. She's terrible with num" (p. 223). Of Kau Dwa, the healer said, "He's blind, but he can see to heal. His num gives him the power to see. And his num is getting stronger as he gets older" (p. 212). Healers such as these dedicate themselves to healing and to nothing else, making them unique among the !Kung, who do not recognize special roles.

!Kung and Isthmus Zapotec healers are similar in that, while they go into trance, they are not possessed by particular gods or spirits. Rather, they are able to travel to the world where the gods live in order to divine causes of illness and, in the case of the !Kung, bargain for the patient's cure. Healers like Ta Feli may speak in the voice of a departed spirit when he summons the spirits of the dead but he does not become that person. He is simply a channel. Balinese possession and Haitian trance, are instances of the gods possessing the person. That person then takes on all the attributes of the particular god. They dance, move, and speak in the manner of the spirit doing the possessing and do so in a way that is unmistakable to other participants.

Altered states, no matter what the culture, are full of risk. The person becomes a medium for power, bringing it to others in order to heal, bargaining for it with spirits who guard their prerogatives zealously, interpreting the will of the spirits to the people as well as of the people to the spirit world. For many, when they are not "in their bodies," but are traveling, they risk losing their souls permanently. When they are pulling sickness from people, that sickness passes through them before it is expelled. Those cultures with active trance practices all have persons whose job it is to watch over those in trance so that they do not hurt themselves and so that they come back. Whether individual healers are modest or boastful, they believe that what they do is essential to the right functioning of the world. If they rest or stop, part of that world will be lost. It is this utter confidence in the importance, even sacredness, of their roles that gives them the power to convince others and to help them. Like all performers, they treat their craft respectfully, mastering everything that it comprises.

It is that discipline that lets them risk stepping outside the universe we know. They bring order to the chaos represented by worlds out of balance. Ta Feli speaks often of those forces that must be balanced. "The young girl [*nisadó*, 'the sea'] who is the guardian of everything from the edge of the sea to as far as you can see on the horizon where the sky begins, gets angry from time to time with human foolishness. She causes the waters in the sea and the rivers to rise and flood, destroying villages and the people in them. Only the wind [*bi*] is stronger than she is. He restores the balance by blowing on the waters to calm them." Feli also tries to keep the balance. He cools the heat of illness in his patients. He and the other healers in their communal "meetings" to which they travel in their altered states hope that their prayers will balance the destructiveness of human beings and so allow the world to continue. Healers are bringers of balance and purveyors of hope. Like others we call performers, they offer us a glimpse of transcendence, crafting it so that we might recognize it in those instants in which they make it present.

Notes

1. I have been working systematically with Ta Feli and other healers as well as independently on the ethnobotany of the Isthmus Zapotec for about eight years. My work with the Isthmus Zapotec encompasses thirty-five years. I remain humble in the face of the knowledge these healers command, and have the greatest respect and admiration for them.

2. One of the most detailed descriptions is that of A. F. Anisimov of the State Museum of Ethnology of St. Petersburg, who documents shamanistic practices of the Evenk. His article, in translation, appears in Schechner and Schuman 1976.

3. *Ju/'hoansi* is the term that the Ju/'hoansi use for themselves. It means "real or genuine people," and while they have always called themselves by it, other terms appear in literature—*Bushmen*, *San*, and *!Kung* are the most common (see Lee and Biesele in Kemper and Royce 2002:162). My discussion of trance and healing is based primarily upon the work of Richard Katz (1982) and Marjorie Shostak (1981, 2000) and they both refer to this people as the !Kung.

CHAPTER TWELVE
AFTERTHOUGHTS

We must never forget that we are interpreters, that we are there to serve the composer and to discharge a very delicate task.

—Maria Callas

What is it that allows certain of our fellow human beings to make a work, a score, a piece of choreography, a dramatic text, or a spirit come alive for us? We allot them the role of interpreters, able to reach back into a disembodied creation, embody it in themselves, and make it meaningful for us who see it only through their art. Performing artists occupy a middle ground between work and public. Their role is to make manifest the work in such a fashion as to be clear and have meaning for an audience. The work has an existence, of course, apart from these interpreter-performers, but in that form it is an existence accessible to very few and certainly not shaped, selected, highlighted, and elucidated by the talents of these mediators. The work is different in its embodied and public manifestation. Two great cellists, Pablo Casals and Janos Starker, have spoken about what they do as re-creation, and they are right.

In a fundamental sense, my fascination with those individuals whose vocation is interpreting and performing springs from my own career as a performer. From the age of seven, when I took my first serious ballet class, until injuries brought my dancing to a halt when I was twenty-seven, my life and passion lay in this classical genre. My days and nights were spent mastering the technique of classical ballet, making my body into the most perfect instrument possible, performing a repertoire, learning how to interpret choreography within the framework of my training and style. With the exception of five years at San Francisco Ballet, all my training came from dancers who had been pupils at the Marinsky Imperial Ballet School in St. Petersburg, primary among them Ludmilla Shollar and Anatol Vilzak.

I had private lessons in classical variations with Madame Shollar, who had danced many of them in their premieres, both in St. Petersburg and with the Diaghilev Ballets Russes in Europe. From those teachers, I learned the classicism of Petipa and the revolutionary style of Michel Fokine. Even the smallest gesture of an arm or a head, when Shollar or Vilzak were teaching, evoked an entire era and style. It was this training in particular that made me aware of something beyond technique, something I have called artistry.

Those generous teachers who most shaped me as a dancer saw technical mastery as a necessary step on the way to the re-creation of the choreography, but only that—a step toward the ultimate goal of making a work live. I reached a level of mastery such that I could forget the technical demands of a piece and think only about the interpretation of it. Much later, when I began taking cello lessons as a total beginner, I understood the frustration of knowing what good playing sounded like but not being able to achieve it. While I made progress, I never reached a level of technique that allowed me to explore the artistic side of music. I could hear others and recognize those two distinct spheres; sitting in lessons and master classes showed me all stages of development. What I did take from that experience was a sense of, first, how the technique was organized and how one began to master it, and, second, what structures of style lay beyond the technique and how one made choices about how and when to use them. My experience of mastering the art of ballet came at a time when I was too young to analyze beyond the level of steps. With the cello, I had a lifetime of being a serious music listener and, as a scholar, I had examined and written about dance and theatre in both their formal and contextual aspects. While knowing all this made learning the cello sometimes a source of great anxiety, I was able to see similarities and differences between music making and dance. Knowing something by the doing of it and knowing something by the thinking about it are quite different experiences. What I have brought together in this book are both those ways of knowing. Some performers have found the time to reflect upon what they do and make their written reflections available to us, but many more have

Anatol Vilzak and Ludmilla Shollar in M. Fokine's Le Carnaval, *Souvenir Program, Ballets Russes season 1922, courtesy of the Harry Ransom Humanities Research Center, The University of Texas at Austin.*

not, caught up in the daily discipline of class, practice, and rehearsal, and nightly presentations. Perhaps this book will give a voice to performers, past and present.

Interpretation: Discipline

There are several major themes that run throughout these pages. The most significant is that of interpretation because it defines what all performers do. I have chosen, where possible, to let performers speak for themselves although I have crafted many of the questions. Elsewhere, I have tried to paint their pictures knowing quite well that words never capture the power of performance. In their performances and in their words, I found striking similarities. All acknowledge the absolute necessity of mastering the technique of their art and of accepting the daily confrontation with its ongoing challenge. Violette Verdy articulated what others would acknowledge, and that is that artistic freedom is found in the rigid discipline of the class or lesson. It is only the confidence of knowing that you have mastered the technique that frees you to think about the artistry. This is the same confidence that allows shamans and healers to venture out into unknown and dangerous territory. I think that it is also making that daily acknowledgment of one's obligation to keep the instrument as perfect as it can be that defines performers to others but also to themselves. In the case of Balinese *sadeg*, the unhurried way in which the gods are accorded their proper respect, no matter how informal or formal the situation, shows the seriousness with which those practitioners regard themselves and what they do.

Interpretation: Stepping Aside

Most performers put their art ahead of their own egos. "It is the music that matters," Starker affirms. For dance, Verdy notes that the dancers know that they fit in a great body of work, and they grow bigger because of the work. They are reticent about their own persona (see chapter two). Conductor Imre Pallo, who has the difficult task of interpreting the composer but doing it through the virtuosity of the musicians in his orchestra, is thoughtful, too, on the topic: "I think the deeper you serve the music, the less you think about—but the more you strive for—perfection. So, if you serve a certain piece of music and try . . . to follow the intentions of the composer, you forget *how* you do it. And then . . . you come closer to a performance that will also convince the people who are listening."[1] Healers, whether they are Isthmus Zapotec or Ju/'hoansi, understand that they are unimportant except as vehicles for the voices of the spirit world. In the case of the West African *griots*, that spirit world and the power of its voice owns them.

A part of putting one's art first is knowing as much as one can about it. I do not mean this in the sense of technique, which we can take for granted, but, rather, in understanding the intentions of the composer, choreographer, or dramatist. Starker put this very clearly: "You are not supposed to interpret a specific work by a composer based on that work alone. You have to learn the language of the composer by gaining a broad familiarity with his entire output, and then you may approximate the intention of the composer. . . . For example, if we are playing a Beethoven cello sonata, we are not supposed to simply learn that sonata, and through that sonata know what Beethoven meant. What we are supposed to learn is the string quartets, the symphonies, and the piano sonatas, and the rest of his work. Then there's a fair chance of becoming familiar with the style, the spirit, the meaning of that particular composer."

Interpretation: Purity, Simplicity, Economy

A third theme that emerges in performers' thinking about their art is the striving for purity, simplicity, and balance, qualities that I see as essential to notions of artistry. Baryshnikov is an excellent example of absolute purity of line and effortlessness of execution. So, too, is Tamasaburo, whether he is performing *onnagata* in traditional Kabuki plays or dancing his own choreography to Bach. Tewa ceremonial is based on simplicity both of steps and of choreography, and Balinese ritual can find an aesthetic in the purity of a single flower. Butoh, as it is embodied by the Sankai Juku company or the solo performances of founder Kazuo Ohno, exemplifies the essential balance between stillness and movement, silence and sound. It is not that ornamentation or elaboration are not allowed; rather, it is that they must be consistent with the formal qualities of the genre. We have all seen performances in which self-indulgence has led to fuzziness and inconsistency instead of clarity and a unifying theme. When Starker talks about the inevitability of a fine interpretation, he is referring to the ability to imagine the whole work and to make each phrase consistent with that image of the whole. This is the brilliance of the choreography of Michel Fokine with its liquid, sweeping phrases. In the same way, Marcel Marceau eliminates all distracting gesture in order to convey complicated and deep meanings with the utmost clarity. Maria Callas, one of the twentieth century's great singers and someone who used ornamentation to stunning effect, said this about the importance of cuts for today's audiences: "The repetition of a melody is usually never good. The sooner you come to the point, the better it is. Never risk a second time. There are exceptions of course. In *Sonnambula* I sang two verses of 'Ah! non giunge,' for it is, frankly, a showpiece, an expression of happiness and joy; pure vocalizing is justified. But when you repeat, you must be careful to vary the music somewhat so that it remains interesting for the public. This is always done, naturally, with good taste and within the style of the composer" (Ardoin 1987:10).

Audience

This statement of Callas's raises the issue of the audience. If the performer stands in the middle, then the audience stands at the end of the re-creative process, away from the creator. Just as performers must strive for the most complete understanding of the creator's intentions, so must they understand the public who receive the embodied work. So their work is threefold—they must understand the intentions of the creator; they must accommodate those intentions to their own abilities and training; finally, they must balance all that with where any given audience may be on any given night. The goal, it seems to me, is not to create the most "accurate" reproduction of a work or to aggrandize one's own performance of it. Neither is it to present a work so rarified and opaque that only a handful in the audience understands it. The goal is to move the audience beyond itself to a place where it can dream or imagine—the goal of all art, shared by creator, interpreter, and most certainly by the people who come to see it.

Through the various examples, we learn that audiences come to performances for different reasons, and, more importantly, with different degrees of knowledge about the genre. Audiences for the commedia dell'arte were radically different when they were members of the court as opposed to a paying public. The players under contract to a royal patron performed at the patron's behest. They were traded around the Italian fiefdoms and sent abroad to perform for royal relatives in France and England, Bavaria and Poland. The point of the entertainment lay not in the story line but in the performance. Because so much of it was improvised and because it incorporated contemporary social and political commentary, it was never the same. Infinite combinations of the *lazzi*, mannerisms, and lines of banter meant that each actor's performance was different every night. And, should a court tire of its own troupe, it could hire the troupe of a neighboring duchy. By the late seventeenth century, theatres for the commedia dell'arte had sprung up so its audience expanded to include the general public. In Venice, for example, the public was composed of the great merchant families who owned boxes in the various theatres and passed them on as part of their estates. Many were as wealthy and powerful as the royal patrons. And, just as having an accomplished commedia troupe was a point of pride for the royalty, owning a box in one of the commedia theatres was a symbol of high status for the wealthy members of the public. The theatre audiences also included, however, the middle classes—bakers, artisans, painters, writers, and so forth. Venetian theatres made available (by law) free tickets to the *gondolieri*, who were quite possessive of their rights. No matter their social status, these audiences knew all the plots, the characters, and the players.

Performance was all, in these improvised dramas. The public knew every gesture, every nuance, every *lazzi*, and every line of their favorite players. They came with a finely honed critical judgment, instantly recognizing a lackluster performance. On the other hand, they also recognized extraordinary performances. Clearly, they had an aesthetic in mind and they measured players and performances by it.

Perhaps because his art is based on narrative but does not use words, Marcel Marceau is keenly aware of when and how audiences understand. In his classic mime, Marceau intentionally crafts meaning into both technique and style in a multilayered fashion that allows many points of access. He performs globally for publics vastly different, not only in their knowledge and sophistication, but also in their cultures. The stories he chooses to tell draw on universal human emotions—the tragedy of a small child who has lost a balloon (*In the Park*) and the tragedy of a soldier in war (*Bip Goes to War)*, the sympathy we feel for the underdog (*The Street*

Musician, The Trial, most of the Bip pantomimes), love (*Remembrances of a Past Love, The Tree*), the horror of being confined (*The Maskmaker, The Cage, The Birdkeeper*)—all these and more are emotions common to all humanity. His programs also balance mimes that are more "simple" with ones that are more complex. Marceau would put *The Liontamer* and *Bip takes the Train* in the first category, and mimes such as *The Tree* and *Fight with an Angel* in the second. Lastly, he frequently crafts individual mimes so that they have all these different layers of meaning—if you wait patiently, you will understand even the most complex piece because of the icons embedded in the technique.

The ritual and ceremonies that arise and take their meaning from a living community have a different relationship to their audience. All Tewa have some knowledge of the ceremonies, which define them as a people and which refine their relationship to the land, its animals, and its plants; to the personages of myth and cosmology; to the all-important wind, rain, sun. All Tewa living in the pueblos and many who return for ceremonials participate, either as performers or as audience. Indeed, the success of the ritual depends on communal investment. The Tewa have changed and they have accommodated their rituals to those changes. What has not changed is the fundamental communal base of all ritual. More rituals are being performed outside the pueblos than before but they still represent the efforts of a community. Tewa audiences appreciate good performances, both in their formal qualities and also in the greater efficacy that comes from a really fine performance. The appreciation may not come in the kind of metalanguage that Western cultures often require of what they call an "aesthetic" but this does not mean that an aesthetic is absent. If the irreducible components of an aesthetic are standards of creation or performance that can be recognized and taught and levels of achievement that go beyond the ordinary, then the Tewa and many other non-Western cultures have an aesthetic whether or not there is a language dedicated to talking about it. This is crucial for us to acknowledge if we hope to reach some broad comparative understanding of artistry and interpretation.

In the case of shamans and healers, there are clearly individuals whose performances are extraordinary. They are recognized by their fellow healers as well as by their communities. It does not demean what they do to call it performance and apply standards of virtuosity and artistry. A healing performance may not cure the patients yet can still be regarded as a good performance. Healers cannot oblige the gods or spirits to respond to their requests; they can only frame them in a voice that is as appropriate as humanly possible. Those who are acknowledged by their communities as the "real" healers are distinguished by the strength of their conviction that they are conduits for the gods, a conviction that allows them to command the attention of patients and community alike.

Audience is implicit in the evolution and definition of genres. The development of the Butoh company Sankai Juku represents choices of content and presentation that engage audiences rather than drive them away as did some of the more radical Butoh performers. While Hiroshima is not a lighthearted topic for a performance, Sankai Juku presents the implications of that event in simple, stark, artistic terms. The message is clearer and more powerful than other, more histrionic choices would have been. In that case, less was certainly more. The founder of Sankai Juku, Ushio Amagatsu, has made clear what he thinks is the obligation of performers to audience: "Acceptance is not gained unless a work is shown that 'allows the audience to gain something.'"[2]

Pilobolus, by adding music to its choreography, accommodated itself to audiences who had defined the company as a dance troupe. Perhaps wanting to maintain something of the initial vision, Moses Pendleton and Alison Chase created Momix, a company that defines itself as a combination of acrobatics, gymnastics, modern dance, and circus. In 1997, Pilobolus announced the founding of the two-person company, Pilobolus TOO. Designed to bring its work to smaller and less well-equipped venues, the company presents full programs of duets and solo pieces. Dancer Rebecca Jung created a work for twelve Radio City Rockettes known as *Rockobolus a.k.a. Pilobolettes.* The dancers and choreographers seem determined to bring their work, in its various manifestations, to many audiences.

My concern with understanding the formal components of performance genres, as evidenced particularly in the discussions of virtuosity and artistry, technique and style, springs initially from my embodied experience as a dancer. I cannot claim to have thought about classical ballet in that way when I was a participant in the studio, in the rehearsal hall, in the theatre. I mastered the technique and could feel comfortable in ballet studios anywhere, wrapped in the confidence that comes with that mastery. I analyzed how my body moved through the classical vocabulary and understood the importance of those extra-technical elements and the characteristics of style. But I was like all dancers, narcissistic in relating everything I knew to my own performance and how to enhance it. The process of becoming an anthropologist encouraged me to move from the personal to the general, from the specific to the abstract. It was especially my growing experience as an ethnographer that made me begin to see the parallel between the performer's role as interpreter and that of the ethnographer as interpreter. In order to tell the stories of other peoples, you must have mastered all the details of lives and hopes, behaviors and reflections, so much so that they become part of your internal repertoire. Then you begin to move past them to the grand themes that distinguish a culture, giving it coherence and will. It strikes me as very close to what Starker describes as crafting an interpretation—moving from the specifics of notes and meter and tempi and phrases and a knowledge of the composer to the big themes of the work, those overarching ideas that give it shape and meaning.

As I began to write about dance, I had to take what was intuitive and deeply embedded or embodied and bring it to consciousness so that I could make sense of it for others. Teaching is another way to give shape to the subconscious. Observing Starker in lessons and master classes, I could see him break down and articulate important elements in ways that never characterize casual conversation or performance. Starker does this better than most because he himself has thought about the technical and stylistic elements of his art, indeed, has written about it in this way.

I was intrigued by the similarities I could see across many genres of dance, quite above the clear differences in the realm of technique. It was challenging to think about why this might be so for the formal structure of genres, but also for the contextual patterns. In order to understand patterns, I thought the genres that would offer the most complete examples would be those that were codified and had long histories of persistence. That thinking led me to the genre I knew best, classical ballet, but also to the commedia dell'arte, Kabuki, mime, classical Indian dance, and the rich ceremonials of native peoples of the Americas.

Of course, I was not just thinking about, reading, and writing about these arts, I was watching performances; following particular artists; watching them teach, rehearse, and record; and talking with them whenever possible. It is probably that intimacy of the individual performer in performance that has sustained me more than anything else. The themes that I explore in the first part of this book—virtuosity, artistry, and transparency—all come from a lifetime of seeing arts in performance. I know the great demands, physical and mental, of performance from the inside out. Perhaps this book puts me in the role of interpreter of the interpreters for a public of which I am also an integral part.

Following performers and genres over long periods of time forces you of necessity to address questions of innovation, change, abandonment, and disappearance. Throughout the long history of the arts of dance, music, and theatre, there have been collaborations, sometimes exemplary and breathtaking. Some of these lasted past the initial excitement of collaboration; here, I offer the example of the Ballets Russes in its glory days under the masterful hand of Sergei Diaghilev. Or we might note the collaborations that created opera as the finest example of *Gesamtkunstwerk*, bringing together virtually all the performing arts as well as painting, literature, and costuming. In the recent decades, aided by the ease of travel and communication, we have seen collaborations that have brought together great artists from quite different genres and continents. Many resulted from the restlessness of accomplished performers who have pushed the boundaries of their own art far past anything audiences could imagine—Mikhail Baryshnikov, Tamasaburo, Yo-Yo Ma—and who go on to create one-of-a-kind performances. It is in those collaborations that the shared elements of artistry are most visible. It is their sharing that makes the collaborations possible.

Some collaborations resulted in new genres that have endured. What seems to be required for an innovation to persist is a recognizable and codified technique. Here, the expectations of audiences about genres become an important factor. There has to be some agreement about the elements of a genre in order for it to last beyond the curiosity of the public. Fokine's radically new style lasted only for the lifetimes of the dancers with whom he worked because the change was not embodied in a corresponding technique. We will never know what might have been the fate of Nijinsky's innovations since his work was tragically abbreviated by his madness, but he seemed to be working toward codifying his changes in technique, something that Fokine did not believe was necessary or desirable.

Believing as I do in aesthetic principles that are common across genres, space, and time, I wanted to examine examples of performance in cultures that may not have a rich metalanguage of aesthetics but that do make artistic judgments,[3] and I wanted to look at performative forms which we do not generally classify as performance. My examination of the Tewa, of their extraordinary complex of rituals and ceremonies, of the details of their choreography and performance, and of the manner in which they assess ability convinced me that their notions of virtuosity and artistry differ little from those of the more clearly theatrical genres—genres that are performed for a paying audience and are discussed in other chapters. My relationship over a number of years with Ta Feli, an extraordinary Zapotec healer, prompted me to look at him and his counterparts elsewhere in the world. Every culture that defines a role for shaman or healer also recognizes differing abilities, singling out those whose gifts mark them as extraordinary beings. Their sense of being intermediaries makes the parallels with performers all the more compelling.

Performers in all guises are exotic beings. Their discipline, accomplishment, and passion separates them from the rest of the world. We praise them, we pry into their lives, and we sometimes resent their single-mindedness and even their talent, but, in the end, we need what they bring us. Through them, we touch a part of our world and of ourselves that is otherwise quite inaccessible. They are the medium through which what matters finds a voice and a means of expression. They heal us—sometimes our physical bodies and sometimes, as importantly, our hearts—and allow us to soar, if only briefly. It is uncomfortable ground for the performer: the daily striving for perfection that is always unattainable, the ephemerality of performance, the necessity of setting aside of ego at the very moment when you are center stage, the loneliness of being set apart. All performers share the element of absolute conviction with their colleagues, the shamans. Whether like the *griots* or the Balinese trancers or the Haitian dancers whose bodies are homes for the gods, all performers understand that they are owned by their passion and driven by the need to master the craft of their art. In this search for common ground in our definitions of artistry and virtuosity lies the hope of greater understanding of performing artists and what they do—those who choose the path of interpretation and so give the world moments of enlightenment couched in the simplicity of imagination.

Notes

1. The comments of Janos Starker, Violette Verdy, and Imre Pallo come from a transcription of the panel discussion "Virtuosity, Artistry, and the Role of In-

terpretation" that I moderated as part of Arts Week 2002, Indiana University, Bloomington.

2. Ushio Amagatsu, choreographer and founder of Sankai Juku, interview by Hiroaki Fujii, president of the Japan Foundation, January 13, 1999, in the office of the president of the Japan Foundation. Available online at www.jpf.go.jp/e/others/whats/9903/03_01.html.

3. I want to propose that most audiences do not have the technical or critical vocabulary with which to frame aesthetic assessments of performance. In that way, they share the same mode of appreciation as the Tewa or the audiences for the seventeenth-century commedia dell'arte. The critics are the ones who have honed their aesthetic vocabulary and who have both the technical knowledge and the comparative and long-term experience with which to essay judgments. There will also be a small number of audience members who are equally competent but who are not critics in the professional sense. Thinking through a performance in the way a critic does forces one to articulate an aesthetic code, albeit a subjective one. As the great *New York Times* music critic Harold Schonberg wrote in that publication on July 8, 1980, "Some critics profess to work according to a set of immutable esthetic and technical laws. They are only fooling themselves. There are no immutable laws. There is only the critic himself: his background, his taste and intuition, his ideals, his literary ability. If style is the man, so is criticism, and his criticism always ends up a reflection of what he is" (in Schonberg's obituary of July 27, 2003, written by Allan Kozinn for the *New York Times*). What Schonberg said is what we all do when we see a performance—we see it through the lens of our own experience and the larger cultural context. In some ways, then, communities that have a cohesiveness across all domains, like the Tewa or like the Zapotec, Balinese, or Ju/'hoansi with their healers, can make judgments that better reflect that sense of a communal aesthetic.

REFERENCES

Abrahams, Roger
1983 *The Man of Words in the West Indies: Performance and the Emergence of Creole Culture*. Baltimore: Johns Hopkins University Press.

Acocella, Joan
1995 *Mark Morris*. 2d ed. New York: Noonday Press/Farrar, Straus and Giroux.

Acocella, Joan, and Lynn Garofala
1991 *André Levinson on Dance: Writings from Paris in the Twenties*. Hanover, N.H.: University Press of New England for the Wesleyan University Press.

Anawalt, Sasha
1996 *The Joffrey Ballet: Robert Joffrey and the Making of an American Dance Company*. New York: Scribner.

Angotti, Vincent L., and Judie L. Herr
1974 "Etienne Décroux and the Advent of Modern Mime," *Theatre Survey* XV: 1–17.

Ardoin, John
1987 *Callas at Julliard: The Masterasses*. New York: Alfred A. Knopf.

Barish, Jonas
1981 *The Antitheatrical Prejudice*. Berkeley and Los Angeles: University of California Press.

Barrault, Jean-Louis.
1951 *Reflections on the Theatre*. Translated by Barbara Wall. London: Rockliff.

Baryshnikov, Mikhail
1978 *Baryshnikov at Work: Mikhail Baryshnikov Discusses His Roles*. Edited and with an introduction by Charles Engell France. New York: Alfred A. Knopf.

Bauman, Richard
1984 *Verbal Art as Performance*. With supplementary essays by Barbara Babcock. Prospect Heights, Ill.: Waveland Press.

Bauman, Richard, and Joel Sherzer, eds.
1989 *Explorations in the Ethnography of Speaking*. New York: Cambridge University Press.

Beck, Jill
1991 "Recalled to Life: Techniques and Perspectives on Reviving Nijinsky's *Faune*." *Choreography and Dance* 1(3):45–79.

REFERENCES

Belo, Jane
  1960 *Trance in Bali*. New York: Columbia University Press.

Benedict, Ruth
  1946 *Patterns of Culture*. New York: Mentor Books.

Berlin, Isaiah
  1993 *The Hedgehog and the Fox: An Essay on Tolstoy's View of History*. Chicago: Ivan R. Dee.

Bland, Alexander
  1976 *The Nureyev Image*. New York: Quadrangle/New York Times Book Company.

Boas, Franz
  1955 *Primitive Art*. New York: Dover Publications.
  1966 *Race, Language, and Culture*. New York: Free Press.

Bochner, Arthur, and Carolyn Ellis, eds.
  2002 *Ethnographically Speaking: Autoethnography, Literature, and Aesthetics*. Walnut Creek, Calif.: AltaMira Press.

Bourdieu, Pierre
  1977 *Outline of the Theory of Practice*. Translated by Richard Nice. New York: Cambridge University Press.

Brown, Jean Morrison, ed.
  1979 *The Vision of Modern Dance*. Princeton, N.J.: Princeton Book Company.

Browning, Barbara
  1995 *Samba: Resistance in Motion*. Bloomington: Indiana University Press.

Brubach, Holly
  1982 "Pilobolus: Fat Gnomes, Hunchbacks, and Tall Ladies." *Vogue* 172 (March):63.

Castiglione, Baldassare
  1959 *The Book of the Courtier*. Translated by Charles Singleton. Garden City, N.Y.: Anchor Books.

Christout, Marie-Françoise
  1992 "Waslaw Nijinsky ou le don de métamorphose." In *Ecrits sur Nijinsky*, edited by Françoise Stanciu-Reiss, 115–23. Paris: Éditions Chiron.

Croce, Arlene
  1987 *Sight Lines*. New York: Alfred A. Knopf.
  2000 *Writing in the Dark: Dancing in the New Yorker*. New York: Farrar, Straus and Giroux.

Daniel, Yvonne
  1995 *Dance and Social Change in Contemporary Cuba*. Bloomington: Indiana University Press.

Davison, Peter
  2000 *Breathing Room: Poems*. New York: Alfred A. Knopf.

Delacroix, Eugène
  1995 *The Journal of Eugène Delacroix*. 3d ed. Edited and with an introduction by Hubert Wellington; translated by Lucy Norton. London: Phaidon Press.

DeMallie, Raymond J., ed.
1984 *The Sixth Grandfather: Black Elk's Teachings Given to John G. Neihardt*. Lincoln: University of Nebraska Press.

Denby, Edwin
1986 *Dance Writings*. Edited by Robert Cornfield and William MacKay. New York: Alfred A. Knopf.

Desjarlais, Robert R.
1992 *Body and Emotion: The Aesthetics of Illness and Healing in the Nepal Himalayas*. Philadelphia: University of Pennsylvania Press.

Fisk, Josiah, and Jeff Nicholas, eds.
1997 *Composers on Music: Eight Centuries of Writings*. 2d ed. Boston: Northeastern University Press.

Fokine, Michel
1961 *Fokine: Memoirs of a Ballet Master*. Translated by Vitale Fokine; edited by Anatole Chujoy. Boston: Little, Brown and Company.

Foucault, Michel
1979 *Discipline and Punish: The Birth of the Prison*. Translated by A. Sheridan. Harmondsworth, England: Penguin Books.

Fraser, John
1988 *Private View: Inside Baryshnikov's American Ballet Theatre*. Photographs by Eve Arnold. New York: Bantam Books.

Geertz, Clifford
1973 *The Interpretation of Cultures*. New York: Basic Books.

Guest, Ann Hutchinson
1991 "Nijinsky's *Faune*." *Choreography and Dance* 1(3):3–34.

Guest, Ann Hutchinson, and Claudia Jeschke
1991 *Nijinsky's Faune Restored: A Study of Vaslav Nijinsky's 1915 Dance Score L'Après-Midi d'un Faune and His Dance Notation System*. Language of Dance 3. Philadelphia: Gordon and Breach.

Gunji, Masakatsu
1970 *Buyo: The Classical Dance*. Translated by Don Kenny, with an introduction by James R. Brandon. New York: John Weatherhill.
1985 *Kabuki*. Photographs by Chiaki Yoshida, with an introduction by Donald Keene. Tokyo: Kodansha International; New York: Kodansha America.

Handelman, Don
1990 *Models and Mirrors: Towards an Anthropology of Public Events*. New York: Cambridge University Press.

Hazzard-Gordon, Katrina
1990 *Jookin': The Rise of Social Dance Formations in African-American Culture*. Philadelphia: Temple University Press.

Herbert, Mimi, with Nur S. Rahardjo
2002 *Voices of the Puppet Masters: The Wayang Golek Theater of Indonesia*. Jakarta, Indonesia: Lontar Foundation; Honolulu: University of Hawai'i Press.

REFERENCES

Herskovits, Melville

1950 "Possession." In *Funk and Wagnalls Standard Dictionary of Folklore, Mythology, and Legend*, edited by Maria Leach and Jerome Fried, 881–82. New York: Funk and Wagnalls.

Hill, Constance Valis

2000 *Brotherhood in Rhythm: The Jazz Tap Dancing of the Nicholas Brothers*. New York: Oxford University Press.

Jacobi, Peter P.

1999 "The Starker Story—A Life in America since 1948." In *Von Budapest nach Bloomington: Janos Starker und die ungarische Cello-Tradition*, edited by Raimund Trenkler, 211–47. Kronberg, Germany: Kronberg Academy Verlag.

Jonas, Gerald

1992 *Dancing: The Pleasure, Power, and Art of Movement*. New York: Harry N. Abrams.

Kallberg, Jeffrey

1996 *Chopin at the Boundaries: Sex, History, and Musical Genre*. Cambridge, Mass.: Harvard University Press.

Karsavina, Tamara

1934 *Les Souvenirs de Tamar Karsavina: Ballets Russes*. Translated by Denyse Clairouin. Paris: Librairie Plon.

Karsavina, Tamara, and Vaslav Nijinsky

1912 "Karsavina-Nijinsky: Leurs souvenirs, racontés par eux-même." *Je Sais Tout* 15 November, 407–20.

Katz, Richard

1982 Boiling Energy: Community Healing among the Kalahari Kung. Cambridge, Mass.: Harvard University Press.

Kemper, Robert V., and Anya Peterson Royce, eds.

2002 *Chronicling Cultures: Long-Term Field Research in Anthropology*. Walnut Creek, Calif.: AltaMira Press.

Kurath, Gertrude Prokosch

1950 "Shaman and shamanism." In *Funk and Wagnalls Standard Dictionary of Folklore, Mythology, and Legend,* edited by Maria Leach and Jerome Fried, 1003–4. New York: Funk and Wagnalls.

1958 "Plaza Circuits of Pueblo Indian Dancers." *El Palacio* 65(1–2):16–25.

Kurath, Gertrude Prokosch, and Antonio Garcia

1970 *Music and Dance of the Tewa Pueblos*. Museum of New Mexico Research Records 8. Santa Fe: Museum of New Mexico Press.

Laufer, Joanna, and Kenneth Lewis

1998 *Inspired Lives*. Woodstock, Vt.: Skylight Paths Publishing.

Lévi-Strauss, Claude

1967 *Structural Anthropology*. Translated by Claire Jacobson and Brooke Grundfest Schoepf. Garden City, N.Y.: Anchor Books.

Lyle, Cynthia

1977 *Dancers on Dancing*. New York: Sterling Publishing Company.

Makarova, Natalia
1979 *A Dance Autobiography*. New York: Alfred A. Knopf.

Meyer, Adolf de
1983 "L'Après-midi d'un faune." In *Vaslav Nijinsky, 1912: Thirty-Three Photographs by Baron Adolf de Meyer*. With an essay by Jennifer Dunning and contributions by Richard Buckle and Ann Hutchinson Guest. London: Dance Books.

Money, Keith
1982 *Anna Pavlova: Her Life and Art*. New York: Alfred A. Knopf.

Neihardt, James
1972 *Black Elk Speaks*. Norman: University of Oklahoma Press.

Ness, Sally Ann
1992 *Body, Movement, and Culture: Kinesthetic and Visual Symbolism in a Philippine Community*. Philadelphia: University of Pennsylvania Press.

Randel, Don Michael, comp.
1978 *Harvard Concise Dictionary of Music*. Cambridge, Mass.: Harvard University Press.

Rilke, Rainer Maria
1985 "Spanish Dancer." In *Rainer Maria Rilke: Selected Poems*. 2d ed. Translated by Albert Ernest Flemming. New York: Methuen.
1995 "To Music." In *Ahead of All Parting: The Selected Poetry and Prose of Rainer Maria Rilke*, edited and translated by Stephen Mitchell, 143. New York: Modern Library.

Ritter, Naomi
1989 *Art as Spectacle: Images of the Entertainer since Romanticism*. Columbia: University of Missouri Press.

Rodríguez, Sylvia
1996 *The Matachines Dance: Ritual Symbolism and Interethnic Relations in the Upper Rio Grande Valley*. Albuquerque: University of New Mexico Press.

Royce, Anya Peterson
1977 *The Anthropology of Dance*. Bloomington: Indiana University Press.
1982 *Ethnic Identity: Strategies of Diversity*. Bloomington: Indiana University Press.
1984 *Movement and Meaning: Creativity and Interpretation in Ballet and Mime*. Bloomington: Indiana University Press.
1986 "The Venetian Commedia: Actors and Masques in the Development of the Commedia dell'Arte." *Theatre Survey* 27(1–2):69–87.
1987a "Limits of Innovation in Dance and Mime." *Semiotica* 65(3–4):269–84.
1987b "Masculinity and Femininity in Elaborated Movement Systems." In *Masculinity/Femininity: Basic Perspectives*, edited by June Machover Reinisch, Leonard A. Rosenblum, and Stephanie A. Sanders, 315–43. New York: Oxford University Press.
1990 "Who Was Argentina? Player and Role in the Late Seventeenth Century Commedia dell'Arte." *Theatre Survey* 30(1–2):45–57.
2002a "From Body as Artifact to Embodied Knowledge: An Introduction to the Reprint Edition." In *The Anthropology of Dance*, repr. ed., by Anya Peterson Royce, xv–xxv. London: Dance Books.
2002b "Learning to See, Learning to Listen: Thirty-five Years of Fieldwork with the Isthmus Zapotec." In *Chronicling Cultures: Long-term Ethnographic Field Research in Anthropology*, edited by Robert V. Kemper and Anya Peterson Royce, 8–33. Walnut Creek, Calif.: AltaMira Press.

REFERENCES

Savigliano, Marta

1995 *Tango: The Political Economy of Passion*. Bloomington: Indiana University Press.

Schechner, Richard, and Mady Schuman, eds.

1976 *Ritual, Play, and Performance: Readings in the Social Sciences and Theatre*. New York: Seabury Press.

Schonberg, Harold C.

1988 *The Virtuosi: Classical Music's Legendary Performers from Paganini to Pavarotti*. New York: Vintage Books.

Schwartzman, Helen B.

1978 *Transformations: The Anthropology of Children's Play*. New York: Plenum Press.

Sherzer, Joel

1990 *Verbal Art in San Blas: Kuna Culture through Its Discourse*. New York: Cambridge University Press.

Shollar, Ludmilla, and Anatole Vilzak

1982 *A Ballerina Prepares: Classical Ballet Variations for the Female Dancer, as Taught by Ludmilla Shollar and Anatole Vilzak*. Notated by Laurencia Klaja. Garden City, N.Y.: Doubleday and Company.

Shostak, Marjorie

1981 *Nisa: The Life and Words of a !Kung Woman*. Cambridge, Mass.: Harvard University Press.

2000 *Return to Nisa*. Cambridge, Mass.: Harvard University Press.

Smakov, Gennady

1981 *Baryshnikov: From Russia to the West*. New York: Farrar, Straus and Giroux.

Starker, Janos

1999 "Recollections of Leó Weiner." In *Von Budapest nach Bloomington: Janos Starker und die ungarische Cello-Tradition*, edited by Raimund Trenkler, 187–89. Kronberg, Germany: Kronberg Academy Verlag.

2001 "Playing for the Master—Starker Speaks: Teaching, Performing, and Golden Moments." *Indiana Alumni Magazine*, May/June.

Stoller, Paul

1989 *Fusion of the Worlds: An Ethnography of Possession among the Songhay of Niger*. Chicago: University of Chicago Press.

1997 *Sensuous Scholarship*. Philadelphia: University of Pennsylvania Press.

2002 "The Griot's Many Burdens—Fiction's Many Truths." In *Ethnographically Speaking: Autoethnography, Literature, and Aesthetics*, edited by Arthur Bochner and Carolyn Ellis, 297–307. Walnut Creek, Calif.: AltaMira Press.

Strathern, Andrew

1996 *Body Thoughts*. Ann Arbor: University of Michigan Press.

Sweet, Jill D.

1985 *Dances of the Tewa Pueblo Indians: Expressions of New Life*. Santa Fe, N.M.: School of American Research Press.

Taylor, Julie

1998 *Paper Tangos*. Durham, N.C.: Duke University Press.

Turner, Victor

1987 *The Anthropology of Performance*. New York: PAJ Publications.

Udall, Sharyn R.
1996 *Contested Terrain: Myth and Meaning in Southwest Art.* Albuquerque: University of New Mexico Press.

Valéry, Paul
1964 *Aesthetics.* Translated by Ralph Manheim. New York: Pantheon Books.

Viala, Jean, and Nourit Masson-Sekine
1988 *Butoh: Shades of Darkness.* Tokyo: Shufunotomo.

Wachtel, Andrew, ed.
1998 *Petrushka: Sources and Contexts.* Evanston, Ill.: Northwestern University Press.

Whitman, William
1947 *The Pueblo Indians of San Ildefonso.* Columbia University Contributions to Anthropology 34. New York: Columbia University Press.

Yamazaki, Kazuko
2001 *Nihon Buyo: Classical Dance of Modern Japan.* Ann Arbor, Mich.: University Microfilms International.

INDEX

ABOUT THE AUTHOR

Anya Peterson Royce in Zobeide, *San Francisco Russian Opera and Ballet, 1967. Photograph by Ronald R. Royce.*

ABOUT THE AUTHOR

Anya Peterson Royce is Chancellor's Professor of Anthropology at Indiana University, Bloomington. She does research and writes in the areas of the anthropology of dance and the performing arts; ethnic identity; and the ethnography of Mexico, especially the Zapotec of Juchitán, Oaxaca, where she has conducted field research for thirty-five years. Her books include *Prestigio y Afiliación en una Comunidad Indígena: Juchitán, Oaxaca*; *Ethnic Identity: Strategies of Diversity*; *The Anthropology of Dance; Movement and Meaning: Creativity and Interpretation in Ballet and Mime;* and *Chronicling Cultures: Long-term Ethnographic Field Research in Anthropology* (edited with Robert V. Kemper). She has also published articles on the history of the commedia dell'arte, innovation in dance and mime, masculinity and femininity in codified movement systems, ethnicity and nationalism, and Zapotec music and dance.

Her poetry has been published in the journal *Qualitative Inquiry* and in the collections *The Linen Weave of Bloomington Poets* and *Five Women Poets: Choice Words*. In a former career in ballet, she danced with the San Francisco Russian Opera and Ballet and the Brooklyn Ballet. That experience and her long-term ethnographic research give her a unique perspective from which to speak about the performing arts as ritual and theatre. She has been a Guggenheim fellow, a Delmas fellow, a Bogliasco fellow, and an American Council of Learned Society fellow, with additional grants and fellowships from the American Philosophical Society, the National Endowment for the Humanities, and the Social Science Research Council. Her teaching has been recognized by four university-wide teaching awards. Her hobbies include tai chi, growing lilies, and herbal medicine.